THE CMO MBA
Your Blueprint to Marketing Excellence

By

Robert N. Jacobs

All rights reserved
Copyright © Robert N. Jacobs, 2025
The right of Robert N. Jacobs to be identified as the author of this
work has been asserted in accordance with Section 78
of the Copyright, Designs and Patents Act 1988
The book cover is copyright to Robert N. Jacobs
This book is published by
Growth Seeker Publishing Ltd.
www.growthseekerpublishing.com

This book is sold subject to the conditions that it shall not, by way of
trade or otherwise, be lent, resold, hired out or otherwise circulated
without the author's or publisher's prior consent in any form of binding
or cover other than that in which it is published and
without a similar condition including this condition being imposed
on the subsequent purchaser.
This book is a work of fiction. Any resemblance to
people or events, past or present, is purely coincidental.
ISBN: 9798282485240

"The role of a CMO has never been more complex or more critical. It's not just about advertising anymore; it's about driving growth, shaping customer experiences, and steering businesses through innovation and transformation. The CMO MBA is your roadmap to mastering these challenges, filled with practical strategies and real-world examples that will sharpen your edge as a marketing leader."

Robert N. Jacobs

Introduction

The role of a Chief Marketing Officer has evolved into one of the most dynamic and strategic positions within the modern business landscape. CMOs are no longer simply responsible for advertising campaigns or creative output; they are the architects of brand purpose, the drivers of customer loyalty, and the catalysts for sustainable growth. Today, the CMO must be both a visionary and a practitioner, balancing the art of storytelling with the science of analytics, all while navigating an ever-changing digital ecosystem.

Whether you're an aspiring marketing leader looking to make your mark or a seasoned CMO seeking fresh perspectives, The CMO MBA is your essential guide to mastering this complex and rewarding role. This book is designed to bridge the gap between theory and practice, offering actionable insights that empower you to thrive in an increasingly customer-centric and data-driven world.

Like many of you, I've wrestled with the challenges of aligning marketing strategies with broader organisational goals, fostering innovation while preserving a brand legacy and achieving measurable impact in an environment of constant change. What sets this book apart is its focus on these real-world challenges. It distils the complexities of modern marketing leadership into practical frameworks and relatable case studies, providing you with a toolkit to tackle everything from crafting effective strategies to leading high-performance teams.

The CMO MBA delves into the critical areas that define marketing excellence today, from harnessing the power of advanced analytics and embracing digital transformation to fostering customer advocacy and championing diversity and inclusion within your brand. It reflects the realities of leading in a role where expectations are as high as the potential for impact.

This book is not just a roadmap for your career; it's a companion on your journey. Whether you're rebranding a global enterprise, navigating the rise of AI and automation, or simply seeking to refine your leadership style, you'll find strategies and insights to guide you every step of the way.

So, as you embark on this transformative journey, I invite you to think big, stay curious, and never stop learning. Marketing is not just about driving business results; it's about inspiring people, shaping culture, and creating lasting value. You have the power to lead that change.

Robert Jacobs
Curious By Design

Table of Contents

Chapter 1
Foundations Of Marketing Leadership 1
1.1 - What is a CMO? Role and Responsibilities 2
1.2 - The Evolution of Marketing Leadership 4
1.3 - Core Skills Every CMO Must Master 7
1.4 - Marketing Basics: From Branding to ROI 12
1.5 - Understanding Marketing's Role in Business Strategy 16
1.6 - Building Effective Communication Skills 21
1.7 - The Importance of Emotional Intelligence in Leadership 26
1.8 - Overview of Marketing Channels and Platforms 30
1.9 - Key Metrics for Early Success 36
1.10 - Case Study: Transitioning to a Marketing Leadership Role. 40

Chapter 2
Crafting a Marketing Strategy 47
2.1 - The Anatomy of a Great Marketing Plan 47
2.2 - Conducting Market Research and Analysis 50
2.3 - Understanding Target Audiences and Segmentation 54
2.4 - Setting Goals: SMART Objectives and KPIs 58
2.5 - Positioning and Messaging Frameworks 63
2.6 - Budget Allocation and Resource Planning 68
2.7 - Competitive Analysis: Tools and Techniques 72
2.8 - Aligning Marketing with Organisational Goals 78
2.9 - Real-World Challenges in Strategic Planning 83
2.10 - Case Study: Building a Winning Strategy from Scratch 89

Chapter 3
Mastering Brand Management 95

3.1 - What is Brand Equity? 95
3.2 - Building a Strong Brand Identity 97
3.3 - The Role of Storytelling in Branding 100
3.4 - Managing Brand Consistency Across Channels 102
3.5 - Brand Crisis Management 105
3.6 - Measuring Brand Health: Tools and Techniques 109
3.7 - Balancing Legacy and Innovation in Branding 113
3.8 - Creating Brand Advocates: Customer Loyalty Programs 117
3.9 - Emerging Trends in Brand Strategy 122
3.10 - Case Study: Rebranding a Global Enterprise 126

Chapter 4
Digital Marketing in the Modern Age 130
4.1 - The Digital Landscape: Trends and Challenges 130
4.2 - Fundamentals of SEO and SEM 133
4.3 - Social Media Strategy: Engagement and Growth 136
4.4 -Content Marketing: Creating Value for Customers 136
4.5- -Leveraging Data for Personalised Campaigns 144
4.6 - Influencer Marketing: Opportunities and Pitfalls 148
4.7 - The Role of AI and Automation in Digital Marketing 153
4.8 - Evaluating Digital Campaign Performance 157
4.9 - Ethical Considerations in Digital Advertising 161
4.10 - Case Study: A Multi-Channel Digital Campaign 165

Chapter 5
Customer-Centric Marketing 172
Understanding the Customer Journey 172
Building Buyer Personas 176
Data-Driven Customer Insights 179
Developing a Customer Retention Strategy 182
Feedback Loops: Listening to Your Audience 185

Nurturing Customer Relationships Through CRM 188

The Role of Customer Experience in Marketing............................. 192

Managing Negative Feedback and Reviews.................................. 195

Creating Memorable Customer Touchpoints................................ 198

Case Study: Transforming Customer Experience 201

Chapter 6

Leading High-Performing Marketing Teams 207

6.1 - Building and Scaling a Marketing Team 208

6.2 - Hiring for Skills and Cultural Fit.. 210

6.3 - Fostering Creativity and Collaboration............................. 213

6.4 - Setting Goals and Accountability Metrics 217

6.5 - Coaching and Mentoring Team Members 220

6.6 - Managing Remote and Global Teams............................... 224

6.7 - Addressing Team Conflict Constructively 228

6.8 - Measuring Team Performance and Productivity 232

6.9 - Celebrating Wins and Learning from Losses................. 235

6.10 - Case Study: Turning Around a Struggling Team.................... 239

Chapter 7

Advanced Analytics and ROI Measurement......................... 245

7.1 - The Importance of Data in Modern Marketing......................... 246

7.2 - Key Metrics and KPIs for CMOs.. 248

7.3 - Understanding Attribution Models 251

7.4 - Advanced Tools for Marketing Analytics........................ 255

7.5 - Creating Dashboards for Executive Reporting........................ 258

7.6 - Balancing Short-Term Results with Long-Term ROI 262

7.7 - Overcoming Challenges in Data Interpretation......................... 266

7.8 - Predictive Analytics and Forecasting.............................. 270

7.9 - Avoiding Common Analytics Pitfalls 274

7.10 - Case Study: Driving ROI Through Data........................ 278

Chapter 8
Innovation and Growth Marketing 284
    8.1 - What is Growth Marketing? 284
    8.2 - Identifying New Market Opportunities 286
    8.3 - Experimentation and A/B Testing 290
    8.4 - Driving Product Innovation Through Marketing 294
    8.5 - The Role of Partnerships and Collaborations 298
    8.6 - Scaling Campaigns: Challenges and Solutions 302
    8.7 - Incorporating Sustainability into Growth Strategies 306
    8.8 - Staying Ahead of Industry Disruptions 310
    8.9 - Tools and Frameworks for Agile Marketing 314
    8.10 - Case Study: Launching a Growth Initiative 318

Chapter 9
Managing Challenges as a CMO 324
    9.1 - Navigating Internal Stakeholder Relationships 324
    9.2 - Managing Up: Communicating with the C-Suite 327
    9.3 - Balancing Marketing and Sales Alignment 330
    9.4 - Handling Budget Cuts and Resource Constraints 334
    9.5 - Dealing with Market Crises and PR Nightmares 339
    9.6 - Keeping Pace with Technological Advancements 343
    9.7 - Managing Burnout and Building Resilience 347
    9.8 - Balancing Creativity and Data-Driven Decisions 351
    9.9 - Ethical Dilemmas in Marketing Leadership 355
    9.10 - Case Study: Overcoming a Major Marketing Challenge 360

Chapter 10
The Future of Marketing Leadership 366
    10.1 - The Evolving Role of the CMO 367
    10.2 - Preparing for the AI-Driven Future 369

10.3 - Mastering Cross-Functional Collaboration............................ 372

10.4 - Global Marketing: Strategies for International Growth....... 376

10.5 - The Importance of Diversity and Inclusion in Marketing.. 381

10.6 - The Role of Purpose-Driven Marketing..................................... 385

10.7 - Lifelong Learning and Professional Development................ 389

10.8 - Becoming a Thought Leader in Your Industry 393

10.9 - Key Predictions for the Next Decade.. 397

10.10 - Case Study: A Visionary CMO's Legacy 403

Thinking About a CMO as a Career Path – Here's What You Need to Do 409

"A Chief Marketing Officer is not just a marketer; they are the architect of brand perception, the strategist of customer connection, and the bridge between creativity and commerce. In a world driven by data and emotion, the CMO translates insights into influence and vision into value."

Robert N. Jacobs

Chapter 1

Foundations Of Marketing Leadership

"A great marketing leader doesn't just follow trends; they set the standard by connecting creativity with strategy and data with purpose."

Robert N. Jacobs

The foundation of effective marketing leadership begins with a deep understanding of the ever-evolving role of the Chief Marketing Officer (CMO). As the bridge between an organisation and its market, the CMO plays a pivotal role in shaping brand identity, driving customer engagement, and aligning marketing strategies with broader business objectives. However, in today's dynamic and technology-driven environment, the expectations for marketing leaders have expanded far beyond traditional responsibilities.

This chapter explores the critical competencies and strategic insights that form the bedrock of marketing leadership, guiding CMOs to not only adapt to industry changes but also to lead with innovation, collaboration, and purpose. From mastering core skills to embracing emerging trends, these principles serve as the foundation for thriving in one of the most challenging and impactful roles in the C-suite.

1.1 - What is a CMO? Role and Responsibilities

The role of the **Chief Marketing Officer (CMO)** has evolved into one of the most crucial leadership positions within any organisation. At its core, the CMO is responsible for overseeing the entire marketing function, shaping how the company interacts with its audience, and driving strategies that align marketing efforts with overall business goals. However, this broad definition barely scratches the surface of what the role entails in practice.

To truly understand what a CMO does, it is important to delve into the diverse responsibilities they carry. At the strategic level, the CMO develops the organisation's overarching marketing strategy. This means defining the brand's identity, creating a roadmap for customer engagement, and determining the marketing channels that will best achieve business objectives. Unlike other leadership roles that may focus exclusively on internal operations, the CMO operates at the intersection of the company and the market. They are responsible for ensuring the brand's messaging resonates with target audiences while simultaneously aligning with the company's mission and values.

Another key responsibility of the CMO is **data-driven decision-making**. Marketing today is as much about numbers as it is about creativity. CMOs must sift through vast amounts of data to uncover actionable insights. For instance, they analyse customer behaviour patterns, measure the effectiveness of campaigns, and forecast market trends. Armed with this information, they make informed decisions that improve ROI and help the business stay competitive in rapidly changing markets.

CMOs also play a pivotal role in **customer experience (CX)**. They oversee the entire customer journey, from the first interaction with the brand to post-purchase support. This involves ensuring consistency across all touchpoints, be it the company website, social media platforms, email campaigns, or physical stores. Today's consumers demand personalised experiences, and it is the CMO's job to ensure these experiences are both meaningful and seamless.

Leadership is another critical dimension of the CMO's responsibilities. They manage teams that span multiple disciplines, including digital marketing, public relations, content creation, and analytics. Leading such a diverse group requires strong communication skills, the ability to inspire creativity and a knack for fostering collaboration. A successful CMO builds a cohesive team where everyone is aligned towards achieving common goals.

Finally, the CMO acts as a **strategic advisor to the CEO and other members of the executive team**. They ensure that marketing is integrated into the company's overall business strategy. For instance, if the company aims to expand into new markets, the CMO provides insights into local consumer behaviour, competitive landscapes, and cultural nuances. This advisory role also extends to crisis management, where the CMO helps protect the brand's reputation during challenging times.

In essence, the modern CMO is much more than a marketing specialist. They are a visionary leader, a data analyst, a customer advocate, and a strategic partner. Their work directly impacts not only the company's revenue but also its long-term success in building meaningful relationships with its audience. As businesses continue to evolve, the role of the CMO will only become more complex, demanding an even greater blend of creativity, strategy, and technical expertise.

Here's the expanded content for the next subheading, **The Evolution of Marketing Leadership**, written in the same detailed format:

1.2 - The Evolution of Marketing Leadership

Marketing leadership has undergone a significant transformation over the last century, shaped by changes in technology, consumer behaviour, and globalisation. The role of the CMO, once narrowly focused on promotional activities, has evolved into a multifaceted position that requires strategic thinking, technological proficiency, and a deep understanding of market dynamics.

In the early 20th century, marketing leadership was primarily about creating awareness. The tools available to marketers were limited to print advertisements, billboards, and radio. CMOs, or their historical equivalents, focused on product-centric messaging that emphasised features over benefits. The emphasis was on reaching the largest possible audience with a singular, one-size-fits-all message. While this approach may have been effective in a time of limited consumer choice, it lacked the nuance required to build lasting relationships with customers.

The post-World War II era saw the emergence of **television advertising**, which revolutionised the way companies communicated with their audiences. The "Mad Men" era of marketing leadership was born, with a heavy focus on creative storytelling and emotional appeal. CMOs during this time were visionaries who understood the power of narrative to influence consumer behaviour. Brands like Coca-Cola and Marlboro became cultural icons, demonstrating the impact of well-executed marketing campaigns. However, even in this golden age of advertising, the role of the marketing leader was largely reactive, focusing on creating demand rather than shaping broader business strategies.

The 1990s marked a pivotal shift with the advent of the **internet**. Suddenly, marketing leaders had access to new channels, such as email and websites, that allowed for direct communication with consumers. This era introduced the concept of **data-driven marketing**, as tools like website analytics provided unprecedented insights into consumer behaviour. CMOs began to leverage this data to personalise their messaging, marking the beginning of the shift from mass marketing to targeted campaigns. However, the internet also brought challenges, including the need to manage a brand's reputation in real-time as consumers gained the ability to share their opinions widely and instantly.

The early 2000s saw the rise of **social media**, which further transformed the responsibilities of marketing leaders. Platforms like Facebook, Twitter, and Instagram became essential tools for engaging with audiences, fostering two-way communication, and building communities around brands. CMOs were now tasked with not only promoting products but also managing brand personas, responding to customer feedback, and navigating the complexities of viral content. The concept of **influencer marketing** emerged, challenging CMOs to rethink traditional advertising strategies.

In recent years, the role of the CMO has become even more dynamic, driven by the explosion of **artificial intelligence (AI)**, automation, and big data. Today, CMOs must integrate technologies like machine learning to predict consumer behaviour, optimise campaigns in real-time, and deliver hyper-personalised experiences. This requires a new level of technological literacy that was unheard of in previous generations of marketing leaders.

Simultaneously, modern CMOs are expected to address societal and ethical issues. Consumers now hold brands accountable for their environmental impact, diversity efforts, and contributions to social justice. Marketing leadership today involves navigating these complex expectations while maintaining authenticity. The shift towards **purpose-driven marketing** has placed the CMO at the forefront of shaping not only how a brand is perceived but also how it contributes to the world.

Another major change is the CMO's role within the C-suite. No longer siloed in the marketing department, CMOs are now integral to shaping overall business strategy. They collaborate closely with the CEO, CFO, and other executives to ensure that marketing efforts align with corporate goals. For instance, CMOs play a key role in product development by providing consumer insights or in business expansion by identifying untapped markets. This strategic alignment underscores the evolution of marketing leadership from a creative function to a business-critical role.

In conclusion, the evolution of marketing leadership reflects broader shifts in technology, consumer expectations, and business priorities. The modern CMO is not just a marketer but a strategist, a technologist, and a cultural steward. As the world continues to change at an accelerating pace, marketing leaders must remain adaptable, innovative, and forward-thinking to stay ahead.

1.3 - Core Skills Every CMO Must Master

The role of the **Chief Marketing Officer (CMO)** requires a unique blend of creativity, strategy, and leadership. As the marketing landscape evolves, so too does the skill set required for CMOs to succeed. Modern CMOs must be versatile and able to navigate complex challenges while driving innovation and achieving measurable results. The following are the core skills every CMO must master to thrive in this demanding role.

1.3.1. Strategic Thinking

At the heart of every successful CMO is the ability to think strategically. This skill enables them to align marketing initiatives with the organisation's overall objectives. Strategic thinking involves seeing the bigger picture, identifying opportunities in the market, and anticipating challenges before they arise. For example, when entering a new market, a CMO must assess local consumer behaviours, cultural nuances, and competitive landscapes to craft an effective strategy. Without a clear vision, marketing efforts risk becoming disjointed and ineffective.

To hone this skill, CMOs must stay informed about industry trends, consumer insights, and economic shifts. They should also cultivate a forward-thinking mindset, focusing on long-term growth rather than short-term wins. Strategic thinking requires both analytical prowess and creative problem-solving, as CMOs must navigate data-driven decisions while remaining open to innovative ideas.

1.3.2. Data Literacy and Analytical Skills

In today's marketing world, data is king. CMOs must be adept at analysing vast amounts of information to uncover insights that drive decision-making. From customer behaviour patterns to campaign performance metrics, data informs every aspect of modern marketing. A skilled CMO understands which metrics matter most, whether it's customer acquisition cost (CAC), customer lifetime value (CLV), or social media engagement, and how to translate these numbers into actionable strategies.

For example, a CMO analysing a dip in website traffic might investigate user behaviour data to identify where visitors are dropping off. This could lead to optimising website design or improving content relevance. Beyond interpreting data, CMOs must also communicate their findings effectively to stakeholders, ensuring the entire organisation understands the value of marketing efforts.

1.3.3. Leadership and Team Building

As leaders, CMOs are responsible for managing diverse teams, often comprising creative, analytical, and technical experts. Building a high-performing team requires not only hiring individuals with the right skills but also fostering an environment where collaboration and innovation thrive. Leadership involves setting clear goals, providing constructive feedback, and recognising achievements to keep the team motivated.

Empathy and emotional intelligence play a significant role in effective leadership. A CMO must understand the strengths and challenges of each team member, offering support and guidance to help them excel. Additionally, they must navigate conflicts and encourage open communication to ensure the team remains cohesive.

1.3.4. Creativity and Innovation

Marketing is an inherently creative field, and a successful CMO must be a champion of innovation. This means not only developing groundbreaking campaigns but also encouraging a culture of creativity within their team. Whether it's brainstorming new ways to engage audiences or experimenting with emerging technologies like augmented reality, CMOs must push the boundaries of traditional marketing.

Creativity, however, must be balanced with practicality. Innovative ideas are only valuable if they achieve the desired outcomes. For example, a bold ad campaign that generates buzz but fails to convert leads may be memorable but ultimately ineffective. The ability to merge creativity with business objectives is what sets exceptional CMOs apart.

1.3.5. Adaptability and Agility

The marketing landscape is constantly changing, with new platforms, trends, and consumer behaviours emerging at a rapid pace. CMOs must be highly adaptable, ready to pivot strategies when circumstances shift. The COVID-19 pandemic, for instance, forced many CMOs to reimagine their approach to consumer engagement, accelerating the adoption of digital channels and virtual experiences.

Agility also means being open to learning and unlearning. CMOs must stay curious, continuously updating their knowledge to remain relevant. This might involve exploring advancements in artificial intelligence, understanding shifts in consumer psychology, or embracing new content formats like interactive videos or live streaming.

1.3.6. Communication Skills

Exceptional communication skills are essential for CMOs, who must articulate their vision to a wide range of stakeholders. Whether it's presenting a marketing plan to the board, rallying the marketing team around a new initiative, or engaging with customers through brand messaging, clear and persuasive communication is key.

Good communication also involves listening. CMOs must actively seek feedback from their teams, customers, and partners, using these insights to refine their strategies. Transparent and consistent communication builds trust and ensures that everyone involved in the marketing process is aligned.

1.3.7. Financial Acumen

Marketing is not just a creative endeavour; it's a significant investment for most organisations. CMOs must demonstrate financial acumen, managing budgets effectively and ensuring a strong return on investment (ROI) for every marketing pound spent. This involves understanding cost structures, forecasting expenses, and allocating resources to maximise impact.

For example, a CMO deciding between investing in a high-profile TV campaign or a series of targeted digital ads must weigh the potential ROI of each option. They must also be prepared to justify their decisions to other members of the executive team, showing how marketing contributes to overall business success.

1.3.8. Technological Proficiency

As technology continues to reshape the marketing landscape, CMOs must be comfortable navigating a wide range of tools and platforms. This includes everything from customer relationship management (CRM) systems and email marketing platforms to advanced analytics software and AI-powered automation tools. Understanding how to leverage technology effectively can streamline workflows, improve campaign performance, and enhance customer experiences.

For instance, using AI to personalise email marketing campaigns can significantly boost engagement rates. However, technological proficiency isn't just about knowing which tools to use; it's also about understanding their limitations and potential ethical implications.

In conclusion, the role of the CMO demands a diverse and evolving skill set, blending strategic vision, creative thinking, and operational excellence. By mastering these core skills, CMOs can not only lead successful marketing initiatives but also drive meaningful business outcomes. As the industry continues to evolve, the most effective CMOs will be those who remain adaptable, curious, and committed to continuous learning.

1.4 - Marketing Basics: From Branding to ROI

At its core, marketing is the art and science of connecting a product or service with its intended audience. While the tools and techniques have evolved dramatically over time, the fundamental principles of marketing remain rooted in understanding human needs, behaviours, and desires. For a **Chief Marketing Officer (CMO)**, mastering these basics is essential, not only to build a strong foundation but also to ensure that all marketing efforts drive meaningful results. In this section, we will explore the importance of branding, the concept of return on investment (ROI), and how the two are intrinsically linked.

Branding is the heart of marketing. It represents the essence of a company's identity, encapsulating what the organisation stands for and how it wishes to be perceived by its audience. A brand is far more than a logo or a tagline, it is the emotional and psychological connection that consumers form with a business. For a CMO, the task of building and maintaining a brand is one of the most strategic and long-term responsibilities.

A well-defined brand provides clarity, consistency, and differentiation. Consider a global company like **Nike**, whose brand is synonymous with athleticism, inspiration, and innovation. The brand's powerful messaging, epitomised by the iconic "Just Do It" slogan, transcends individual marketing campaigns and resonates universally. This level of branding success does not happen by chance; it is the result of meticulous planning, deep consumer insights, and consistent execution.

For CMOs, the challenge often lies in balancing brand consistency with the need to adapt to local markets or changing trends. For example, a luxury fashion brand targeting affluent customers in London may need to communicate exclusivity and sophistication, while the same brand entering a growing market like India might focus on accessibility and aspirational appeal. Maintaining the core essence of the brand while tailoring its expression to different contexts is an ongoing challenge for marketing leaders.

In the modern business environment, marketing is no longer seen as a creative endeavour alone; it is also a significant investment. As such, CMOs are under constant pressure to demonstrate a **return on investment (ROI)** for their marketing efforts. Simply put, ROI is a measure of the value generated from a marketing campaign relative to its cost. It answers the critical question: Was this marketing effort worth it?

Measuring ROI can be both straightforward and complex, depending on the nature of the campaign. For example, a digital advertising campaign aimed at driving e-commerce sales might have a clear metric: the revenue generated directly from the ads compared to the cost of running them. On the other hand, measuring the ROI of a brand awareness campaign, which focuses on intangible outcomes like improved recognition or sentiment, requires a more nuanced approach.

For CMOs, understanding ROI goes beyond numbers. It involves setting clear objectives for each campaign, choosing the right metrics to track success, and analysing the results to inform future strategies. Key performance indicators (KPIs) such as **customer acquisition cost (CAC)**, **customer lifetime value (CLV)**, and **conversion rates** are critical in this process. However, CMOs must also recognise that not all marketing efforts yield immediate results; some, like building brand loyalty or improving reputation, are long-term investments.

One of the most significant challenges for CMOs is aligning branding efforts with measurable ROI. Branding is inherently qualitative, focusing on perception, trust, and emotional connection. ROI, on the other hand, is quantitative, demanding hard data and financial justification. Yet, these two aspects of marketing are not mutually exclusive; they are, in fact, deeply interconnected.

For example, a strong brand can directly impact ROI by reducing customer acquisition costs. When consumers are already familiar with and trust a brand, they are more likely to make a purchase without requiring extensive persuasion. Similarly, a positive brand reputation can lead to higher customer retention rates, increasing the overall lifetime value of customers. On the flip side, poorly executed branding efforts, such as an ad campaign that contradicts the company's core values, can erode trust and damage long-term profitability.

CMOs must find ways to bridge the gap between these two dimensions. This often involves using data to quantify the impact of branding efforts. For instance, tracking changes in **brand equity** (the perceived value of a brand) over time can provide insights into the effectiveness of branding initiatives. Tools like **Net Promoter Score (NPS)** or sentiment analysis on social media can also offer valuable indicators of brand health.

Despite its importance, achieving and measuring ROI in marketing is not without challenges. One of the biggest obstacles is the sheer complexity of today's marketing landscape. With so many channels available, from social media and search engines to traditional outlets like TV and print, determining the precise contribution of each channel to overall results can be daunting. This is where **attribution modelling** comes into play, allowing CMOs to assign value to different touchpoints in the customer journey.

Another challenge lies in balancing short-term and long-term goals. While performance marketing campaigns like pay-per-click (PPC) ads might deliver immediate results, they may not contribute significantly to brand equity. Conversely, brand-building activities like storytelling or sponsorships often take years to yield tangible returns. CMOs must manage stakeholder expectations by clearly communicating the purpose and timeline of different marketing efforts.

In conclusion, understanding the basics of marketing, particularly the interplay between branding and ROI is essential for any CMO. Branding lays the foundation for building trust and emotional connection with consumers, while ROI ensures that marketing efforts deliver measurable value. By mastering these fundamentals, CMOs can not only drive immediate business results but also create sustainable growth and resilience for their organisations. In today's competitive and ever-changing environment, these skills are no longer optional; they are the bedrock of effective marketing leadership.

1.5 - Understanding Marketing's Role in Business Strategy

Foundations Of Marketing Leadership

Marketing is often viewed as the engine of any organisation's growth. However, its role extends far beyond creating eye-catching advertisements or crafting witty social media posts. For a business to thrive in today's competitive and ever-changing market, marketing must be deeply integrated into the organisation's broader strategy. The **Chief Marketing Officer (CMO)** plays a pivotal role in ensuring this alignment, acting as a bridge between the customer and the company. This section explores the strategic importance of marketing and how it intersects with various aspects of business planning and execution.

At its core, marketing connects a business with its customers. It involves understanding customer needs, identifying how a product or service can meet those needs, and creating a compelling narrative that resonates with the target audience. However, marketing is not just about outward communication; it is also a critical tool for shaping business decisions.

For instance, the insights gathered through **market research**, such as trends in consumer behaviour, preferences, and purchasing patterns, can inform product development, pricing strategies, and even operational priorities. A CMO who understands the market deeply can help the organisation anticipate shifts in demand, identify untapped opportunities, and mitigate risks associated with disruptive competitors.

Consider a technology company planning to launch a new product. The marketing team's research might reveal that potential customers are more interested in sustainability features than cutting-edge performance. Armed with this insight, the product team can adjust their approach, ensuring the final offering aligns with consumer expectations. In this way, marketing plays a strategic role not only in promoting products but also in shaping them.

One of the most significant challenges CMOs face is aligning marketing efforts with the organisation's overarching goals. This requires a clear understanding of the company's mission, vision, and priorities. For example, a start-up focused on rapid growth might prioritise customer acquisition, requiring a marketing strategy that emphasises reach and volume. On the other hand, a well-established brand aiming to solidify its market position might focus on customer retention and loyalty, calling for a different set of tactics.

Achieving alignment also involves close collaboration with other departments. The relationship between **marketing and sales** is particularly critical. While marketing generates leads and builds brand awareness, sales teams close deals and nurture client relationships. Misalignment between these two functions can result in wasted resources and missed opportunities. A skilled CMO fosters collaboration by ensuring that both teams share common goals, metrics, and workflows.

Another key partnership is with the **finance department**. CMOs must work closely with the Chief Financial Officer (CFO) to allocate budgets effectively and demonstrate the ROI of marketing efforts. By aligning marketing strategies with financial objectives, CMOs can ensure that their initiatives contribute meaningfully to the company's bottom line.

In addition to supporting existing goals, marketing often acts as a catalyst for innovation. By keeping a finger on the pulse of the market, CMOs can identify emerging trends and propose new directions for the business. For example, the rise of plant-based diets in recent years has prompted many food companies to develop alternative protein products. Marketing teams were instrumental in recognising this shift and advocating for investment in new product lines.

Innovation also extends to how companies communicate with their audiences. The emergence of new platforms and technologies, such as **TikTok**, **podcasts**, or **augmented reality**, offers fresh opportunities for engagement. CMOs must continuously experiment with these tools, balancing the potential rewards of innovation against the risks of overextending resources.

A critical aspect of integrating marketing into business strategy is balancing short-term and long-term objectives. Short-term goals, such as boosting quarterly sales, often require performance marketing campaigns with immediate results. These might include targeted digital ads, limited-time promotions, or influencer partnerships. While these tactics are effective in generating quick wins, they may not contribute significantly to the brand's long-term health.

Conversely, long-term goals, such as building brand equity or expanding into new markets, demand sustained investment. These initiatives often yield results over months or years rather than days or weeks. A CMO must communicate the importance of these efforts to stakeholders, ensuring they understand the value of patience and strategic vision.

Despite its strategic importance, marketing often faces challenges in gaining recognition as a central pillar of business strategy. One common issue is the perception of marketing as a cost centre rather than a revenue driver. To overcome this, CMOs must demonstrate the tangible impact of marketing efforts, using metrics such as ROI, customer lifetime value, and market share growth.

Another challenge is the siloed nature of many organisations. When marketing operates in isolation from other departments, its potential to influence broader business decisions is limited. Breaking down these silos requires proactive communication, cross-departmental collaboration, and a willingness to advocate for marketing's role at the executive table.

Finally, marketing serves as the storyteller of an organisation's strategy. The way a company presents itself to the world, its branding, messaging, and campaigns reflects its core values and priorities. For instance, a business committed to sustainability might highlight its environmental initiatives through marketing content, reinforcing its positioning as an eco-conscious brand.

CMOs are responsible for ensuring that this narrative is not only compelling but also consistent across all touchpoints. From advertising and public relations to employee communications and investor relations, marketing acts as the voice of the organisation. This consistency helps build trust and credibility with stakeholders, which is crucial for achieving long-term success.

In conclusion, understanding and integrating marketing's role in business strategy is fundamental to the success of any organisation. Marketing is no longer a standalone function; it is a strategic partner that informs decision-making, drives innovation, and aligns with organisational goals. For CMOs, mastering this integration requires a deep understanding of both the market and the business, as well as the ability to communicate the value of marketing to all stakeholders. By embedding marketing into the fabric of the company's strategy, CMOs can ensure sustainable growth, resilience, and relevance in an ever-changing world.

1.6 - Building Effective Communication Skills

Effective communication is the cornerstone of leadership, and for a **Chief Marketing Officer (CMO)**, it is a non-negotiable skill. Marketing is a discipline that thrives on storytelling, persuasion, and collaboration, all of which rely on clear and impactful communication. Whether it's articulating a vision to a marketing team, presenting a strategy to the board of directors, or engaging with customers through brand messaging, a CMO's ability to communicate effectively can determine the success or failure of its initiatives. This section explores why communication is so critical for CMOs and how they can build and refine this vital skill.

For a CMO, communication operates on multiple levels. Internally, they must align their teams around a unified vision, ensuring that every member understands their role in executing the organisation's strategy. Externally, they are the voice of the brand, responsible for crafting messages that resonate with diverse audiences, including customers, investors, and the media.

A skilled communicator bridges gaps between departments, resolves conflicts, and fosters a culture of transparency and collaboration. For example, the marketing and sales teams often have overlapping but distinct goals, which can lead to misunderstandings or friction. A CMO who communicates effectively can mediate these differences, ensuring both teams work towards shared objectives.

Moreover, CMOs frequently interact with stakeholders outside the marketing function, such as the **CEO**, **CFO**, and board members. In these settings, their ability to present data-driven insights in a clear and compelling manner is crucial. For instance, explaining the ROI of a brand awareness campaign to a finance-focused audience requires not just technical knowledge but also the ability to tell a persuasive story.

Effective communication involves several key elements, all of which CMOs must master to excel in their roles.

Foundations Of Marketing Leadership

1. **Clarity and Precision:** In a fast-paced business environment, clarity is essential. CMOs must ensure that their messages are easily understood, avoiding jargon or overly complex explanations. This is particularly important when communicating with non-marketing stakeholders, who may not be familiar with technical terms or concepts.

2. **Active Listening:** Communication is not just about speaking; it's also about listening. A CMO who actively listens to their team, customers, and peers gains valuable insights that can inform their strategies. For example, listening to customer feedback on social media can reveal pain points or opportunities that might otherwise go unnoticed.

3. **Empathy:** Understanding the emotions and perspectives of others is a critical component of communication. Empathy allows CMOs to connect with their audience on a deeper level, whether they're addressing employee concerns or crafting a campaign that resonates with customers.

4. **Adaptability:** Different audiences require different communication styles. A presentation to the board might focus on high-level strategy and financial metrics, while a team meeting might involve more detailed discussions about campaign execution. CMOs must adapt their tone, language, and delivery to suit each context.

5. **Storytelling:** At its heart, marketing is about telling stories that captivate and inspire. CMOs must not only excel at crafting brand narratives but also apply storytelling principles to internal communications. For instance, framing a new initiative as part of a larger organisational journey can help rally teams around a common goal.

Despite its importance, effective communication is not without challenges. One of the most common obstacles CMOs face is **information overload**. With so many data points, campaigns, and stakeholders to manage, it can be difficult to distil the most critical information into a concise message. CMOs must prioritise what matters most and resist the temptation to overwhelm their audience with unnecessary details.

Another challenge is **navigating conflicts**. Disagreements are inevitable in any organisation, and CMOs often find themselves in the middle of competing priorities. For example, a product development team might push for an aggressive launch timeline, while the marketing team requires more time to craft a cohesive campaign. In such situations, the CMO's communication skills are put to the test as they work to find a resolution that satisfies all parties.

Developing effective communication skills is an ongoing process, even for seasoned CMOs. Here are some practical steps they can take to enhance their abilities:

- **Seek Feedback**: Regularly soliciting feedback from colleagues, team members, and stakeholders can provide valuable insights into how well a CMO's communication is being received. This might involve conducting surveys, holding one-on-one meetings, or simply asking for candid input.
- **Invest in Training**: Public speaking courses, leadership workshops, and communication coaching can help CMOs refine their skills. These resources offer techniques for

structuring messages, improving delivery, and managing challenging conversations.

- **Practice Active Listening**: Actively engaging with others during conversations by asking questions, paraphrasing their points, and showing genuine interest builds rapport and ensures a deeper understanding of their needs and concerns.
- **Leverage Technology**: Tools like collaborative software, video conferencing platforms, and analytics dashboards can enhance communication by making it easier to share information and gather insights. However, CMOs must use these tools judiciously to avoid creating barriers to personal interaction.

When CMOs communicate effectively, the benefits extend far beyond their immediate team. Clear and transparent communication fosters trust, which is critical for building strong relationships with employees, customers, and other stakeholders. It also enhances collaboration, enabling cross-functional teams to work together seamlessly towards common goals.

Moreover, a CMO who excels at communication can amplify the organisation's brand. Whether delivering a keynote speech at an industry event, participating in media interviews, or engaging with customers on social media, their ability to represent the company with confidence and authenticity strengthens their reputation.

In conclusion, building effective communication skills is not just a necessity for CMOs; it is a fundamental aspect of their role as leaders and brand ambassadors. By mastering clarity, empathy, adaptability, and storytelling, CMOs can inspire their teams, influence stakeholders, and create meaningful connections with their audience. In an increasingly complex and fast-paced world, the ability to communicate effectively is what sets exceptional marketing leaders apart from the rest.

1.7 - The Importance of Emotional Intelligence in Leadership

In the fast-paced and high-stakes world of marketing, technical skills and strategic thinking are critical. However, an often overlooked trait that separates exceptional leaders from the rest is **emotional intelligence (EI)**. For a **Chief Marketing Officer (CMO)**, EI is not just a "nice-to-have" quality; it is a fundamental skill that shapes how they interact with their teams, stakeholders, and customers. This section explores why emotional intelligence is so vital for CMOs, how it manifests in leadership, and how it can be developed and applied in the context of modern marketing.

Emotional intelligence refers to the ability to recognise, understand, and manage one's own emotions while also empathising with the emotions of others. Psychologist Daniel Goleman, a pioneer in the field, identified five key components of EI: **self-awareness**, **self-regulation**, **motivation**, **empathy**, and **social skills**. For CMOs, these components come into play in various aspects of their work, from decision-making and conflict resolution to team building and customer engagement.

Unlike technical expertise or strategic acumen, EI is inherently relational. It influences how leaders perceive and respond to challenges, communicate with their teams, and foster a positive organisational culture. In the context of marketing, where creativity, collaboration, and adaptability are paramount, EI becomes a powerful tool for driving success.

The role of a CMO is inherently people-centric. Whether it's inspiring a creative team, aligning with other executives, or connecting with customers, effective marketing leadership depends on building strong relationships. EI enables CMOs to navigate these relationships with empathy and authenticity, fostering trust and loyalty.

1. **Building Strong Teams**: Marketing teams often comprise individuals with diverse skill sets and personalities, from data analysts to designers. A CMO with high EI can recognise and appreciate these differences, creating an environment where everyone feels valued and motivated. For example, if a team member is struggling with burnout, an emotionally intelligent leader will address the issue with sensitivity, offering support and solutions that prioritise the individual's well-being.

2. **Managing Conflict**: In a dynamic and high-pressure field like marketing, conflicts are inevitable. Whether it's a disagreement over creative direction or tension between marketing and sales teams, conflicts can derail progress if not handled effectively. A CMO with strong EI can mediate such situations by understanding the emotions and

perspectives of all parties involved. This not only resolves the immediate issue but also strengthens relationships in the long term.

3. **Enhancing Customer Engagement**: Marketing is ultimately about understanding and addressing customer needs. Emotional intelligence helps CMOs connect with their audience on a deeper level, crafting campaigns that resonate emotionally. For example, a brand that demonstrates genuine empathy during a crisis, such as offering flexible policies or charitable support during a global event, can build lasting goodwill with its customers.

4. **Navigating Change and Uncertainty**: The marketing landscape is constantly evolving, with new technologies, trends, and challenges emerging at a rapid pace. Change can be unsettling for teams, leading to resistance or anxiety. A CMO with high EI can guide their team through such transitions with confidence and compassion, addressing concerns while maintaining focus on the bigger picture.

Emotional intelligence is not an abstract concept; it has tangible applications in the daily work of a CMO. Here are a few examples of how EI can be leveraged to enhance marketing leadership:

- **Leading with Empathy**: Imagine a scenario where a campaign underperforms, leading to disappointment among the team. A leader with high EI will acknowledge the team's feelings, provide constructive feedback, and focus on learning from the experience rather than assigning blame. This approach fosters resilience and encourages continuous improvement.

- **Influencing Stakeholders**: CMOs often need to secure buy-in from other executives or investors for their initiatives. By understanding the priorities and concerns of these stakeholders, an emotionally intelligent CMO can tailor their communication to address specific needs, increasing the likelihood of approval.

- **Fostering Creativity**: Creativity thrives in an environment where individuals feel safe to take risks and express their ideas. A CMO who demonstrates emotional intelligence will encourage open dialogue, celebrate diverse perspectives, and create a culture where innovation is rewarded.

- **Responding to Crisis**: During a public relations crisis, emotions run high both within the organisation and among its audience. A CMO with strong EI can remain calm under pressure, making thoughtful decisions while addressing the concerns of employees, customers, and the media.

While some individuals may have a natural aptitude for emotional intelligence, it is a skill that can be cultivated through deliberate practice. For CMOs looking to enhance their EI, the following steps can be helpful:

1. **Practice Self-Awareness**: Regularly reflect on your emotions, triggers, and behavioural patterns. Consider keeping a journal or seeking feedback from trusted colleagues to gain deeper insights into your strengths and areas for improvement.

2. **Enhance Empathy**: Make a conscious effort to listen actively and understand the perspectives of others. This might involve asking open-ended questions, observing

non-verbal cues, or putting yourself in someone else's shoes during a disagreement.

3. **Improve Self-Regulation**: Learn to manage your emotions, especially in high-pressure situations. Techniques like mindfulness, meditation, or breathing exercises can help you stay composed and focused.

4. **Develop Social Skills**: Building strong relationships requires effective communication, collaboration, and conflict resolution skills. Invest time in developing these abilities through training, mentorship, or real-world practice.

5. **Stay Motivated**: Cultivate a sense of purpose and passion for your work. Leaders with high intrinsic motivation are not only more resilient but also more inspiring to their teams.

In conclusion, emotional intelligence is a critical yet often underappreciated aspect of marketing leadership. For CMOs, it enables them to build strong teams, connect with customers, and navigate the complexities of a constantly evolving industry. By cultivating self-awareness, empathy, and social skills, CMOs can lead with authenticity and impact, creating a lasting legacy for their organisations. In an increasingly competitive and human-centric marketplace, emotional intelligence is not just a differentiator; it is a necessity.

1.8 - Overview of Marketing Channels and Platforms

Marketing channels and platforms are the vehicles through which a company communicates its messages to its target audience. For a **Chief Marketing Officer (CMO)**, understanding these channels and platforms and how to use them effectively is fundamental to crafting strategies that resonate with customers and achieve organisational goals. The modern marketing landscape is diverse, dynamic, and constantly evolving, presenting both opportunities and challenges for marketing leaders. This section explores the various types of marketing channels, their unique roles, and the considerations CMOs must keep in mind when leveraging them.

Marketing channels can broadly be divided into two categories: **traditional channels** and **digital channels**. Each has its own strengths, weaknesses, and contexts in which it excels.

1. **Traditional Channels** Traditional marketing channels include print media (newspapers, magazines), broadcast media (television, radio), outdoor advertising (billboards, posters), and direct mail. These channels have been the cornerstone of marketing for decades, offering mass reach and credibility.

For instance, a television ad during a major sporting event can reach millions of viewers simultaneously, making it an effective tool for building brand awareness. Similarly, a well-designed billboard in a high-traffic area can create lasting impressions. However, traditional channels often come with higher costs and less precise targeting compared to digital alternatives.

2. **Digital Channels**: Digital channels, including social media, search engines, email, and websites, have revolutionised marketing by enabling targeted, measurable, and cost-effective communication. **For example:**

- **Social Media Platforms**: Channels like Facebook, Instagram, LinkedIn, and TikTok allow brands to engage directly with their audiences through content, conversations, and advertisements. Social media's interactive nature makes it ideal for building relationships and fostering brand loyalty.
- **Search Engine Marketing (SEM)**: Platforms like Google Ads enable businesses to target users actively searching for specific products or services. SEM campaigns are highly measurable and offer an excellent return on investment (ROI) when executed correctly.
- **Email Marketing**: Despite being one of the oldest digital channels, email remains one of the most effective. Personalised, well-timed emails can drive conversions, nurture leads, and strengthen customer relationships.
- **Websites and Blogs**: A company's website is often its digital storefront, serving as a central hub for information, transactions, and customer engagement. Blogs, on the other hand, are powerful tools for establishing thought leadership and driving organic traffic through search engine optimisation (SEO).

The marketing landscape is constantly evolving, and new channels continue to emerge. For CMOs, staying ahead of these trends is crucial for maintaining a competitive edge. Some of the most promising emerging platforms include:

- **Podcasts**: With their growing popularity, podcasts offer a unique way to engage audiences through storytelling and in-depth discussions. Sponsorships and branded content on popular podcasts can enhance brand awareness and credibility.

- **Augmented Reality (AR) and Virtual Reality (VR)**: Technologies like AR and VR provide immersive experiences that can captivate audiences. For example, a furniture retailer might use AR to allow customers to visualise products in their homes before making a purchase.

- **Voice Search and Smart Devices**: With the rise of voice assistants like Alexa and Google Assistant, optimising content for voice search is becoming increasingly important. Voice-activated ads and skills are also emerging as potential marketing tools.

One of the key challenges for CMOs is ensuring that all marketing channels work together cohesively. This is where the concept of **integrated marketing communications (IMC)** comes into play. IMC involves creating a unified message across all channels, ensuring consistency in branding and maximising the impact of marketing efforts.

For example, a product launch might involve a combination of traditional and digital channels: a TV commercial to build awareness, social media ads to drive engagement, email campaigns to nurture leads, and an SEO-optimised landing page for conversions. By integrating these efforts, the CMO ensures that every touchpoint reinforces the same message, creating a seamless customer experience.

Selecting the right marketing channels requires a thorough understanding of the target audience, campaign objectives, and available resources. Here are some key considerations for CMOs:

1. **Audience Preferences**: Different demographics favour different channels. For instance, younger audiences might engage more with TikTok and Instagram, while older professionals may prefer LinkedIn or traditional print media.

2. **Budget Constraints**: Each channel comes with its own cost structure. While digital channels often offer more affordable options with measurable results, traditional channels can be expensive but impactful for mass reach.

3. **Campaign Goals**: The choice of channels depends on whether the goal is to build awareness, generate leads, drive conversions, or nurture customer relationships. For example, social media is excellent for engagement, while email is more effective for lead nurturing.

4. **Measurement and Analytics**: Channels that provide robust analytics capabilities allow CMOs to track performance and optimise campaigns in real-time. This is particularly important in digital marketing, where data-driven decisions are key to success.

While the abundance of marketing channels offers flexibility, it also presents challenges. One major issue is the risk of **fragmentation**, where messages become inconsistent or disconnected across platforms. Another challenge is the increasing complexity of managing campaigns across multiple channels, each with its own metrics, tools, and audience behaviours.

Additionally, the rapid pace of technological advancements can make it difficult for CMOs to keep up with new platforms and trends. Staying informed and agile is critical to ensuring the organisation remains competitive in this dynamic environment.

As technology continues to evolve, so too will the opportunities for marketing. Artificial intelligence (AI) and machine learning are expected to play an increasingly prominent role in optimising channel performance, personalising customer experiences, and predicting future trends. Meanwhile, the rise of decentralised platforms and blockchain technology could reshape how brands interact with consumers.

In conclusion, understanding and leveraging marketing channels and platforms is a core responsibility of any CMO. By mastering the strengths and limitations of traditional and digital channels, exploring emerging platforms, and adopting an integrated approach, CMOs can create impactful campaigns that drive business success. In an increasingly complex landscape, the ability to navigate these channels effectively is not just a skill; it is a strategic advantage.

For a **Chief Marketing Officer (CMO)**, understanding and measuring success is critical, especially during the early stages of a marketing strategy or campaign. Metrics are more than just numbers, they tell a story about how well marketing efforts are resonating with the target audience, achieving organisational goals, and delivering a return on investment (ROI). In this section, we will explore the essential metrics that CMOs should focus on when evaluating the initial success of their initiatives.

Metrics are the foundation of data-driven decision-making, enabling CMOs to assess what's working, identify areas for improvement, and make informed adjustments in real-time. While creativity and intuition are important in marketing, relying solely on them without quantifiable measures can lead to wasted resources and missed opportunities. Metrics provide an objective way to evaluate performance and justify marketing investments to stakeholders.

However, not all metrics are created equal. Focusing on the wrong ones, commonly referred to as "vanity metrics", can lead to misleading conclusions. For instance, high website traffic might look impressive, but without corresponding conversions or engagement, it offers little value. Therefore, CMOs must prioritise metrics that align with their strategic goals and provide actionable insights.

1.9 - Key Metrics for Early Success

The following metrics are essential for measuring the early impact of marketing efforts. Each provides a unique perspective on performance, allowing CMOs to gain a holistic understanding of their campaigns.

1. **Customer Acquisition Cost (CAC)**: CAC measures the cost of acquiring a new customer, including expenses related to advertising, sales efforts, and promotions. This metric is particularly important in the early stages of a campaign when the focus is on attracting new customers. A lower CAC indicates greater efficiency in converting leads into paying customers.

For example, if a company spends £10,000 on a digital advertising campaign that generates 500 new customers, the CAC is £20 per customer. CMOs can use this data to compare the effectiveness of different campaigns or channels, identifying which provides the best value for money.

2. **Conversion Rate**: The conversion rate tracks the percentage of users who take a desired action, such as signing up for a newsletter, making a purchase, or downloading a resource. It is a direct indicator of how effectively marketing efforts are driving engagement and achieving specific objectives.

For instance, if a landing page receives 1,000 visitors and 100 of them complete a sign-up form, the conversion rate is 10%. By analysing this metric, CMOs can optimise elements like call-to-action (CTA) design, messaging, and user experience to improve results.

3. **Return on Investment (ROI)**: ROI is a fundamental metric that evaluates the financial impact of marketing efforts. It calculates the revenue generated relative to the costs incurred, offering a clear picture of a campaign's profitability.

The formula for ROI is: **ROI (%) = (Revenue - Cost) ÷ Cost × 100**

For example, if a social media campaign costs £5,000 and generates £15,000 in revenue, the ROI is 200%. High ROI indicates that marketing activities are effectively contributing to the organisation's bottom line.

4. **Customer Lifetime Value (CLV)**: CLV estimates the total revenue a customer will generate over the course of their relationship with the company. Understanding this metric

early on allows CMOs to assess the long-term impact of customer acquisition efforts.

For example, if a subscription-based service acquires a customer for £50 and expects them to stay for two years, spending £300 annually, the CLV is £600. Comparing CLV to CAC provides insights into the profitability of marketing efforts.

5. **Engagement Metrics**: Engagement metrics, such as click-through rates (CTR), social media likes, shares, and comments, indicate how well content resonates with the target audience. While these metrics may not directly correlate to revenue, they are valuable for gauging interest and building relationships during the early stages of a campaign.

For example, a high CTR on a paid search ad suggests that the messaging and targeting are effective, prompting further investment in similar strategies.

6. **Lead Generation Metrics**: For campaigns aimed at generating leads, metrics like the number of leads captured, cost per lead, and lead quality are critical. CMOs must ensure that the leads generated are not only numerous but also relevant and likely to convert into customers.

For instance, a campaign that generates 1,000 leads with a conversion rate of 2% may be less effective than one that generates 500 leads with a conversion rate of 10%.

7. **Website Performance Metrics**: Website performance metrics, such as bounce rate, average session duration, and pages per visit, provide insights into user behaviour and the effectiveness of the site in supporting marketing goals.

For example, a high bounce rate (the percentage of visitors who leave the site after viewing only one page) may indicate issues with page load time, content relevance, or navigation.

8. **Brand Awareness Metrics**: Early in a campaign, building brand awareness is often a priority. Metrics such as social media reach, share of voice, and brand recall surveys can help CMOs assess how well their efforts are increasing visibility and recognition.

   For example, tracking the growth of social media followers or the number of mentions in media coverage provides a snapshot of brand awareness progress.

9. **Email Marketing Metrics**: For email campaigns, open rates, click-through rates, and unsubscribe rates are key indicators of success. High open rates suggest effective subject lines, while high click-through rates indicate engaging content and CTAs.

   For instance, an email campaign with a 25% open rate and a 10% click-through rate demonstrates strong audience interest and relevance.

10. **Sales Metrics**: Ultimately, the success of many marketing campaigns is measured by their impact on sales. Metrics such as revenue growth, average order value (AOV), and sales velocity provide a direct link between marketing efforts and business outcomes.

    For example, tracking the correlation between a promotional campaign and a spike in sales can highlight the effectiveness of the marketing strategy.

While metrics are essential for evaluating success, they come with challenges. One common issue is **attribution**, determining which touchpoints in a multi-channel campaign deserve credit for conversions. For example, should a sale be attributed to a social media ad that initiated interest, an email that nurtured the lead, or a retargeting ad that sealed the deal? CMOs must use advanced attribution models to overcome this complexity.

Another challenge is ensuring that metrics are aligned with strategic goals. It's easy to get distracted by vanity metrics, such as the number of social media followers, that may not directly contribute to business objectives.

In conclusion, key metrics for early success provide CMOs with a roadmap for evaluating and optimising their marketing efforts. By focusing on meaningful, actionable data, such as CAC, ROI, and engagement rates, CMOs can demonstrate the value of their initiatives, refine their strategies, and build a foundation for long-term success. In an increasingly data-driven world, mastering these metrics is not just a skill; it's a necessity for effective marketing leadership.

1.10 - Case Study: Transitioning to a Marketing Leadership Role

Becoming a **Chief Marketing Officer (CMO)** is a significant career milestone, representing the pinnacle of marketing leadership. However, transitioning into this role comes with unique challenges and opportunities. This case study examines the journey of a fictional character, Sarah, as she navigates her first year as a CMO, highlighting the hurdles she faced, the strategies she employed, and the lessons she learned along the way.

Background

Sarah was a seasoned marketing professional with over 15 years of experience in various roles, including brand management, digital marketing, and customer analytics. Before her promotion, she served as the Head of Digital Strategy at a mid-sized technology company, where she led a team responsible for driving a 40% increase in online sales over two years. Her innovative approach and proven track record earned her the opportunity to step into the CMO role at a larger, fast-growing retail organisation.

Despite her expertise, Sarah recognised that the CMO position required a significant shift in mindset and responsibilities. No longer was she just executing campaigns or managing a team; she now had to oversee the entire marketing function, align it with organisational goals, and influence the company's strategic direction. The following highlights the key challenges Sarah faced and how she addressed them.

Challenge 1: Building Credibility as a New Leader

As a new CMO, Sarah knew she needed to earn the trust and respect of her team, peers, and the executive board. She faced initial resistance from some team members who were sceptical of her ability to lead a retail-focused organisation, given her technology background. Additionally, some senior executives were more familiar with traditional marketing approaches and questioned her data-driven and digital-first mindset.

Strategy: To build credibility, Sarah prioritised active listening and relationship-building during her first 90 days. She conducted one-on-one meetings with her team members to understand their strengths, challenges, and aspirations. By demonstrating genuine interest in their perspectives, she began to foster trust and collaboration.

At the executive level, Sarah presented a clear, data-backed vision for the marketing function, outlining how her approach aligned with the company's growth objectives. She used examples from her previous successes to illustrate her ability to deliver results, bridging the gap between her past experience and the retail industry's unique demands.

Lesson Learned: Establishing credibility requires a combination of humility, transparency, and confidence. By listening first and acting strategically, new leaders can overcome scepticism and build trust.

Challenge 2: Aligning Marketing with Organisational Goals

One of Sarah's first tasks as CMO was to create a marketing strategy that aligned with the company's ambitious goal of doubling revenue within three years. However, she quickly realised that the existing marketing team operated in silos, with minimal collaboration between branding, digital, and in-store marketing efforts. This fragmentation hindered the company's ability to present a cohesive brand message.

Strategy: Sarah introduced the concept of **integrated marketing communications (IMC)** to the organisation, emphasising the importance of a unified approach. She facilitated cross-departmental workshops to encourage collaboration, break down silos, and align teams around common objectives.

To ensure alignment with broader organisational goals, Sarah worked closely with the Chief Financial Officer (CFO) to secure buy-in for a revamped budget allocation. She proposed reallocating funds from low-impact campaigns to high-growth initiatives, such as targeted digital advertising and personalised customer experiences. By presenting a detailed ROI forecast, she convinced the executive team of the value of her approach.

Lesson Learned: Effective CMOs must act as integrators, ensuring that marketing efforts are aligned internally and externally. Collaboration and alignment are essential for achieving strategic goals.

Challenge 3: Navigating a Changing Market

Midway through Sarah's first year, the retail industry faced a significant disruption: a competitor launched a price-slashing campaign, capturing market share and creating downward pressure on profit margins. This development forced Sarah to rethink her strategy in real-time.

Strategy: Rather than engaging in a price war, Sarah focused on differentiating the brand through **customer experience (CX)**. She launched a loyalty programme that rewarded repeat purchases and personalised the shopping journey using data analytics. For example, customers received tailored recommendations and exclusive discounts based on their purchase history.

Additionally, Sarah ramped up storytelling efforts, creating emotionally resonant campaigns that highlighted the brand's commitment to sustainability and community impact. These initiatives not only reinforced the company's value proposition but also deepened customer loyalty.

Lesson Learned: CMOs must remain agile, adapting strategies to market conditions without compromising long-term brand equity.

Challenge 4: Managing Team Morale and Burnout

As the marketing team adapted to Sarah's new vision and the external pressures of a competitive market, morale began to dip. The ambitious goals and rapid pace of change led to signs of burnout among team members.

Strategy: Recognising the importance of emotional intelligence, Sarah prioritised the well-being of her team. She implemented flexible work arrangements, provided additional training resources, and celebrated small wins to maintain motivation. Quarterly off-site retreats allowed the team to recharge, brainstorm new ideas, and strengthen their sense of camaraderie.

Lesson Learned: A successful CMO must not only drive performance but also nurture their team. Investing in employee well-being pays dividends in productivity and creativity.

Challenge 5: Demonstrating Results to Stakeholders

By the end of her first year, Sarah faced the challenge of proving the effectiveness of her strategies to the board. The company's leadership team wanted tangible evidence that her initiatives were contributing to revenue growth and brand value.

Strategy: Sarah prepared a comprehensive report that combined quantitative metrics (e.g., increased online sales, higher conversion rates, improved customer retention) with qualitative insights (e.g., customer testimonials and brand sentiment analysis). She also highlighted key milestones, such as the successful launch of the loyalty programme and the measurable impact of her sustainability campaigns.

By framing her report as a narrative of progress rather than just a collection of numbers, Sarah demonstrated her ability to think strategically and execute effectively.

Lesson Learned: CMOs must communicate their impact in a way that resonates with stakeholders, balancing data with storytelling to make a compelling case.

Conclusion

Sarah's journey highlights the complexities of transitioning into a CMO role. From building credibility and aligning marketing with business goals to navigating market challenges and managing team morale, her experience underscores the multifaceted nature of marketing leadership. By leveraging emotional intelligence, fostering collaboration, and maintaining a focus on measurable outcomes, Sarah not only established herself as a capable leader but also set the stage for long-term success.

Chapter 2

Crafting a Marketing Strategy

> *"A marketing strategy without clear objectives is like setting sail without a destination; motion without progress."*
> **Robert N. Jacobs**

In the dynamic world of marketing, a well-crafted strategy is more than a roadmap; it is the engine driving business success. For Chief Marketing Officers (CMOs), crafting a marketing strategy involves striking a delicate balance between creativity and data-driven precision, ensuring that every campaign aligns with organisational goals while resonating deeply with target audiences.

This chapter delves into the essential components of strategic planning, from understanding market dynamics to setting measurable objectives and building a compelling messaging framework. By exploring these foundational elements, CMOs can transform abstract visions into actionable plans, navigating challenges and seizing opportunities in an ever-evolving marketplace.

2.1 - The Anatomy of a Great Marketing Plan

A **marketing plan** is the cornerstone of a successful strategy, acting as both a blueprint and a guide for the marketing team. It outlines objectives, allocates resources, and establishes a framework for measuring success. For a **Chief Marketing Officer (CMO)**, creating a marketing plan is a balancing act between creativity and structure, ensuring the team's efforts align with broader organisational goals while remaining flexible enough to adapt to market shifts.

A well-crafted marketing plan is not just a collection of ideas; it is a document with purpose and clarity. At its core, the plan serves as a unifying document that ensures every member of the marketing team, as well as other stakeholders, understands the direction and intent of campaigns. Without it, marketing efforts can become fragmented, inefficient, and misaligned with the company's strategic priorities.

The foundation of any great marketing plan starts with an **executive summary**. This section offers a concise overview of the plan, highlighting key objectives, strategies, and anticipated outcomes. While brief, it is one of the most critical components, particularly for presenting to senior leadership or external stakeholders who need a snapshot of the plan without delving into the minutiae. This section serves as a persuasive tool, demonstrating that the marketing team has a clear and structured approach to achieving results. Next comes the **market analysis**, which provides a comprehensive overview of the current landscape. A strong market analysis should cover the industry's key trends, competitive dynamics, and customer insights. For example, if the plan focuses on launching a new product, understanding how competitors have positioned similar products can inform the brand's differentiation strategy. This analysis also identifies potential challenges, such as emerging competitors or regulatory changes, enabling the team to prepare accordingly.

Defining the **target audience** is another essential component of the plan. Here, the marketing team segments the audience based on demographics, psychographics, and behaviours, ensuring that campaigns are tailored to resonate with specific groups. For instance, a luxury brand targeting high-net-worth individuals would need a very different messaging approach than one aimed at environmentally conscious millennials. Understanding these nuances allows the team to craft more relevant and impactful campaigns.

At the heart of the plan lies the **strategy and tactics** section, where the team outlines how objectives will be achieved. Strategies define the overarching approach, such as increasing brand awareness or driving lead generation, while tactics break this down into actionable steps. For example, a strategy to increase brand awareness might include tactics like leveraging influencer partnerships, creating high-quality video content, and running targeted social media ads. This section also identifies the channels and platforms most appropriate for reaching the target audience, ensuring consistency across all touchpoints.

A robust marketing plan also includes a detailed **budget**. This section outlines how resources will be allocated across various campaigns and activities, prioritising initiatives with the greatest potential ROI. Transparency in budgeting is crucial for gaining buy-in from stakeholders, particularly in organisations where marketing expenditure is heavily scrutinised.

Finally, the plan must incorporate a system for **measuring success**. Defining key performance indicators (KPIs) ensures that progress can be tracked and adjustments made when necessary. Metrics such as conversion rates, customer acquisition costs, and website traffic are commonly used to evaluate the effectiveness of campaigns. Regular performance reviews not only help the team stay on track but also provide valuable insights for future planning.

A great marketing plan is not static. It evolves in response to market dynamics, customer feedback, and campaign performance. For CMOs, the ability to create and adapt this plan is a testament to their strategic thinking and leadership. By ensuring the plan is both detailed and actionable, the CMO provides the team with a clear roadmap to success, fostering collaboration and accountability at every step.

2.2 - Conducting Market Research and Analysis

Market research and analysis are fundamental to crafting a marketing strategy that is both informed and impactful. For a **Chief Marketing Officer (CMO)**, this process is not simply about collecting data but understanding its implications to drive decisions that resonate with the audience and achieve organisational objectives. By delving deeply into market trends, customer behaviours, and competitive dynamics, CMOs can create strategies that are grounded in reality and designed for success.

At its essence, market research is about uncovering the needs, preferences, and behaviours of your target audience. This insight is the foundation of every marketing decision, from defining a product's value proposition to selecting the most effective communication channels. Without it, strategies are built on assumptions, risking misalignment with customer expectations and market opportunities.

To begin, **primary research** plays a crucial role in gathering fresh, first-hand insights. This can take many forms, including surveys, focus groups, interviews, and observational studies. For example, an e-commerce brand might conduct focus groups to explore how customers perceive its website's user experience, while surveys could gather quantitative data on purchasing habits. Primary research provides the brand with unique and actionable insights that are directly relevant to its goals.

On the other hand, **secondary research** involves analysing existing data from external sources such as industry reports, competitor case studies, and government statistics. This type of research is particularly valuable for understanding broader market trends and benchmarking performance against competitors. For instance, a start-up entering the renewable energy sector could use industry reports to identify growth areas and potential barriers, allowing it to position itself strategically.

However, collecting data is only part of the equation; the real value lies in the analysis. This is where the **SWOT framework**, Strengths, Weaknesses, Opportunities, and Threats become invaluable. By using SWOT, CMOs can assess their market position comprehensively:

- **Strengths**: Identify internal advantages, such as strong brand equity or proprietary technology.

- **Weaknesses**: Highlight areas that require improvement, such as limited customer awareness or outdated digital tools.

- **Opportunities**: Recognise external factors, such as emerging customer segments or new market trends, that could be leveraged.

- **Threats**: Understand potential risks, such as increasing competition or economic instability.

For example, a tech company conducting a SWOT analysis might identify its innovative product features as a strength while recognising a lack of customer trust as a weakness. The rise in remote work could present an opportunity, while the threat of larger competitors copying features demands proactive counter-strategies.

In addition to SWOT, **segmentation analysis** is critical for identifying and categorising target audiences. Segmenting customers based on demographics, psychographics, or behaviours allows for more tailored and effective marketing efforts. For instance, a fitness brand might segment its audience into younger consumers seeking aesthetic benefits and older individuals prioritising health and mobility. By understanding these distinct groups, the brand can create messaging that speaks directly to each segment's motivations.

Technology has revolutionised market research, providing CMOs with tools to analyse data at scale and in real-time. Platforms such as Google Analytics, SEMrush, and CRM systems enable organisations to track customer behaviour, assess campaign performance, and uncover trends that would otherwise remain hidden. For example, analysing website traffic data might reveal that most visitors come from mobile devices, prompting the brand to prioritise mobile-friendly design in its next campaign.

Yet, market research is not without its challenges. One common issue is **data overload**, having too much information and not enough clarity. CMOs must focus on identifying the data points that are most relevant to their objectives, avoiding distractions from less impactful metrics. Another challenge is ensuring data accuracy and timeliness. Outdated or poorly sourced data can lead to flawed decisions, so CMOs must prioritise data quality and continuous updates.

Moreover, research is not a one-time activity but an ongoing process. Consumer behaviours, market conditions, and competitive landscapes evolve, often rapidly. CMOs must commit to continuous monitoring and adaptation, using tools like sentiment analysis or real-time social media tracking to stay informed.

In conclusion, conducting market research and analysis is a vital skill for any CMO. It enables them to understand the intricacies of their market, identify opportunities, and make informed decisions that drive results. By combining primary and secondary research, leveraging advanced tools, and applying analytical frameworks, CMOs can ensure their strategies are not only creative but also grounded in evidence. In a world where data drives decisions, mastering the art of market research is essential for staying ahead of the curve.

2.3 - Understanding Target Audiences and Segmentation

At the heart of every successful marketing strategy is a profound understanding of the **target audience**. For a **Chief Marketing Officer (CMO)**, knowing the audience goes beyond surface-level demographics; it requires a deep dive into behaviours, needs, aspirations, and motivations. Equally important is the art of **segmentation**, which involves dividing the audience into distinct groups to tailor messaging, offers, and strategies effectively. Understanding target audiences and segmentation is not just a tactical requirement; it is a strategic imperative for creating meaningful connections and driving measurable results.

Understanding the target audience is the cornerstone of relevance; in a world where consumers are inundated with information, brands that fail to address specific needs or preferences risk being ignored. By truly knowing the audience, CMOs can ensure that every aspect of their marketing, from product development to messaging, resonates on a personal level.

For example, consider a skincare brand launching a new line of anti-ageing products. Without understanding its audience, the brand might create generic campaigns that fail to capture attention. However, if the brand identifies that its primary audience comprises women aged 35–50 who value natural ingredients and sustainability, it can craft campaigns that highlight these attributes, leading to stronger engagement and loyalty.

Segmentation is the process of dividing a broad audience into smaller, more manageable groups based on shared characteristics. This allows CMOs to create targeted strategies that address the unique needs of each segment. The most effective segmentation approaches are based on a combination of the following:

1. **Demographic Segmentation**: This is the most basic form of segmentation, focusing on attributes such as age, gender, income, education, and occupation. For example, a luxury car brand may target high-income individuals aged 35–55, tailoring its campaigns to highlight exclusivity and performance.

2. **Psychographic Segmentation**: Psychographic segmentation goes beyond demographics to explore consumers' values, lifestyles, and personalities. For instance, an eco-friendly clothing brand might target environmentally conscious individuals who prioritise sustainable living, crafting messaging around ethical production practices and carbon neutrality.

3. **Behavioural Segmentation**: This approach groups consumers based on their interactions with the brand or product, such as purchase history, loyalty, or usage patterns. For example, a streaming service might segment its audience into heavy users who binge-watch series and light users who prefer films, offering personalised recommendations for each group.

4. **Geographic Segmentation**: Geographic segmentation considers the physical location of the audience, which can influence preferences and behaviours. For example, a beverage company might promote iced drinks in warmer climates and hot beverages in colder regions.

Steps to Understanding and Segmenting Audiences

1. **Gather Data**: The first step in understanding your audience is collecting data. This can be done through surveys, interviews, focus groups, and digital analytics. For example, a beauty brand might survey customers to understand their skincare routines and preferences.

2. **Identify Patterns**: Analyse the data to uncover trends and similarities among customers. For instance, a fitness app might find that its users fall into two primary segments: young professionals looking for quick workouts and older individuals seeking low-impact exercises.

3. **Create Personas**: Build detailed customer personas that represent each segment. These personas should include demographic details, goals, pain points, and behaviours. For example, a travel agency might create a persona like "Adventure-Seeking Anna," a 30-year-old who values unique experiences and spontaneity.

4. **Tailor Messaging**: Develop targeted messaging for each segment based on their unique needs and preferences. For example, a tech company launching a new laptop might emphasise speed and functionality for professionals while highlighting portability and style for students.

5. **Monitor and Refine**: Segmentation is not a one-time process. Consumer behaviours and market dynamics

evolve, so CMOs must regularly review and adjust their segmentation strategy. For example, a retail brand might notice shifts in purchasing behaviour during economic downturns, prompting a focus on value-oriented segments.

Despite its importance, segmentation comes with challenges. Over-segmentation can lead to fragmented efforts and inefficiency, while under-segmentation risks generic campaigns that fail to resonate. Additionally, ensuring data accuracy and timeliness is a constant challenge, as outdated insights can lead to misaligned strategies.

Another common pitfall is neglecting the emotional aspect of consumer decision-making. While data provides a wealth of information, it is equally important to understand the intangible factors that influence behaviour, such as trust, loyalty, and cultural values.

Understanding target audiences and segmentation has real-world applications across industries; for example:

- **E-Commerce**: Online retailers use behavioural data to personalise product recommendations, increasing conversion rates.
- **Healthcare**: Pharmaceutical companies tailor campaigns to specific patient demographics, ensuring that messaging is both relevant and compliant.
- **Automotive**: Car manufacturers target different segments with distinct models, such as electric vehicles for eco-conscious drivers and SUVs for families.

Understanding target audiences and segmentation is a fundamental skill for CMOs, enabling them to create marketing strategies that are both precise and impactful. By leveraging data, building detailed personas, and tailoring messaging, CMOs can ensure their campaigns resonate with the right people at the right time. In an increasingly competitive landscape, the brands that succeed will be those that prioritise understanding over assumption, creating deeper connections with their audiences and driving long-term loyalty.

2.4 - Setting Goals: SMART Objectives and KPIs

The ability to set clear, actionable goals is one of the most critical skills for a **Chief Marketing Officer (CMO)**. Goals provide direction, structure, and a way to measure the success of marketing initiatives. Without them, marketing teams risk wasting resources on activities that fail to contribute to the broader objectives of the organisation. By using the **SMART framework**, ensuring that goals are **Specific, Measurable, Achievable, Relevant, and Time-bound**, CMOs can craft objectives that are both realistic and impactful. Paired with well-defined **Key Performance Indicators (KPIs)**, these goals become the cornerstone of a results-driven marketing strategy.

Goals are more than just aspirations; they are the foundation of effective planning and execution. They serve several essential purposes:

- **Clarity**: Goals provide a clear sense of direction, ensuring that all team members understand what needs to be achieved.

- **Focus**: Well-defined goals help prioritise efforts, directing resources toward activities that have the greatest impact.

- **Motivation**: Achievable yet challenging goals inspire teams to perform at their best.

- **Accountability**: Goals establish benchmarks for success, allowing CMOs to track progress and make data-driven adjustments.

For example, a vague goal like "increase sales" offers little guidance. However, a SMART goal such as "increase online sales by 20% within six months through targeted email campaigns and retargeting ads" provides clarity and focus.

Breaking Down the SMART Framework

1. **Specific**: A specific goal clearly defines what needs to be achieved. It answers questions like:
   - What are we trying to accomplish?
   - Why is this important?
   - Who is responsible for achieving it?

Example: Instead of saying, "improve social media engagement," a specific goal would be to "increase Instagram engagement rates by 15% through interactive content, including polls, quizzes, and live Q&A sessions."

2. **Measurable**: Measurability ensures that progress can be tracked and evaluated. Metrics like percentages, numbers, or ratios make goals quantifiable.

Example: "Generate 5,000 new leads through a pay-per-click (PPC) campaign within three months" is a measurable goal, allowing the team to track how many leads are generated weekly.

3. **Achievable:** Goals should be ambitious yet realistic, given the resources and constraints of the organisation. Setting unattainable goals can demotivate teams, while overly simple ones may fail to drive growth.

Example: A start-up might aim to "grow email subscribers by 10% per month" rather than attempting to triple its subscriber base in the same timeframe.

4. **Relevant:** Goals must align with the organisation's broader objectives, ensuring that marketing efforts directly contribute to business success.

Example: For a company focused on expanding into new markets, a relevant goal might be to "increase website traffic from international audiences by 25% over the next quarter."

5. **Time-Bound:** Setting a deadline creates urgency and accountability, motivating teams to stay on track.

Example: "Launch a rebranding campaign by the end of Q3, including a new logo, updated website, and refreshed social media profiles."

Defining Key Performance Indicators (KPIs)

KPIs are the metrics used to measure progress toward achieving goals. For CMOs, selecting the right KPIs is critical for tracking success and identifying areas for improvement. Effective KPIs are specific, actionable, and tied directly to the goal they measure.

Examples of KPIs by Objective:

1. **Brand Awareness:**
   - Social media reach
   - Website traffic growth
   - Number of press mentions

2. **Lead Generation:**
   - Number of new leads
   - Cost per lead (CPL)
   - Lead-to-customer conversion rate

3. **Customer Retention:**
   - Churn rate
   - Repeat purchase rate
   - Net Promoter Score (NPS)

4. **Revenue Growth:**
   - Monthly recurring revenue (MRR)
   - Average order value (AOV)
   - Customer lifetime value (CLV)

For instance, if the goal is to "increase email open rates by 15% within six months," the relevant KPI would be the email open rate. Tracking this metric allows the team to gauge the effectiveness of subject lines, timing, and segmentation.

Challenges in Setting Goals and KPIs

Despite the simplicity of the SMART framework, setting goals and KPIs comes with challenges. One common pitfall is focusing on **vanity metrics**, data points that look impressive but offer little insight into real performance. For example, while a high number of social media followers may seem positive, it does not necessarily correlate with engagement or conversions.

Another challenge is ensuring that goals remain flexible enough to adapt to changing circumstances. For example, during economic downturns, a company's focus might shift from growth to cost optimisation, requiring a recalibration of marketing objectives.

Lastly, maintaining alignment between short-term and long-term goals is often tricky. While short-term goals deliver immediate results, long-term goals, such as brand building or market penetration, ensure sustained success. Balancing the two requires a nuanced approach.

In practice, SMART objectives and KPIs can transform marketing strategies:

- A subscription box service aiming to boost customer retention might set a SMART goal to "reduce churn by 5% within six months through enhanced loyalty programs and personalised emails." KPIs would include churn rate and customer satisfaction scores.
- A tech start-up launching a new app might set a SMART goal to "achieve 10,000 downloads in the first three months, with a 30% conversion rate from free to premium

users." Relevant KPIs would include download numbers and conversion rates.

Setting goals using the SMART framework and defining relevant KPIs are essential components of an effective marketing strategy. For CMOs, these tools provide a clear roadmap for success, ensuring that every campaign and initiative contributes to the organisation's objectives. By combining specificity, measurability, and alignment, CMOs can inspire their teams, track progress, and deliver tangible results. In an increasingly competitive and data-driven environment, mastering the art of goal-setting is a skill that distinguishes exceptional marketing leaders from the rest.

2.5 - Positioning and Messaging Frameworks

Effective **positioning and messaging frameworks** are the backbone of any successful marketing strategy. These tools define how a brand communicates its value and resonates with its target audience. For a **Chief Marketing Officer (CMO)**, mastering the art of positioning and messaging is not only about crafting compelling narratives but also about ensuring these narratives are consistent, relevant, and aligned with the company's goals. This section explores the importance of positioning, the key elements of a messaging framework, and how CMOs can create and implement these critical tools to establish a competitive advantage.

Positioning is the process of creating a unique and memorable identity for a brand in the minds of its target audience. It answers a simple yet powerful question: *Why should someone choose this* *brand over its competitors?* Effective positioning ensures that the brand stands out while addressing the specific needs and preferences of its audience.

Strong positioning is built on three core principles:

1. **Relevance**: The brand must address a genuine need or desire within the target audience.
2. **Differentiation**: The brand must offer something unique that competitors cannot easily replicate.
3. **Clarity**: The brand's value proposition must be simple and easy to understand.

For example, consider a boutique coffee company entering a market dominated by global chains. Instead of competing on price or convenience, the company might position itself as the purveyor of ethically sourced, artisan-crafted blends. This positioning appeals to socially conscious consumers seeking premium experiences, setting the brand apart from mass-market alternatives.

While positioning defines *what* a brand stands for, the **messaging framework** determines *how* that story is told. A messaging framework provides a structured approach to crafting consistent and impactful communications across all channels, ensuring that every interaction reinforces the brand's identity.

Key elements of a messaging framework include:
- **Core Message**: The overarching statement that encapsulates the brand's essence. For example, Patagonia's

core message, "We're in business to save our home planet," clearly communicates its commitment to environmental sustainability.

- **Supporting Messages**: Secondary messages that elaborate on the core message, tailored to different audience segments or product categories. For instance, a financial services firm might highlight affordability for millennials while emphasising reliability for older customers.

- **Proof Points**: Evidence that validates the brand's claims, such as testimonials, case studies, or data. A skincare brand might showcase clinical trial results or customer reviews to back its promise of effectiveness.

- **Tone and Voice**: Guidelines for how the brand communicates, including its style, tone, and vocabulary. A playful tone might work for a children's toy brand, while a professional and authoritative voice is more appropriate for a law firm.

Creating an effective positioning and messaging framework is a multi-step process that requires deep insights into the market, the audience, and the brand itself.

1. **Conduct Market Research**: Understanding the competitive landscape is critical. CMOs must identify what competitors are offering, how they position themselves, and where gaps exist. For instance, if most competitors in a tech market emphasise speed and innovation, a brand might differentiate itself by focusing on user-friendliness and customer support.

2. **Define the Target Audience**: Detailed audience segmentation is essential for crafting relevant messages.

By understanding the demographics, psychographics, and behaviours of their audience, CMOs can ensure that messaging aligns with customer needs and preferences. For example, a luxury travel agency might tailor its messaging to affluent retirees seeking unique, once-in-a-lifetime experiences.

3. **Develop the Value Proposition**: The value proposition is the foundation of positioning, articulating what the brand offers, who it serves, and why it matters. A strong value proposition is concise, specific, and focused on benefits rather than features. For example, a meal kit delivery service might position itself as "helping busy families enjoy healthy, home-cooked meals without the hassle."

4. **Craft the Messaging Hierarchy**: The messaging hierarchy organises the brand's communication, starting with the core message and branching into supporting messages, proof points, and calls to action. This structure ensures consistency while allowing flexibility for different campaigns and channels.

5. **Test and Refine**: Positioning and messaging are not static. CMOs should test their frameworks with real audiences, gathering feedback to refine and optimise the approach. A/B testing, focus groups, and surveys are valuable tools for evaluating how messages resonate.

Positioning and messaging frameworks can encounter several challenges:

- **Overcrowded Markets**: In competitive industries, finding a unique angle can be difficult. CMOs must focus on niche opportunities or untapped audience segments.

- **Internal Misalignment**: Ensuring that all departments understand and adhere to the messaging framework is crucial. Misalignment can dilute the brand's identity and confuse customers.
- **Evolving Consumer Preferences**: As customer behaviours and expectations change, CMOs must continuously revisit and update their frameworks to stay relevant.

Positioning and messaging frameworks have broad applications:

- **Product Launches**: A clear framework ensures that new products are introduced with consistent, compelling messaging.
- **Rebranding Efforts**: During rebrands, the framework helps communicate changes while preserving the brand's core identity.
- **Crisis Communication**: In challenging times, a strong framework ensures that the brand responds authentically and consistently.

For example, during the COVID-19 pandemic, many brands adjusted their messaging to focus on empathy, safety, and community support, reinforcing their relevance in uncertain times.

In conclusion, positioning and messaging frameworks are indispensable tools for CMOs, enabling them to differentiate their brands, connect with audiences, and drive strategic success. By crafting clear, compelling narratives and ensuring consistency across all touchpoints, CMOs can build stronger relationships with customers and establish a competitive edge. In an increasingly crowded marketplace, mastering these frameworks is not just an advantage; it is a necessity for sustained growth and relevance.

2.6 - Budget Allocation and Resource Planning

For any **Chief Marketing Officer (CMO)**, the effective allocation of budgets and resources is not just a matter of financial management; it is a strategic exercise that determines the success of marketing initiatives. Marketing departments often operate with finite budgets, making it critical to ensure that every pound spent delivers maximum value. Similarly, resource planning involves optimising the use of human talent, technology, and time to execute campaigns effectively. Together, budget allocation and resource planning form the backbone of a results-driven marketing strategy.

Budget allocation is more than just dividing up funds; it is about aligning financial resources with the organisation's strategic priorities. A well-structured budget ensures that the marketing team can achieve its objectives without overspending or compromising quality. However, this requires a careful balance of several factors, including short-term goals, long-term investments, and contingencies for unforeseen challenges.

To begin, CMOs must align the marketing budget with the company's overarching goals. For example, if the organisation aims to expand into new markets, a significant portion of the budget might be allocated to market research, localisation efforts, and awareness campaigns. Conversely, a company focused on retaining existing customers may invest more heavily in loyalty programs and personalised communication.

A successful budget allocation also involves prioritising high-impact channels and initiatives. This requires a clear understanding of the target audience and how they interact with different platforms. For instance, a fashion brand targeting Gen Z consumers might prioritise social media platforms like Instagram and TikTok, while a B2B software company might allocate more funds to LinkedIn advertising and industry webinars.

Steps in Budget Allocation

1. **Define Objectives:** Start by identifying the primary objectives of the marketing strategy. Whether the goal is to increase brand awareness, generate leads, or drive conversions, the budget should be tailored to support these aims.

2. **Analyse Past Performance**: Review the performance of previous campaigns to identify which channels and tactics delivered the best ROI. For example, if email marketing consistently generates high conversion rates, it might warrant a larger share of the budget.

3. **Allocate Funds Across Channels**: Divide the budget among different channels based on their potential impact. This might include digital advertising, content creation, events, influencer marketing, and traditional media.

4. **Reserve Funds for Testing and Innovation**: Allocate a portion of the budget to experimenting with new platforms

or strategies. This allows the team to stay ahead of trends and discover untapped opportunities.

5. **Plan for Contingencies**: Set aside a contingency fund, typically 5–10% of the total budget, to address unexpected needs, such as responding to a crisis or capitalising on emerging trends.

While budget allocation focuses on financial resources, **resource planning** ensures the optimal use of personnel, technology, and time. Effective resource planning is essential for executing campaigns on time, maintaining quality, and avoiding burnout among team members.

1. **Human Resources:** Marketing teams are made up of diverse roles, from creative professionals and data analysts to project managers and strategists. CMOs must assess the skills and capacity of their team to ensure they can handle current and future workloads. If gaps exist, outsourcing or hiring specialised talent may be necessary.

For example, a company planning a video-heavy campaign might collaborate with a production agency to handle the workload efficiently. Alternatively, investing in upskilling employees through training programs can enhance in-house capabilities.

2. **Technology Resources:** Modern marketing relies heavily on technology, from analytics platforms to automation tools. CMOs must allocate resources to acquire and maintain the tools that will drive efficiency and insights. For instance:
   - **Customer Relationship Management (CRM)** software enables effective lead tracking and nurturing.

- **Analytics Platforms like Google Analytics** provide valuable insights into campaign performance.

- **Marketing Automation Tools** streamline repetitive tasks, such as email scheduling and social media posting.

3. **Time Management:** Time is a finite resource that requires careful planning. CMOs must ensure that campaigns are launched on schedule and that team members have sufficient time to deliver high-quality work. Project management tools, such as Asana or Trello, can help track tasks, deadlines, and dependencies, ensuring smooth execution.

Budget allocation and resource planning are not without challenges:

1. **Limited Budgets**: CMOs often face pressure to achieve ambitious goals with constrained budgets. This requires prioritising initiatives with the highest potential ROI and being creative in stretching resources.

2. **Competing Priorities**: Balancing long-term investments, such as brand-building campaigns, with immediate revenue-driving activities can be difficult.

3. **Market Uncertainty**: Economic fluctuations, competitive pressures, and emerging trends can disrupt plans, requiring frequent adjustments.

4. **Team Overload**: Without proper planning, teams can become overwhelmed, leading to reduced productivity and burnout.

Strategies to Overcome Challenges

1. **Adopt a Data-Driven Approach**: Use analytics to guide decision-making, ensuring that budgets are allocated based on measurable impact rather than intuition.
2. **Collaborate Across Departments**: Work closely with finance, sales, and product teams to align resources and objectives, creating a unified approach.
3. **Leverage Partnerships**: Collaborate with agencies, freelancers, or technology providers to access specialised skills and tools without overburdening internal teams.
4. **Monitor and Adjust Regularly**: Continuously track performance and adjust budgets and resource plans as needed. For instance, reallocating funds from underperforming campaigns to successful ones can maximise ROI.

In conclusion, budget allocation and resource planning are pivotal responsibilities for CMOs, directly influencing the success of marketing strategies. By aligning budgets with organisational goals, prioritising high-impact initiatives, and optimising the use of human and technological resources, CMOs can deliver results while maintaining efficiency. In an era of increasing competition and economic uncertainty, the ability to manage budgets and resources effectively is not just a skill but a strategic advantage. Through careful planning and adaptability, CMOs can ensure that every investment contributes meaningfully to the organisation's success.

2.7 - Competitive Analysis: Tools and Techniques

In today's highly competitive and fast-evolving business landscape, understanding what competitors are doing is not just advantageous, it is essential. **Competitive analysis** equips a **Chief Marketing Officer (CMO)** with the insights needed to make informed strategic decisions, differentiate the brand, and seize opportunities before competitors do. This process goes far beyond observing rivals; it involves systematically gathering, analysing, and applying information to craft strategies that drive growth and innovation.

Competitive analysis provides a clear picture of where a brand stands relative to its competitors. It identifies strengths to leverage, weaknesses to address, and market gaps to exploit. For CMOs, it offers several critical benefits:

1. **Informed Decision-Making**: By understanding competitor strategies, CMOs can make data-driven choices about pricing, product development, and marketing.

2. **Strategic Differentiation**: Competitive analysis reveals how to position the brand uniquely, ensuring that it stands out in a crowded market.

3. **Proactive Adaptation**: Monitoring competitors allows CMOs to anticipate changes in the market and adjust strategies accordingly.

For example, a fintech company analysing a competitor's customer reviews might identify dissatisfaction with customer support, creating an opportunity to position itself as the most customer-centric brand in the industry.

Steps in Conducting Competitive Analysis

1. **Identify Competitors:** Begin by categorising competitors into three types:

- **Direct Competitors**: Brands offering similar products or services to the same audience (e.g., Nike vs. Adidas).

- **Indirect Competitors**: Brands addressing the same customer need but with different solutions (e.g., a fitness app vs. a personal trainer).

- **Emerging Competitors**: New players or substitutes that could disrupt the market.

For example, an energy drink company might identify direct competitors like Red Bull, indirect competitors like coffee brands, and emerging competitors in the form of wellness beverages.

2. **Gather Data**: Collect information on competitors' strategies, operations, and performance. Key areas to investigate include:

    - **Products and Services:** Features, pricing, and innovation.

    - **Marketing and Branding:** Campaigns, messaging, and tone of voice.

    - **Customer Experience:** Online reviews, testimonials, and social media engagement.

    - **Financial Performance:** Revenue, market share, and growth trends.

This data can be collected through:

- **Public Sources**: Websites, social media, press releases, and financial reports.

- **Customer Feedback**: Insights from customers who have used competitors' products.

- **Third-Party Tools**: Analytics platforms and market research reports.

3. **Analyse Strengths and Weaknesses**: Use a SWOT framework (Strengths, Weaknesses, Opportunities, Threats) to evaluate competitors:

   - **Strengths**: What do they do well? For instance, strong brand recognition or advanced technology.

   - **Weaknesses**: Where do they fall short? Examples include poor customer service or limited product variety.

   - **Opportunities**: What gaps exist in their offering that your brand can exploit?

   - **Threats**: What risks do their strategies pose to your market share?

4. **Evaluate Market Positioning**: Assess how competitors position themselves in the market. Are they focusing on affordability, premium quality, or innovation? This analysis helps identify ways to differentiate your brand.

5. **Track Competitor Activity Over Time**: Competitive analysis is not a one-time activity. CMOs must monitor competitors continuously to stay informed about changes in their strategies, such as new product launches, rebranding efforts, or expansions into new markets.

Tools for Competitive Analysis

Several tools can streamline and enhance competitive analysis, providing actionable insights quickly and efficiently:

1. **SEMrush** is a comprehensive platform for analysing competitors' online presence. It provides insights into keywords, search engine rankings, and paid ad performance, making it invaluable for digital marketing strategies.

2. **BuzzSumo** tracks competitors' content performance, highlighting the topics, formats, and channels driving the most engagement. For instance, a brand can discover which blog posts or social media campaigns resonate most with audiences.

3. **SimilarWeb** offers detailed data on website traffic, audience demographics, and referral sources. This tool is particularly useful for benchmarking your online performance against competitors.

4. **Social Media Analytics Tools:** Platforms like Hootsuite and Sprout Social enable CMOs to monitor competitors' social media activity, including post frequency, audience engagement, and sentiment analysis.

5. **Owler** provides business intelligence, such as competitors' funding rounds, partnerships, and market expansions, giving CMOs a strategic edge.

Despite its importance, competitive analysis comes with challenges:

- **Information Overload**: With so much data available, it can be difficult to focus on what truly matters. CMOs must prioritise insights that directly impact strategic goals.

- **Dynamic Markets**: Competitors' strategies evolve rapidly, requiring constant monitoring and adaptability.

- **Avoiding Imitation**: While it is important to learn from competitors, blindly copying their strategies can dilute your brand's uniqueness.

To overcome these challenges:

- **Define Clear Objectives**: Focus the analysis on specific questions, such as "What pricing strategy will give us a competitive edge?" or "Which audience segments are underserved?"
- **Balance Competitive and Internal Focus**: Use competitive insights to complement, not overshadow, your brand's own strengths and vision.

Competitive analysis drives decisions across various aspects of marketing:

- **Product Development**: A tech start-up identifying gaps in competitors' offerings might introduce features that address unmet customer needs.
- **Pricing Strategies**: An e-commerce company might adjust its pricing based on competitor benchmarks to remain competitive without eroding profitability.
- **Campaign Optimisation**: A fashion brand monitoring competitors' social media campaigns could identify trends, such as the rising popularity of user-generated content, and incorporate them into its strategy.

In conclusion, competitive analysis is an indispensable tool for CMOs, providing the insights needed to navigate complex markets and build winning strategies. By leveraging effective tools, systematically gathering data, and focusing on actionable insights, CMOs can ensure their brand remains relevant, differentiated, and ahead of the competition. In a world where change is constant, the ability to analyse and respond to competitors' moves is not just a skill but a necessity for sustained success.

2.8 - Aligning Marketing with Organisational Goals

For any business to succeed, it is critical that its marketing efforts are not only effective but also fully aligned with the organisation's overarching goals. For a **Chief Marketing Officer (CMO)**, this alignment ensures that every campaign, initiative, and budget allocation contributes meaningfully to the broader objectives of the company. Misalignment, on the other hand, can lead to wasted resources, fragmented strategies, and missed opportunities. Aligning marketing with organisational goals is a dynamic, ongoing process that requires strategic foresight, collaboration, and adaptability.

Marketing does not exist in isolation; it is a vital function that supports the business's ambitions. When marketing is aligned with organisational goals:

- **Focus is Enhanced**: Teams work on initiatives that directly impact the company's success.
- **Efficiency Increases**: Resources are allocated where they deliver the most value.
- **Accountability is Strengthened**: Results can be measured against specific business objectives.
- **Collaboration is Improved**: Marketing becomes an integrated partner across departments, ensuring cohesion and unity.

Crafting a Marketing Strategy

For instance, if an organisation aims to expand into new geographic markets, the marketing team's role may include creating awareness in those regions, developing culturally relevant campaigns, and supporting localised sales efforts.

Steps to Align Marketing with Organisational Goals

1. **Understand the Organisation's Strategic Objectives:** The first step for any CMO is to gain a deep understanding of the company's long-term vision and immediate priorities. These might include revenue growth, market expansion, brand recognition, or customer retention. Once these objectives are clear, marketing strategies can be designed to support them.

2. For example, a SaaS company with a goal to increase annual recurring revenue (ARR) by 25% would require marketing to focus on lead generation, customer acquisition, and upselling initiatives.

3. **Collaborate Across Departments:** Alignment requires collaboration with other key functions such as sales, finance, product development, and customer service. Each department provides unique insights and plays a role in achieving organisational goals:

   - **Sales**: Collaborating with sales ensures that marketing generates leads that are both high-quality and aligned with the sales team's priorities.

   - **Finance**: Working with finance helps marketing teams align budgets with revenue expectations and demonstrate ROI.

- **Product Development**: Marketing can use insights from customer feedback to inform product improvements or highlight key features in campaigns.

- **Customer Service**: Understanding customer pain points and satisfaction levels allows marketing to create initiatives that enhance loyalty.

For instance, a CMO at an e-commerce company might work closely with sales to refine targeting strategies and with customer service to address common complaints through proactive content.

4. **Develop Marketing Goals that Mirror Organisational Objectives:** Using the **SMART framework**, CMOs can translate organisational objectives into actionable marketing goals. These goals should be specific, measurable, achievable, relevant, and time-bound. Examples include:

    - **Organisational Goal:** Achieve 15% revenue growth.

    - **Marketing Goal:** Generate 20,000 qualified leads in Q1 through targeted digital campaigns and email marketing.

    - **Organisational Goal**: Improve customer retention by 10%.

    - **Marketing Goal**: Increase loyalty program participation by 25% through personalised offers and communication.

5. **Communicate Marketing's Role:** CMOs must articulate how marketing contributes to the organisation's goals, ensuring alignment and buy-in from stakeholders. This includes presenting data that links marketing activities to tangible outcomes, such as increased sales, improved customer satisfaction, or enhanced brand visibility.

For example, a CMO might present a report showing how a recent digital campaign drove a 30% increase in website traffic, leading to a 10% uplift in conversions.

6. **Ensure Consistency in Messaging:** Alignment extends to how the brand communicates its vision, mission, and values. Consistent messaging across all marketing channels reinforces the organisation's identity and resonates with its audience. For example, a company focused on sustainability must reflect this in every touchpoint, from advertising to packaging.

7. **Monitor and Adapt Strategies:** Markets evolve, customer behaviours shift, and business priorities change. Regularly reviewing marketing strategies ensures they remain aligned with organisational goals. If a company's focus shifts from acquisition to retention, marketing should pivot accordingly by prioritising loyalty programs and personalised communication.

Despite its importance, aligning marketing with organisational goals presents several challenges:

1. **Siloed Departments**: Lack of communication and collaboration across departments can lead to conflicting priorities. For instance, sales may prioritise immediate revenue, while marketing focuses on long-term brand building.

2. **Changing Priorities**: Organisational goals may shift due to market conditions, leadership changes, or economic factors, requiring marketing to adapt quickly.

3. **Proving ROI**: Marketing efforts, particularly those focused on brand awareness or customer engagement, may take

time to show measurable results, leading to challenges in demonstrating their value.

Strategies to Overcome Challenges

1. **Foster a Culture of Collaboration:** Regular cross-departmental meetings and shared planning sessions can break down silos and ensure alignment. For example, joint planning between marketing and sales can synchronise lead generation efforts with sales capacity.

2. **Adopt an Agile Approach:** Building flexibility into marketing plans allows teams to pivot quickly in response to changing organisational priorities. For instance, a sudden shift in focus from growth to cost efficiency might prompt marketing to optimise existing campaigns rather than launching new ones.

3. **Leverage Data and Technology:** Tools like customer relationship management (CRM) systems and analytics platforms help track the impact of marketing activities, providing data-driven insights that align with organisational goals.

Consider a telecommunications company aiming to increase customer retention by 20%. The CMO aligned marketing efforts by:

- Launching personalised email campaigns targeting at-risk customers with exclusive offers.
- Enhancing the loyalty program to reward long-term subscribers.
- Collaborating with customer service to address common pain points highlighted in surveys.

As a result, the company not only achieved its retention target but also improved customer satisfaction scores, demonstrating the power of alignment.

In conclusion, aligning marketing with organisational goals is a fundamental responsibility of any CMO. It ensures that every campaign and initiative contributes directly to the company's success, creating a cohesive and focused approach to growth. By fostering collaboration, setting clear objectives, and remaining adaptable, CMOs can bridge the gap between strategy and execution, delivering measurable results that resonate across the organisation. In today's competitive business environment, alignment is not just beneficial; it is essential for sustained success.

2.9 - Real-World Challenges in Strategic Planning

Strategic planning is a cornerstone of effective marketing, providing the roadmap for achieving organisational goals. However, in the real world, the process of crafting and executing a marketing strategy is fraught with challenges. For a **Chief Marketing Officer (CMO)**, these challenges are compounded by constantly evolving markets, diverse stakeholder expectations, and resource constraints. Successfully navigating these obstacles requires a combination of foresight, adaptability, and a deep understanding of the business landscape.

Challenge 1: Rapidly Changing Market Conditions

One of the most significant challenges in strategic planning is dealing with the unpredictability of market conditions. Economic downturns, emerging competitors, technological advancements, and shifts in consumer behaviour can render even the most carefully crafted strategies obsolete.

For instance, during the COVID-19 pandemic, businesses across industries were forced to adapt quickly to changing circumstances. Retailers had to pivot from in-store experiences to online shopping, while travel companies focused on maintaining brand loyalty despite reduced demand. CMOs who could adapt their strategies to these changing conditions, such as leveraging e-commerce or creating virtual experiences, were better positioned to weather the storm.

Solution:

- **Agility**: Build flexibility into marketing plans, allowing for quick adjustments in response to external changes. For example, shorter planning cycles (e.g., quarterly reviews) enable teams to reassess priorities more frequently.

- **Scenario Planning**: Develop contingency plans for potential disruptions, such as economic downturns or supply chain issues, so the organisation is prepared for a range of outcomes.

- **Real-Time Monitoring**: Use analytics tools to track market trends and customer sentiment, enabling proactive decision-making.

Challenge 2: Balancing Short-Term and Long-Term Goals

Marketing strategies often need to balance the pursuit of immediate results with investments in long-term brand building.

This tension can create conflicts, particularly when stakeholders demand quick returns.

For example, a company under pressure to meet quarterly revenue targets may prioritise aggressive sales promotions, which can undermine brand equity if overused. Conversely, focusing solely on long-term goals like brand awareness might neglect the immediate need for cash flow.

Solution:

- **Portfolio Approach**: Allocate resources across a mix of short-term and long-term initiatives. For instance, dedicate a portion of the budget to performance marketing for immediate lead generation, while investing in content marketing to build authority over time.

- **Transparent Communication**: Educate stakeholders about the importance of balancing short-term gains with sustainable growth. Use data to demonstrate how long-term investments contribute to the organisation's overall success.

- **Integrated Metrics**: Track KPIs that reflect both short-term outcomes (e.g., sales conversions) and long-term impact (e.g., customer lifetime value).

Challenge 3: Siloed Departments

In many organisations, strategic planning is hindered by a lack of collaboration between departments. Marketing, sales, product development, and finance often operate in silos, leading to misaligned goals and inefficient resource allocation.

For instance, a marketing team might focus on generating high volumes of leads without consulting the sales team about lead quality. This disconnect can result in wasted effort and strained relationships between departments.

Solution:

- **Cross-Functional Collaboration**: Establish regular meetings and shared planning sessions between departments to ensure alignment on goals and strategies.
- **Unified KPIs**: Develop metrics that reflect the contributions of multiple departments, such as revenue growth or customer acquisition costs, fostering shared accountability.
- **Integrated Tools**: Use collaborative platforms like CRM systems to improve communication and data sharing between teams.

Challenge 4: Limited Resources

Resource constraints, whether financial, technological, or human, are a common challenge in strategic planning. CMOs must often make difficult decisions about where to allocate limited budgets and talent to achieve the greatest impact.

For example, a start-up with a small marketing budget may struggle to compete with larger, more established players. In such cases, prioritising high-ROI activities, like targeted social media ads or influencer partnerships, becomes essential.

Solution:

- **Prioritisation**: Focus on initiatives that deliver the highest ROI. For instance, invest in channels that have consistently driven results in the past, such as email marketing or paid search.
- **Outsourcing and Partnerships**: Collaborate with external agencies or freelancers to access specialised skills without overburdening internal teams.
- **Automation and Technology**: Use tools like marketing automation platforms to streamline workflows and improve efficiency.

Challenge 5: Stakeholder Resistance

Securing buy-in from stakeholders, such as executives, board members, and other department heads, can be a significant hurdle. Resistance often stems from a lack of understanding about the value of marketing or a reluctance to change established practices.

For example, a CMO proposing a shift from traditional advertising to digital channels might face pushback from stakeholders accustomed to older methods. Without buy-in, implementing the strategy becomes an uphill battle.

Solution:

- **Data-Driven Advocacy**: Present clear evidence, such as case studies or performance metrics, to demonstrate the effectiveness of proposed strategies.
- **Early Engagement**: Involve stakeholders in the planning process from the outset, ensuring their perspectives are considered and building a sense of ownership.
- **Pilot Projects**: Start with small-scale initiatives to prove the viability of new approaches before scaling them.

Challenge 6: Keeping Up with Technology

The rapid pace of technological innovation presents both opportunities and challenges for CMOs. Staying ahead of trends like artificial intelligence (AI), augmented reality (AR), and voice search is essential, but integrating these technologies into a strategy requires expertise and resources.

For instance, while AI-driven personalisation can significantly enhance customer experiences, implementing it effectively demands robust data infrastructure and skilled personnel.

Solution:

- **Continuous Learning**: Invest in training programs to upskill the marketing team on emerging technologies.
- **Strategic Partnerships**: Collaborate with technology providers or consultants to implement advanced solutions.
- **Prioritised Adoption**: Focus on technologies that align closely with organisational goals rather than adopting every trend indiscriminately.

In conclusion, strategic planning in marketing is a complex process, made more challenging by rapidly changing markets, resource limitations, and competing priorities. For CMOs, overcoming these real-world challenges requires a combination of adaptability, collaboration, and strategic focus. By addressing issues such as siloed departments, stakeholder resistance, and technological advancements, CMOs can ensure their strategies remain effective and aligned with organisational goals. In the end, it is not the absence of challenges but the ability to navigate them that defines exceptional marketing leadership.

2.10 - Case Study: Building a Winning Strategy from Scratch

Creating a marketing strategy from the ground up is a formidable challenge, particularly for organisations navigating competitive markets or launching new products. For a **Chief Marketing Officer (CMO)**, the task demands strategic thinking, creativity, and a deep understanding of the target audience. This case study illustrates how Sarah, a newly appointed CMO at an emerging sustainable fashion brand, developed a winning marketing strategy that transformed the company's market position and delivered measurable success.

Background

Sarah joined the sustainable fashion brand, "EcoThreads," during a critical growth phase. Despite offering ethically sourced and environmentally friendly products, the company struggled to gain traction in a competitive market dominated by fast-fashion giants and premium sustainable labels. Key challenges included:

- **Minimal Brand Awareness**: EcoThreads lacked visibility in a crowded marketplace.
- **Limited Budget**: The company operated on a lean marketing budget, restricting its ability to compete with larger brands.
- **Diverse Audience Segments**: The target audience ranged from environmentally conscious millennials to fashion-forward Gen Z consumers, requiring tailored messaging.

Crafting a Marketing Strategy

EcoThreads aimed to increase sales by 30% within the first year, establish itself as a trusted sustainable brand, and build a loyal customer base. Sarah's task was to design a marketing strategy to achieve these objectives.

Step 1: Conducting Research

Sarah began by conducting extensive research to understand the market landscape and EcoThreads' target audience. Her approach included:

1. **Competitor Analysis**: She identified key competitors, analysing their positioning, messaging, and pricing strategies. This revealed gaps in the market, such as limited options for mid-range sustainable fashion that combined affordability with style.

2. **Customer Insights**: Using surveys and focus groups, Sarah uncovered two distinct audience segments:

    - **Sustainability Advocates**: Consumers motivated by environmental and ethical concerns.

    - **Style Seekers**: Younger buyers who valued trendy, sustainable clothing but were less focused on ethical production processes.

3. **Industry Trends**: Research highlighted a growing demand for transparency in supply chains and personalisation in shopping experiences, which informed Sarah's strategic decisions.

Step 2: Defining Positioning and Messaging

Crafting a Marketing Strategy

Armed with insights, Sarah crafted a clear and compelling positioning statement for EcoThreads: **"Sustainable fashion that fits your style and your values."**

She developed a messaging framework tailored to the brand's audience:

1. **Core Message**: EcoThreads offers affordable, stylish clothing made with ethical materials and transparent practices.

2. **Supporting Messages**:
   - For Sustainability Advocates: "Every purchase helps reduce waste and support fair labour."
   - For Style Seekers: "Look good while doing good."

3. **Proof Points**: Certifications (e.g., Fair Trade, GOTS-certified fabrics) and transparency reports detailing the supply chain.

Step 3: Allocating Resources Strategically

Given the limited budget, Sarah prioritised high-impact, cost-effective channels:

1. **Social Media Marketing**: She focused on Instagram and TikTok to target style-conscious Gen Z and millennial consumers. Engaging content, such as "behind-the-scenes" videos of the production process, highlighted the brand's transparency and ethical practices.

2. **Influencer Partnerships**: Collaborations with micro-influencers in the sustainable fashion space provided authentic endorsements at a fraction of the cost of celebrity partnerships.

3. **Content Marketing**: Sarah launched a blog featuring articles on sustainable fashion trends, tips for eco-friendly

living, and customer stories, driving organic traffic to the website.

4. **Email Campaigns**: Personalised emails segmented by audience (e.g., product recommendations for Sustainability Advocates vs. trend alerts for Style Seekers) enhanced engagement and conversions.

Sarah allocated 40% of the budget to social media, 30% to influencer collaborations, 20% to content creation, and 10% to email marketing.

Step 4: Setting SMART Objectives and KPIs

Sarah established clear, measurable goals aligned with the company's objectives:

- **Goal 1**: Increase website traffic by 50% within six months.

KPI: Monthly unique visitors.

- **Goal 2**: Achieve a 20% email open rate and a 5% click-through rate.

KPI: Email engagement metrics.

- **Goal 3**: Drive a 15% conversion rate from social media campaigns.

KPI: Purchases originating from social media platforms.

- **Goal 4**: Build a social media following of 50,000 across platforms within a year.

KPI: Number of followers and engagement rates.

Step 5: Executing and Monitoring the Strategy

Sarah implemented the strategy in phases:

1. **Awareness Phase**: Social media campaigns and influencer partnerships created buzz, with hashtags like #EcoThreadsMovement encouraging user-generated content.

2. **Engagement Phase**: Interactive polls, Q&A sessions, and live-streamed events fostered community engagement and reinforced brand values.

3. **Conversion Phase**: Limited-time discounts and referral programs incentivised purchases, while retargeting ads re-engaged users who visited the website but didn't convert.

Using analytics tools, Sarah tracked performance in real-time, identifying what worked and making adjustments. For example, when TikTok videos consistently outperformed Instagram posts, she reallocated resources to prioritise TikTok content.

Results and Impact

Sarah's strategy delivered remarkable results:

- **Website Traffic**: Increased by 60% within six months, exceeding the initial goal.

- **Sales Growth**: Achieved a 35% increase in annual sales, surpassing the company's target.

- **Social Media Growth**: Gained 70,000 followers across platforms, driving higher engagement and brand awareness.

- **Customer Loyalty**: Repeat purchases rose by 25%, driven by personalised email campaigns and loyalty incentives.

EcoThreads not only gained a foothold in the sustainable fashion market but also built a loyal community of customers who became brand advocates, amplifying its message organically.

Lessons Learned

1. **Data-Driven Decisions**: Research and analytics were critical to tailoring the strategy and ensuring every effort was aligned with audience needs.

2. **Resource Prioritisation**: By focusing on high-impact, cost-effective channels, Sarah maximised the budget's effectiveness.

3. **Agility**: Regular monitoring and adjustments allowed the strategy to remain relevant and responsive to audience behaviour.

Conclusion

This case study demonstrates the transformative power of a well-crafted marketing strategy, even in the face of resource constraints and stiff competition. For CMOs, the ability to build a strategy from scratch requires a blend of creativity, strategic thinking, and executional excellence. Sarah's success with EcoThreads highlights the importance of clear positioning, tailored messaging, and data-driven decision-making in achieving impactful results. In today's competitive landscape, the brands that succeed are those that understand their audience, prioritise resources wisely, and stay agile in their approach.

Chapter 3

Mastering Brand Management

> *"Your brand isn't what you say it is; it's what your customers believe it to be, shaped by every experience you deliver."*
> **Robert N. Jacobs**

In an increasingly dynamic and competitive marketplace, a brand is more than just a logo or a tagline; it is the heart and soul of a business, representing its values, vision, and promises to its audience. For Chief Marketing Officers (CMOs), mastering brand management is not just about maintaining consistency or building recognition; it is about creating a powerful narrative that resonates with consumers, fosters loyalty, and drives growth.

This chapter explores the fundamental pillars of brand management, from cultivating brand equity and crafting compelling stories to navigating crises and balancing legacy with innovation. Through practical insights and real-world examples, it provides CMOs with the tools to transform brands into lasting icons of trust and value.

3.1 - What is Brand Equity?

Brand equity refers to the value a brand holds in the minds of its customers and stakeholders. This value is not solely based on tangible assets like products or services but also on intangible elements such as reputation, trust, and emotional connections. A brand with high equity often enjoys greater customer loyalty, the ability to charge premium prices, and resilience during market disruptions. For a **Chief Marketing Officer (CMO)**, understanding and nurturing brand equity is essential for driving growth and securing long-term success.

Brand equity is a dynamic construct encompassing various elements that work together to create overall value. At its core, brand equity includes **awareness**, which ensures the brand is recognised by its target audience. Awareness acts as a foundation because customers can only choose what they know exists. For example, Coca-Cola has leveraged its global recognition to dominate the beverage market for over a century. Beyond awareness, brand equity also includes **associations**, which refer to the thoughts, feelings, and emotions customers connect to a brand. These associations can be positive, such as trust and innovation, or negative, such as unreliability or insincerity.

Another crucial component is **perceived quality**, which shapes customers' expectations and decisions. When a brand is synonymous with high quality, such as Apple in the technology sector, customers are willing to pay a premium for its products. Lastly, **brand loyalty** ties directly to equity. Loyal customers not only drive repeat business but also advocate for the brand, increasing its reach organically.

Building brand equity is a long-term process that requires consistent investment. Companies must ensure that their products deliver on their promises, their messaging aligns with customer expectations, and their actions reflect their stated values. However, managing brand equity is not without challenges. A single misstep, such as a public relations crisis or a failed product launch, can erode years of trust. For instance, brands like Volkswagen faced significant setbacks in equity following revelations about emissions scandals.

The financial implications of brand equity are equally significant. Companies with strong brand equity often command higher market valuations. In fact, intangible assets, including brand equity, account for a substantial portion of many corporations' overall value. Brands like Amazon, Google, and Microsoft exemplify this, as their equity drives customer retention, attracts top talent, and fosters investor confidence.

In conclusion, brand equity is an invaluable asset that transcends the functional aspects of a business. For CMOs, the task of building and maintaining equity involves balancing consistent messaging, delivering exceptional experiences, and staying attuned to market dynamics. In an increasingly competitive and fast-changing environment, brand equity is not just a differentiator, it is a vital driver of sustained success.

3.2 - Building a Strong Brand Identity

A **strong brand identity** is the foundation upon which a company builds trust, loyalty, and differentiation. It is more than a logo or a tagline; it is the combination of visual, verbal, and emotional elements that collectively define how a brand is perceived by its audience. For a **Chief Marketing Officer (CMO)**, creating a brand identity that resonates with customers and aligns with business goals is a complex yet essential task. A well-executed brand identity ensures consistency across touchpoints, fosters an emotional connection with consumers, and serves as a guiding framework for all marketing and operational activities.

At its core, brand identity communicates who the brand is, what it stands for, and why it matters to its audience. This involves a deep understanding of the company's mission, vision, and values, which serve as the philosophical backbone of the brand. For example, **Nike**'s identity revolves around empowering athletes to push their limits, as encapsulated in its iconic tagline, "Just Do It." This identity resonates universally, connecting with both elite athletes and everyday individuals seeking self-improvement.

Building a strong brand identity begins with visual elements that make the brand instantly recognisable. This includes the logo, colour palette, typography, and imagery. These components should not only be aesthetically pleasing but also reflective of the brand's personality and positioning. Take **Coca-Cola**, for instance: its red-and-white colour scheme and distinctive script logo evoke feelings of happiness, tradition, and familiarity, reinforcing its status as a global icon.

However, brand identity extends beyond visuals. The tone of voice and messaging style also play a critical role. Whether a brand adopts a formal, authoritative tone like **Rolex** or a friendly, conversational tone like **Innocent Drinks**, consistency is key. This consistency builds familiarity, ensuring that customers have a seamless experience, whether they interact with the brand via social media, customer service, or packaging.

Emotional resonance is another critical aspect of a strong brand identity. People remember how brands make them feel, and a powerful identity leverages this to forge connections. **Apple**, for example, evokes innovation, simplicity, and aspiration, which has allowed it to cultivate a fiercely loyal customer base. Similarly, brands like **Patagonia** inspire trust and admiration by aligning their identity with their commitment to environmental sustainability.

Challenges in building a strong brand identity often stem from fragmentation or inconsistency, particularly for companies operating in multiple markets. Global brands must strike a balance between maintaining a cohesive identity and adapting to local cultural nuances. For instance, **McDonald's** preserves its global branding elements while tailoring its menu and advertising to regional preferences, such as offering vegetarian options in India.

Maintaining a strong brand identity also requires regular evaluation and evolution. While consistency is crucial, stagnation can make a brand appear out of touch. Periodic refreshes, whether through updated logos, modernised messaging, or new product offerings, ensure that the brand remains relevant without losing its essence. **Burberry**, for example, rejuvenated its identity by blending its British heritage with modern digital-first campaigns, resulting in a resurgence of its luxury status.

In conclusion, building a strong brand identity is both an art and a science. It requires CMOs to harmonise visual design, messaging, and emotional resonance to create a cohesive and compelling presence. A robust identity not only attracts customers but also engenders loyalty, ensuring that the brand stands out in a crowded marketplace. For brands aiming for longevity, a strong identity is not optional; it is indispensable.

3.3 - The Role of Storytelling in Branding

Storytelling is one of the most powerful tools in a CMO's arsenal, transforming brands from faceless entities into relatable, memorable characters. In branding, storytelling is not simply about narrating a company's history; it is about creating an emotional connection with the audience by weaving a narrative that reflects their values, aspirations, and experiences. A well-crafted story elevates a brand from a product provider to a meaningful presence in people's lives, fostering loyalty and advocacy.

At its heart, storytelling in branding serves to humanise a company. People connect with stories more deeply than they do with facts or statistics. A story can communicate a brand's mission and values in a way that resonates emotionally, making it more likely to be remembered. Consider **Airbnb**, which built its brand around the concept of "belonging anywhere." Instead of focusing solely on accommodations, Airbnb tells the stories of its hosts and guests, highlighting unique, personal experiences that inspire connection and trust.

A compelling brand story typically answers three key questions: *Who are we? What do we stand for? Why do we matter?* The answers must be authentic and relevant to the target audience. Authenticity is particularly important in an age where consumers are quick to detect and criticise insincerity. A brand story that is inconsistent with its actions or values can backfire, damaging trust and credibility.

The structure of a good story often mirrors that of a narrative arc, with a beginning, a conflict or challenge, and a resolution. The conflict provides tension, making the story engaging, while the resolution offers hope, satisfaction, or inspiration. For example, **Nike's** storytelling often revolves around athletes overcoming adversity, turning their struggles into triumphs. These narratives not only align with the brand's core message of empowerment but also inspire and motivate audiences.

Technology has expanded the avenues for storytelling, enabling brands to engage with their audience in more interactive and immersive ways. From social media platforms to augmented reality experiences, brands can now tell their stories across multiple formats and channels. For instance, **IKEA** uses augmented reality to let customers visualise how furniture will look in their homes, blending storytelling with practicality.

However, storytelling in branding is not without its challenges. A poorly executed story can come across as contrived or disconnected from the brand's identity. Furthermore, maintaining consistency across channels while adapting to diverse cultural contexts requires careful planning and execution. Brands must also ensure that their storytelling evolves with changing customer expectations and societal norms to remain relevant.

In conclusion, storytelling is a cornerstone of modern branding, enabling brands to connect with their audiences on a deeper level. By crafting authentic, engaging narratives that reflect their identity and values, brands can inspire trust, loyalty, and advocacy. In a marketplace where emotional resonance often drives purchasing decisions, storytelling is not just an asset; it is a necessity for brands seeking to thrive in the long term.

3.4 - Managing Brand Consistency Across Channels

Consistency is the cornerstone of effective brand management. A **brand** is more than a logo or a tagline; it is the cumulative experience a customer has across all touchpoints. Ensuring that this experience remains consistent, regardless of the channel or medium, is critical for building trust, enhancing recognition, and maintaining loyalty. For a **Chief Marketing Officer (CMO)**, managing brand consistency across channels involves creating a seamless and unified representation of the brand that reinforces its identity and values.

A consistent brand experience ensures that customers know what to expect when they interact with the company. Whether it's browsing a website, engaging on social media, visiting a physical store, or contacting customer service, the brand's messaging, tone, and visuals must align. This cohesion strengthens brand equity by fostering familiarity and reliability, making the brand more memorable and trustworthy. For example, **Apple** has mastered brand consistency across its channels, maintaining a sleek, minimalist aesthetic and tone in its advertising, packaging, in-store environments, and digital platforms. This unified approach reinforces the brand's identity as a leader in innovation and design.

Managing brand consistency begins with the establishment of clear **brand guidelines**. These guidelines serve as a blueprint for all communications, detailing specifications for visual elements (logos, colours, typography), tone of voice, and messaging frameworks. For example, **Coca-Cola** ensures that its red and white colour scheme and iconic script logo are consistently applied across everything from billboards to social media posts. Such guidelines eliminate ambiguity and ensure that internal teams, agencies, and external partners represent the brand correctly.

While consistency in visual identity is important, consistency in tone and messaging is equally crucial. The tone of voice should reflect the brand's personality and values, whether it is formal and authoritative, playful and conversational, or something in between. For instance, **Nike** maintains a motivational and empowering tone across all channels, whether it's a social media post celebrating an athlete's achievement or an email promoting its latest product line. This uniformity ensures that every interaction reinforces the brand's core message.

In today's digital-first world, ensuring brand consistency across multiple online platforms presents unique challenges. Social media, websites, email marketing, and paid advertising each require distinct strategies, but the underlying brand identity must remain consistent. A humorous tone that works on Twitter may not translate to a corporate website, but the messaging should still align with the brand's overall personality and values. Tools like **content management systems** and **social media scheduling platforms** can help ensure that messaging remains on-brand while adapting to the nuances of each channel.

Challenges in maintaining brand consistency often arise in global markets, where cultural differences and language barriers must be addressed. Brands must balance the need for localisation with the imperative to maintain a unified identity. For example, **McDonald's** adapts its menu and advertising to local tastes while preserving its global branding elements, such as the golden arches and the "I'm Lovin' It" tagline. This approach allows the brand to resonate with diverse audiences while retaining its universal appeal.

Another challenge is ensuring alignment across internal teams and external partners. Discrepancies can arise when departments work in silos or when third-party agencies fail to adhere to brand guidelines. Regular training, clear communication, and collaboration are essential to prevent inconsistencies. Designating a **brand steward** or team responsible for overseeing brand representation can also help maintain alignment across channels.

Measuring the impact of brand consistency is critical for continuous improvement. Tools like sentiment analysis, customer surveys, and brand audits provide insights into how the brand is perceived and whether inconsistencies exist. For example, tracking customer feedback on social media can reveal whether the brand's tone aligns with customer expectations, while a brand audit can identify discrepancies in visual identity across marketing materials.

The benefits of managing brand consistency are significant. A consistent brand experience builds trust, as customers feel confident that their expectations will be met. It enhances recognition, making the brand more memorable and increasing its impact in a crowded marketplace. Consistency also improves customer loyalty, as a cohesive experience reinforces emotional connections with the brand. For example, **Starbucks** has cultivated a loyal customer base by delivering a consistent experience across its stores, mobile app, and loyalty program, all of which reflect its focus on quality, community, and personalisation.

In conclusion, managing brand consistency across channels is an essential aspect of brand management. By maintaining a unified identity in visuals, tone, and messaging, CMOs can ensure that every customer interaction reinforces the brand's values and strengthens its equity. While challenges exist, particularly in global markets or diverse digital platforms, strategic planning, clear guidelines, and continuous monitoring can help overcome these obstacles. In a world where customers engage with brands across multiple touchpoints, consistency is not just a competitive advantage; it is a necessity for building trust, loyalty, and long-term success.

3.5 - Brand Crisis Management

No matter how carefully a brand is managed, crises are inevitable. Whether it is a product recall, a public relations mishap, or a data breach, the way a brand responds in a crisis can make or break its reputation. For a **Chief Marketing Officer (CMO)**, **brand crisis management** is not just about damage control; it is about demonstrating leadership, transparency, and a commitment to the brand's values. Handled well, a crisis can even strengthen customer loyalty and trust. Handled poorly, it can result in long-term damage to the brand's equity and credibility.

A brand crisis typically arises from one of several common scenarios: product defects, corporate misconduct, social media missteps, or ethical violations. For instance, in 2018, **Facebook** faced a major crisis when the Cambridge Analytica scandal revealed that user data had been improperly accessed for political purposes. The company's delayed response and perceived lack of transparency initially exacerbated the backlash, highlighting the importance of swift and decisive action during a crisis.

The first step in effective crisis management is **preparation**. Brands must anticipate potential risks and create a comprehensive crisis management plan that includes defined roles and responsibilities, communication protocols, and a decision-making framework. For example, assigning a crisis response team comprising representatives from marketing, public relations, legal, and executive leadership ensures a coordinated response. Additionally, conducting scenario planning can help brands rehearse their responses to various crises, ensuring that teams are prepared when real challenges arise.

When a crisis occurs, the **speed of response** is critical. The longer a brand remains silent, the greater the likelihood of speculation and misinformation spreading. A prompt initial statement acknowledging the issue and expressing concern can help manage public perception. For example, when a crisis breaks on social media, responding within hours, even if only to say that the issue is being investigated, can demonstrate that the brand is proactive and attentive.

Transparency is another cornerstone of effective crisis management. Customers value honesty, and any attempt to obscure or downplay the situation can erode trust. A successful response involves acknowledging mistakes, taking responsibility, and outlining clear steps to resolve the issue. For instance, during the 2018 romaine lettuce E. coli outbreak, brands that transparently communicated recalls and safety measures were better able to retain customer trust than those that offered vague responses.

Empathy is equally important. Brands must show that they understand the impact of the crisis on their customers and are committed to making things right. This might include issuing refunds, offering support, or providing solutions that address customer concerns. For example, when a cybersecurity breach affects customer data, offering free credit monitoring services demonstrates accountability and concern for affected individuals.

Effective communication during a crisis also involves tailoring messages to different stakeholders. While customers need reassurance, employees, investors, and regulators may require detailed updates. Using appropriate channels for each audience, such as press releases for the public, internal emails for staff, and direct meetings with investors, ensures that the right message reaches the right people.

Monitoring public sentiment throughout the crisis is essential for guiding the brand's response. Social media listening tools, customer feedback platforms, and sentiment analysis can provide real-time insights into how the public perceives the brand's actions. These insights allow CMOs to adjust messaging and address emerging concerns. For example, if a public apology is met with criticism for lacking sincerity, a follow-up statement with greater depth and specific commitments may be necessary.

Once the immediate crisis has been addressed, brands must focus on **rebuilding trust**. This involves not only resolving the issue but also taking steps to prevent similar incidents in the future. Communicating these preventive measures to stakeholders demonstrates a commitment to improvement. For example, after the Volkswagen emissions scandal, the company invested heavily in electric vehicle development and marketing, aiming to reposition itself as a leader in sustainability.

However, crises are not without their challenges. One common difficulty is the tension between responding quickly and ensuring accuracy. An incomplete or inaccurate statement can lead to further backlash, but prolonged silence can appear negligent. Similarly, managing misinformation in the age of social media can be overwhelming, as false narratives can spread rapidly and damage a brand's reputation.

Despite these challenges, a well-managed crisis can ultimately strengthen a brand's standing. For instance, in 1982, **Tylenol** faced a devastating crisis when cyanide-laced capsules caused several deaths. The company's swift and transparent response, pulling all products from shelves, cooperating with authorities, and introducing tamper-proof packaging, set a new standard for crisis management and restored customer trust.

In conclusion, brand crisis management is an essential skill for CMOs. By preparing in advance, responding swiftly and transparently, and prioritising empathy and accountability, brands can navigate crises effectively and emerge stronger. In a world where reputations are fragile, the ability to manage crises with integrity and precision is not just an advantage; it is a necessity for sustaining trust, loyalty, and long-term success.

3.6 - Measuring Brand Health: Tools and Techniques

For any organisation, understanding the state of its **brand health** is critical for long-term success. **Brand health** refers to how well a brand performs in terms of awareness, reputation, loyalty, and overall impact in the marketplace. It is not just a reflection of financial performance but also a measure of how customers perceive, engage with, and trust the brand. For a **Chief Marketing Officer (CMO)**, regularly evaluating brand health ensures that the brand remains relevant, competitive, and aligned with customer expectations. Measuring brand health involves a combination of quantitative metrics, qualitative insights, and strategic tools to create a comprehensive view.

Brand health is multifaceted, encompassing several dimensions. **Brand awareness** is one of the foundational components; it gauges how familiar customers are with the brand and its offerings. Awareness can be further divided into aided and unaided awareness. Aided awareness refers to customers recognising the brand when prompted, while unaided awareness measures whether the brand comes to mind without any cues. For example, when customers think of smartphones, brands like Apple and Samsung often dominate unaided awareness due to their market leadership and consistent visibility.

Another key dimension is **brand perception**, which captures how customers feel about the brand and the associations they make with it. Perception goes beyond functionality; it includes attributes like trustworthiness, quality, and innovation. Sentiment analysis tools, surveys, and social media listening platforms provide valuable insights into brand perception, allowing CMOs to identify areas of strength and opportunities for improvement. For instance, a luxury brand like Louis Vuitton may measure perception by assessing how customers view its exclusivity and craftsmanship.

Customer loyalty is another critical indicator of brand health. Loyal customers not only drive repeat business but also act as advocates, promoting the brand to others. Metrics like the **Net Promoter Score (NPS)** are commonly used to assess loyalty.

NPS measures how likely customers are to recommend the brand to others, categorising them as promoters, passives, or detractors. A high NPS indicates strong loyalty and advocacy, while a low score signals areas that require attention.

Engagement metrics are increasingly vital in the digital age. These metrics measure how actively customers interact with the brand across various channels, such as social media, websites, and email campaigns. High engagement often signals that the brand is resonating with its audience. Tools like Google Analytics, Hootsuite, and CRM platforms provide detailed insights into metrics like website traffic, click-through rates, and social media interactions. For example, a brand launching a new product might track how many users click on promotional emails or engage with related social media posts.

Another crucial aspect of brand health is **market share**, which indicates how well the brand performs relative to competitors. A growing market share often reflects strong brand equity and customer preference. This metric is particularly important in competitive industries, where even small gains can translate into significant financial impact.

Brand equity, a broader concept, measures the overall value that the brand adds to its products or services. This value can be quantified through metrics like price premium (how much more customers are willing to pay for the brand compared to competitors), financial valuation models, and customer surveys. For instance, a brand like Tesla enjoys high brand equity because customers associate it with innovation, sustainability, and cutting-edge technology, allowing it to command premium pricing.

While quantitative metrics are invaluable, qualitative insights provide context and depth. Customer interviews, focus groups, and open-ended survey questions reveal the emotions, motivations, and experiences that drive customer behaviour. These insights help brands understand why customers feel the way they do, offering guidance for strategic adjustments.

To measure brand health effectively, CMOs must leverage a mix of tools and techniques. Surveys and NPS are widely used for gathering direct feedback, while social media listening tools like Brandwatch and Sprout Social monitor online conversations to gauge sentiment and trends. Analytics platforms like Google Analytics track engagement metrics, while CRM systems like Salesforce provide insights into customer loyalty and lifetime value.

Despite its importance, measuring brand health comes with challenges. One common issue is **data fragmentation**, where insights are scattered across multiple platforms and teams. Consolidating data into a centralised dashboard helps create a unified view of brand performance. Another challenge is ensuring that metrics align with business goals. For instance, tracking social media likes may not be meaningful if the brand's primary objective is to increase sales.

Additionally, **external factors** such as economic conditions, competitive pressures, and cultural shifts can influence brand health, making it difficult to isolate the impact of specific initiatives. Regular monitoring and benchmarking against competitors can help brands adapt to these changes.

The benefits of measuring brand health are significant. A strong understanding of brand performance allows CMOs to identify risks and opportunities, optimise campaigns, and make data-driven decisions. It also ensures that the brand remains aligned with customer expectations, fostering loyalty and driving growth. For example, a technology company noticing a decline in brand perception might launch a campaign to highlight its commitment to innovation, addressing concerns and strengthening its position.

In conclusion, measuring brand health is an essential practice for CMOs aiming to build and sustain successful brands. By tracking awareness, perception, loyalty, and engagement and using the right tools to analyse these dimensions, brands can ensure they remain competitive and relevant. In a rapidly changing marketplace, brand health is not just a metric; it is a reflection of how well a brand connects with its audience and adapts to its evolving needs.

3.7 - Balancing Legacy and Innovation in Branding

For a brand to remain relevant in an ever-evolving marketplace, it must strike a delicate balance between preserving its **legacy** and embracing **innovation**. Legacy represents a brand's history, values, and achievements, attributes that establish trust and loyalty among customers. Innovation, on the other hand, ensures the brand adapts to changing consumer preferences, market dynamics, and technological advancements. For a **Chief Marketing Officer (CMO)**, achieving this balance is both an art and a science, requiring strategic vision and precise execution.

Legacy is a cornerstone of many established brands. It reflects the trust built over years, sometimes decades, of consistent performance. Legacy-based branding evokes nostalgia and loyalty, particularly among long-time customers who value stability and tradition. For example, **Harley-Davidson** leverages its legacy of freedom and rebellion to maintain a loyal customer base. Its heritage, deeply rooted in motorcycle culture, is a significant driver of its appeal. Similarly, luxury brands like **Rolex** and **Hermès** use their long histories and craftsmanship to justify their exclusivity and premium pricing.

However, relying solely on legacy can lead to stagnation. Brands that resist innovation risk becoming irrelevant, particularly in industries where disruption is constant. For instance, the retail landscape has been transformed by e-commerce, requiring even legacy brands to rethink their strategies. While department stores like **Sears** struggled to adapt and ultimately declined, **Macy's** embraced digital channels and omnichannel strategies to stay competitive.

Innovation is the lifeblood of a brand's future. It enables companies to meet evolving customer needs, differentiate themselves from competitors, and explore new markets. For example, **Tesla**, though a relatively young brand, has established itself as an innovator in electric vehicles and sustainable energy solutions. Its ability to disrupt traditional automotive norms has positioned it as a leader in its industry.

That said, over-innovation can alienate a brand's core audience. If changes stray too far from the brand's identity, loyal customers may feel disconnected. For instance, when **Gap** abruptly changed its logo in 2010, it faced immediate backlash from customers who felt the new design lacked a connection to the brand's heritage. The company quickly reverted to its original logo, highlighting the risks of disregarding legacy.

The key to balancing legacy and innovation lies in understanding what defines the brand's identity. Legacy elements, such as core values, iconic products, and recognisable aesthetics, should serve as a foundation for innovation rather than a constraint. For example, **Burberry**, a British luxury fashion house, successfully modernised its image by integrating digital campaigns and targeting younger audiences. At the same time, it preserved its core identity, exemplified by its iconic trench coat and British heritage.

A successful approach to balancing legacy and innovation also involves listening to customers. By understanding their evolving preferences, brands can make informed decisions about which elements of their legacy to emphasise and where to innovate. For example, **Levi's**, a brand steeped in denim history, reintroduced its vintage styles to capitalise on the growing trend for retro fashion while simultaneously embracing sustainability by using eco-friendly materials.

Technology plays a pivotal role in bridging the gap between legacy and innovation. Digital transformation allows brands to modernise customer experiences without compromising their heritage. For instance, **Lego**, a company with over 90 years of history, embraced technology by introducing augmented reality (AR) apps and robotics kits. These innovations complemented its traditional building blocks, attracting new generations of customers while retaining its legacy.

Challenges in balancing legacy and innovation are inevitable. Internal resistance is common, as stakeholders may fear that innovation will dilute the brand's heritage. Conversely, rapid innovation can disrupt organisational structures and processes. To address these challenges, CMOs must foster a culture of adaptability within the organisation, emphasising the value of both legacy and forward-thinking initiatives.

Additionally, global brands face the challenge of maintaining consistency while appealing to diverse markets. What resonates as a legacy in one region may not hold the same significance in another. For example, **Coca-Cola** tailors its messaging and product offerings to local tastes but ensures its core identity, happiness and refreshment, remains intact.

One strategy for managing this balance is incremental innovation, where changes are introduced gradually rather than all at once. This approach allows brands to test new ideas without overwhelming their audience. For instance, **Nike** regularly updates its iconic sneakers with new materials and designs, ensuring the product remains relevant while retaining its core identity.

Another effective strategy is leveraging storytelling to connect legacy and innovation. A compelling narrative can highlight how the brand's history informs its future direction. For example, **Ford** leveraged the legacy of its Mustang brand while introducing the all-electric Mustang Mach-E, blending tradition with sustainability and technology.

In conclusion, balancing legacy and innovation is a critical aspect of brand management that requires careful consideration and strategic execution. For CMOs, the challenge lies in preserving what makes the brand unique while embracing change to meet the demands of modern consumers. By honouring their heritage and using it as a springboard for innovation, brands can remain relevant, resilient, and admired. In an era where both tradition and transformation are valued, the ability to balance these forces is not just a competitive advantage; it is essential for long-term success.

3.8 - Creating Brand Advocates: Customer Loyalty Programs

In a competitive marketplace where acquiring new customers is far more expensive than retaining existing ones, cultivating customer loyalty is critical for long-term success. But loyalty is not just about repeat purchases; it is about transforming satisfied customers into enthusiastic **brand advocates** who actively promote the brand to others. For a **Chief Marketing Officer (CMO)**, a well-designed **customer loyalty program** is one of the most powerful tools for fostering advocacy, driving engagement, and strengthening emotional connections between customers and the brand.

At its core, a loyalty program rewards customers for their continued engagement with the brand. However, a successful program goes beyond transactional incentives, creating an ecosystem where customers feel valued, connected, and motivated to share their positive experiences. Brand advocates play a pivotal role in this ecosystem, as their genuine enthusiasm enhances credibility and expands the brand's reach through word-of-mouth, social media, and personal recommendations.

To design an effective loyalty program, the first step is to define its objectives. While many programs aim to increase customer retention, the best ones also focus on driving advocacy. For example, **Sephora's Beauty Insider** program not only rewards customers for purchases but also encourages them to share reviews, create social media content, and participate in the brand's community. This holistic approach transforms loyal customers into passionate advocates who amplify the brand's message.

The structure of a loyalty program significantly impacts its effectiveness. Programs must strike a balance between simplicity and engagement, ensuring they are easy to understand yet compelling enough to sustain participation. Popular structures include:

- **Points-Based Systems**: Customers earn points for every purchase, which can be redeemed for discounts, free products, or exclusive experiences. For example, **Starbucks Rewards** allows customers to earn points for each transaction, redeemable for drinks and food, fostering frequent visits.

- **Tiered Programs**: These reward customers based on their level of engagement, offering increasing benefits as they ascend tiers. Tiered programs, like **Delta Airlines' SkyMiles**, create a sense of achievement and exclusivity, motivating customers to deepen their relationship with the brand.

- **Subscription Models**: Paid loyalty programs, such as **Amazon Prime**, offer members exclusive benefits like free shipping and access to premium content. These programs often drive higher engagement due to the perceived value of membership.

While financial incentives like discounts and freebies are effective, the most successful loyalty programs incorporate **personalisation** to create meaningful connections. Personalisation ensures that rewards and communications align with individual customer preferences, enhancing the overall experience. For instance, **Netflix** leverages its customer data to recommend content tailored to individual viewing habits, creating a sense of relevance and value.

In addition to personalisation, offering non-monetary rewards can significantly enhance advocacy. Recognising and celebrating customers through gestures like birthday messages, exclusive previews, or shoutouts on social media fosters emotional loyalty. For example, **Nike Membership** offers members access to exclusive events, personalised training plans, and early product launches, building a community of engaged advocates.

Encouraging advocacy within the program is another crucial element. Referral incentives, where both the referrer and the new customer receive benefits, can turn loyal customers into brand ambassadors. For example, **Dropbox** experienced rapid growth through a referral program that rewarded users with additional storage for each successful recommendation. Similarly, rewarding customers for creating and sharing content, such as reviews or social media posts, amplifies the brand's visibility and credibility.

Technology plays a vital role in managing loyalty programs and fostering advocacy. Mobile apps, customer relationship management (CRM) systems, and analytics tools enable brands to track customer behaviour, deliver personalised rewards, and monitor program performance. For example, apps like the **Starbucks Rewards** app provide seamless access to rewards, track points, and allow customers to redeem them instantly, enhancing convenience and engagement.

Despite their benefits, loyalty programs come with challenges. Over-saturation in certain industries means customers often participate in multiple programs, making it difficult for a brand to stand out. To address this, programs must offer unique value propositions, whether through exclusive rewards, exceptional experiences, or a strong sense of community. Another challenge is balancing program costs with profitability. CMOs must ensure that the program delivers a clear return on investment (ROI) by driving retention, upselling, and advocacy.

Metrics such as customer lifetime value (CLV), redemption rates, and Net Promoter Score (NPS) help measure a program's effectiveness. High redemption rates indicate active engagement, while an increasing NPS suggests that customers are likely to recommend the brand to others. Regularly reviewing these metrics allows brands to refine their programs and ensure they continue to resonate with customers.

Examples of successful loyalty programs underscore the importance of combining tangible rewards with emotional engagement. **Apple's ecosystem**, for instance, creates loyalty by offering seamless integration between its products and services, such as iCloud and Apple Music, fostering an enduring connection with its users. Meanwhile, **Tesco Clubcard** rewards customers with personalised discounts and exclusive deals, reinforcing its value proposition as a customer-centric retailer.

In conclusion, customer loyalty programs are a powerful mechanism for transforming satisfied customers into brand advocates. By designing programs that go beyond transactional rewards to deliver personalised, meaningful experiences, brands can foster deeper connections, encourage advocacy, and drive sustained growth. For CMOs, loyalty programs are not just tools for retention; they are strategies for creating ambassadors who amplify the brand's voice and help build a loyal community. In an era where trust and relationships are paramount, fostering advocacy through loyalty programs is a critical pathway to long-term success.

3.9 - Emerging Trends in Brand Strategy

The world of branding is constantly evolving, driven by advancements in technology, shifting consumer expectations, and cultural changes. For a **Chief Marketing Officer (CMO)**, staying ahead of these **emerging trends in brand strategy** is not just an option; it is a necessity for maintaining relevance and fostering long-term success. These trends provide new opportunities to connect with customers, differentiate from competitors, and create meaningful brand experiences. However, they also require adaptability, creativity, and a willingness to innovate.

One of the most significant trends shaping brand strategy today is the increasing demand for **personalisation**. Modern consumers expect brands to understand their preferences, behaviours, and needs, delivering tailored experiences across all touchpoints. Personalisation has evolved from simple name customisation in emails to sophisticated, AI-driven recommendations and dynamic content. For instance, **Spotify's Wrapped** campaign offers users a personalised summary of their listening habits, creating a highly engaging and shareable experience. Personalisation not only enhances customer satisfaction but also fosters loyalty by making customers feel valued as individuals.

Another critical trend is the rise of **purpose-driven branding**. Consumers, particularly younger generations, increasingly prioritise brands that align with their values. Sustainability, inclusivity, and social responsibility have become central to purchasing decisions. Brands like **Patagonia**, which actively champion environmental causes, have successfully differentiated themselves by embedding purpose into their core identity. Purpose-driven branding goes beyond marketing; it requires genuine actions and transparency to avoid accusations of greenwashing or virtue signalling.

Sustainability as a standalone trend is also reshaping brand strategies. As concerns about climate change and resource depletion grow, brands are adopting eco-friendly practices, from reducing packaging waste to using renewable energy in production. Companies like **Unilever** have committed to making all their plastic packaging reusable or recyclable by 2025, a move that resonates with environmentally conscious consumers. Brands that embrace sustainability not only meet regulatory requirements but also build trust and loyalty among eco-minded audiences.

Digital transformation continues to drive significant changes in branding. The rise of digital-first consumers has shifted the focus to online experiences, making it essential for brands to optimise their digital presence. This includes everything from e-commerce platforms and social media engagement to virtual and augmented reality. For example, **IKEA** has integrated augmented reality into its mobile app, allowing customers to visualise how furniture will look in their homes. These immersive experiences enhance engagement and help brands stand out in a crowded digital landscape.

Community-centric branding is another emerging trend that focuses on building relationships and fostering a sense of belonging. Customers no longer want to be passive consumers; they seek opportunities to engage with brands and like-minded individuals. Companies like **Peloton** excel at creating vibrant communities where customers feel part of something larger. By integrating social features into their products and services, such brands strengthen loyalty and advocacy.

The integration of **technology and AI** is revolutionising how brands operate and interact with their customers. From chatbots and AI-powered customer service to predictive analytics and machine learning, technology enables brands to deliver faster, smarter, and more efficient solutions. **Netflix**, for example, uses advanced algorithms to recommend personalised content, enhancing user satisfaction and retention. As AI tools become more accessible, even smaller brands can leverage them to compete with larger players.

Another significant trend is the **rise of experiential branding**. In an era where digital interactions dominate, consumers crave memorable, real-world experiences that create emotional connections with brands. Experiential branding focuses on creating immersive events, pop-ups, or activations that allow customers to engage directly with the brand. For instance, **Adidas** has hosted running events and workshops that align with its mission to promote an active lifestyle. These experiences not only generate buzz but also build deeper emotional ties with participants.

Inclusivity and representation have also become central to brand strategies. Modern consumers expect brands to reflect the diversity of their audience in marketing campaigns, product offerings, and internal practices. Brands like **Fenty Beauty** have set a high standard by offering inclusive product ranges that cater to all skin tones. Inclusivity is not just a moral imperative; it is a strategic advantage that broadens a brand's appeal and fosters loyalty among underrepresented groups.

Finally, the shift to **direct-to-consumer (DTC)** models is transforming traditional retail dynamics. By bypassing intermediaries, brands can establish direct relationships with their customers, gaining valuable insights and delivering personalised experiences. Companies like **Warby Parker** and **Dollar Shave Club** have disrupted their industries by focusing on DTC strategies, offering convenience, value, and transparency.

Despite the opportunities these trends present, they come with challenges. For example, personalisation requires significant investment in data collection and analysis, raising concerns about privacy and security. Similarly, purpose-driven branding demands authenticity and consistency; any misstep can lead to accusations of hypocrisy. Navigating these challenges requires a thoughtful approach that prioritises transparency, integrity, and customer-centricity.

For CMOs, embracing these trends means staying agile and forward-thinking. It involves experimenting with new technologies, listening to customer feedback, and aligning brand strategies with evolving societal values. Measuring the impact of these trends is equally important, with metrics such as customer engagement, loyalty, and brand equity providing insights into their effectiveness.

In conclusion, the emerging trends in brand strategy offer exciting opportunities for innovation and growth. From personalisation and sustainability to community building and experiential branding, these trends enable brands to connect with customers in more meaningful ways. However, they also require a commitment to authenticity, adaptability, and continuous learning. For CMOs, staying ahead of these trends is not just about keeping up; it is about leading the way in shaping the future of branding.

3.10 - Case Study: Rebranding a Global Enterprise

Rebranding a multinational corporation is a complex process that requires strategic vision, a unifying purpose, and the courage to redefine existing perceptions. The stakes are particularly high for a Chief Marketing Officer (CMO), as a successful rebrand can reshape market positioning, strengthen customer loyalty, and set new expectations across global markets. One of the most notable examples of a successful rebrand is Microsoft's transformation from a legacy software provider to a leader in cloud computing, collaboration tools, and integrated services.

Background

Microsoft's brand identity was traditionally associated with its Windows operating system and Office productivity suite. While these products dominated their segments, the brand struggled to resonate with a younger, mobile-first audience. By the late 2000s, Microsoft's image as a desktop-bound, complex platform no longer aligned with the shifting landscape of consumer technology, nor did it reflect the company's emerging strengths in cloud infrastructure and cross-platform solutions.

The Approach

The rebrand was not limited to visual changes but included a comprehensive overhaul of Microsoft's mission, culture, and strategy. Central to the rebranding was the adoption of a refreshed corporate mission: to empower every person and organisation on the planet to achieve more. This mission redefined the company's goals, emphasising inclusivity, global reach, and cutting-edge innovation.

Steps

1. **Mission Alignment**: Leaders communicated the new mission internally to ensure that employees understood how their roles aligned with the company's broader goals. This internal cultural shift was critical for external consistency.

2. **Visual Identity Refresh**: Microsoft introduced a modernised logo, maintaining its iconic four-colour design but with cleaner lines and a contemporary aesthetic. Product interfaces, such as the Office suite, were also

updated to reflect the new brand ethos, emphasising integration and accessibility.

3. **Strategic Partnerships and Acquisitions**: Microsoft leveraged strategic alliances and acquisitions to reinforce its mission. Investments in cloud computing, artificial intelligence, and enterprise solutions positioned the company as a robust provider of end-to-end services.

4. **Communication and Narrative**: The rebranding strategy emphasised a cohesive narrative. Through public announcements, media engagements, and product events, Microsoft communicated its evolution from a PC-centric company to a multifaceted technology innovator.

The Results

Microsoft's rebranding efforts were a resounding success. The company emerged as a leader in cloud computing and collaboration tools, with products like Azure, Teams, and OneDrive redefining its market presence. The refreshed mission and visual identity resonated with both existing and new audiences, driving sustained growth and innovation. Revenue from cloud services significantly increased, solidifying Microsoft's competitive edge in the tech industry.

Lessons Learned

- **Unified Direction is Essential**: Aligning internal culture with external messaging ensures consistent delivery of the brand's new identity.

- **Mission-Driven Branding Works**: A clear and inspiring mission creates alignment across stakeholders and fosters trust.

- **Evolve Without Losing Legacy**: Microsoft retained its legacy strengths while boldly embracing innovation, demonstrating how to balance tradition with transformation.

Conclusion

Microsoft's rebranding illustrates how a global enterprise can redefine itself to meet the demands of a changing market. Through strategic leadership, a compelling mission, and cohesive communication, Microsoft transitioned from a dated identity to a forward-thinking technology powerhouse. For CMOs undertaking similar challenges, this case underscores the importance of aligning internal values, embracing innovation, and maintaining a unified brand narrative.

Chapter 4

Digital Marketing in the Modern Age

> *"In the digital age, brands don't just tell stories; they invite their audiences to become part of the narrative."*
> **Robert N. Jacobs**

In today's hyper-connected world, digital marketing has emerged as the cornerstone of how brands engage with their audiences, foster relationships, and drive growth. With the rapid evolution of technology, shifting consumer behaviours, and an ever-expanding digital landscape, mastering digital marketing has become both an opportunity and a challenge for Chief Marketing Officers (CMOs).

This chapter delves into the critical components of digital marketing, from leveraging data-driven strategies and mastering SEO to navigating social media dynamics and implementing ethical advertising practices. Through a blend of insights, strategies, and real-world examples, it equips CMOs with the tools to thrive in a competitive, digitally driven marketplace.

4.1 - The Digital Landscape: Trends and Challenges

The **digital landscape** has become a vast and intricate ecosystem where brands and consumers interact at an unprecedented scale. For a **Chief Marketing Officer (CMO)**, navigating this dynamic environment requires a firm grasp of its emerging trends, persistent challenges, and the shifting expectations of a digitally connected audience. With technological advancements continually reshaping the rules of engagement, a forward-thinking approach is essential to thrive in this competitive space.

One of the most significant trends in digital marketing today is the rise of **personalisation**. Consumers no longer respond to generic, one-size-fits-all messages. Instead, they demand tailored experiences that align with their unique preferences and needs. This shift is driven by the availability of data, enabling brands to deliver highly targeted messages across channels. However, the challenge lies in balancing personalisation with privacy concerns. Customers are more aware of how their data is collected and used, and brands must operate transparently to avoid eroding trust. Adopting stringent data protection measures and communicating clearly about how data benefits the customer is now a core aspect of any ethical digital strategy. Another key trend is the growing dominance of **video content**. Platforms like YouTube, TikTok, and Instagram have made video the most engaging format online. Whether through live streams, short-form clips, or long-form narratives, video allows brands to convey complex ideas in a visually compelling way. However, creating high-quality video content requires investment in production and creativity, making it a resource-intensive endeavour. Marketers must find innovative ways to produce content that stands out in an oversaturated market without exhausting their budgets.

Voice search optimisation is also gaining traction, particularly with the increasing adoption of voice-activated devices such as Amazon Alexa and Google Home. Voice queries often differ from typed searches, typically being longer and more conversational. Brands must optimise their content for these natural language queries to remain relevant as voice search continues to grow. This shift highlights the need for marketers to anticipate changes in consumer behaviour and adapt accordingly.

The **omnichannel experience** is another area of focus, as consumers expect seamless interactions across multiple touchpoints. Whether browsing on mobile, engaging on social media, or visiting a physical store, customers want a cohesive journey that reflects their preferences. This requires brands to integrate their channels effectively, using data and technology to ensure a unified experience. However, achieving this level of integration can be challenging, particularly for legacy brands with disparate systems and processes.

At the same time, **ethical considerations** are reshaping the digital marketing landscape. Consumers increasingly value authenticity and responsibility, scrutinising brands for their environmental and social impact. Marketers must ensure that their campaigns reflect genuine commitments rather than hollow statements. For example, promoting sustainability initiatives requires concrete action, not just buzzwords. Brands that fail to align their messaging with their practices risk damaging their credibility.

Despite these opportunities, the digital space presents several persistent challenges. **Algorithm changes** on platforms like Google, Facebook, and Instagram can significantly impact a brand's reach and visibility. Marketers must stay agile, continuously monitoring and adapting to these changes to maintain their competitive edge. Additionally, the sheer volume of content produced daily creates **content fatigue** among consumers. Capturing and retaining attention requires creative strategies and a deep understanding of the target audience.

In conclusion, the digital landscape offers immense potential for growth and engagement, but it demands a proactive and ethical approach. By staying attuned to emerging trends, addressing challenges head-on, and prioritising authentic connections with consumers, CMOs can position their brands for sustained success in the digital age.

4.2 - Fundamentals of SEO and SEM

The **fundamentals of SEO (Search Engine Optimisation) and SEM (Search Engine Marketing)** form the backbone of any effective digital marketing strategy. These tools enable brands to enhance their visibility on search engines, driving traffic and ultimately improving conversions. For a **Chief Marketing Officer (CMO)**, understanding the mechanics and nuances of SEO and SEM is crucial for building a strong online presence. Although they operate differently, SEO and SEM are complementary strategies that work together to achieve both short- and long-term goals.

SEO is the process of optimising a website to achieve higher rankings in **organic search results**. It focuses on improving the relevance and authority of a website, ensuring that search engines like Google recognise it as a valuable resource for specific queries. The foundation of SEO lies in **keyword research**. This involves identifying the words and phrases that users type into search engines when looking for products, services, or information. However, successful SEO goes beyond merely inserting these keywords into content. The content must be high-quality, engaging, and address the intent behind the user's search. For instance, an individual searching for "best running shoes for beginners" is likely seeking detailed reviews or guides rather than a generic product listing.

In addition to content, **technical SEO** plays a critical role. Search engines favour websites that offer a seamless user experience, which includes fast loading speeds, mobile responsiveness, secure connections (HTTPS), and intuitive site navigation. If a site takes too long to load or isn't optimised for mobile devices, users are likely to leave, increasing the **bounce rate** and negatively impacting rankings. Furthermore, earning backlinks and links from other reputable websites to your site remains a key factor in improving domain authority and credibility. A well-executed content strategy often naturally attracts these backlinks, as others link to valuable, original resources.

While SEO is a long-term investment, **SEM** delivers quicker results by leveraging paid advertising. Using platforms like Google Ads, SEM enables brands to bid for placement on search engine results pages (SERPs). These placements typically appear above organic results, giving them prime visibility. SEM campaigns are highly customisable, allowing marketers to target specific demographics, locations, and even times of day. For instance, a local coffee shop could use SEM to promote an early-morning offer, ensuring their advert appears when potential customers search for "coffee near me" between 6 am and 9 am.

One of the strengths of SEM is its immediacy. While SEO can take months to yield noticeable results, SEM campaigns can go live in minutes and begin driving traffic almost immediately. However, SEM requires careful management to ensure cost efficiency. Marketers must monitor **cost per click (CPC)**, ensure that ad copy aligns with user intent and direct traffic to optimised landing pages that convert visitors into customers. Failure to align these elements can lead to wasted ad spend and low ROI.

The interplay between SEO and SEM offers a powerful combination. SEM insights can inform SEO strategies by highlighting high-performing keywords and audience behaviours. For instance, if an SEM campaign identifies a keyword with strong engagement, this keyword can become the focus of an SEO-driven content strategy. Conversely, SEO successes can reduce dependency on paid ads over time, creating a sustainable traffic source.

Despite their effectiveness, both SEO and SEM come with challenges. SEO requires continuous adaptation to **algorithm updates** as search engines refine their criteria to prioritise user-focused content. Similarly, SEM campaigns must be monitored and optimised regularly to account for changes in competition, bidding dynamics, and audience preferences. Ignoring these aspects can lead to declining performance over time.

Measuring success in SEO and SEM involves tracking key performance indicators (KPIs). For SEO, these might include **organic traffic**, **keyword rankings**, and **click-through rates (CTR)**. SEM metrics, on the other hand, focus on **impressions**, **conversion rates**, and **return on ad spend (ROAS)**. A detailed analysis of these metrics allows marketers to identify what's working, adjust strategies, and ensure that resources are allocated effectively.

In summary, the fundamentals of SEO and SEM lie in their shared goal: to connect brands with audiences at critical moments in the decision-making process. While SEO builds a foundation of credibility and sustainability, SEM provides the agility to capture immediate opportunities. For CMOs, leveraging these strategies in tandem is essential to achieving both long-term growth and short-term success in a competitive digital landscape.

4.3 - Social Media Strategy: Engagement and Growth

A well-executed **social media strategy** is an essential component of any digital marketing plan. Social media platforms provide unparalleled opportunities for brands to connect directly with their audience, foster meaningful engagement, and drive sustained growth. For a **Chief Marketing Officer (CMO)**, crafting a social media strategy that aligns with the brand's values and business goals while resonating with diverse audiences is a dynamic and ongoing challenge.

The foundation of any successful social media strategy lies in understanding the brand's **target audience**. Each platform attracts distinct demographics with varying preferences, behaviours, and expectations. For instance, Instagram is a visually driven space popular among younger audiences, while LinkedIn caters to professionals seeking thought leadership and networking opportunities. Tailoring content to match the unique characteristics of each platform ensures relevance and maximises engagement. A CMO must ensure that the brand's voice and tone adapt seamlessly to these platforms while remaining consistent with its overarching identity.

Another cornerstone of social media success is **authenticity**. Users on these platforms value brands that show genuine personalities, admit their imperfections, and connect on a human level. Posting polished, overly promotional content often alienates audiences, whereas relatable, interactive posts encourage dialogue. For example, sharing behind-the-scenes videos of a product's development process or showcasing the team behind the brand humanises the organisation and builds trust. Likewise, responding promptly and sincerely to comments, questions, or concerns fosters a sense of community and demonstrates the brand's commitment to its followers.

A robust social media strategy also hinges on **content variety**. Different formats, such as short videos, live streams, carousel posts, and stories, cater to various user preferences and ensure that the content remains fresh and engaging. For instance, a fashion brand might use Instagram Reels to showcase styling tips, post high-quality images of new collections, and host live Q&A sessions to discuss sustainability initiatives. This multifaceted approach allows the brand to reach broader audiences and keep followers intrigued.

Strategic use of **hashtags and trending topics** can amplify reach. Hashtags categorise content and make it discoverable to users interested in specific themes. For example, a fitness brand launching a campaign around at-home workouts could use popular fitness hashtags like #HomeWorkoutTips or create its own branded hashtag to encourage user-generated content. Joining trending conversations, provided they align with the brand's values, can further enhance visibility and relevance. However, brands must exercise caution when engaging with trends to avoid appearing opportunistic or out of touch.

Another critical aspect of social media strategy is fostering **user-generated content (UGC)**. Encouraging customers to share their experiences with the brand, through photos, testimonials, or reviews, not only boosts credibility but also reduces the burden of content creation. A beauty brand, for instance, might incentivise customers to post selfies using its products by offering discounts or featuring their photos on its official account. UGC transforms satisfied customers into brand advocates, strengthening the connection between the brand and its audience.

While organic content is essential, **paid social media advertising** offers additional opportunities for targeted reach and growth. Platforms like Facebook, Instagram, and TikTok provide sophisticated tools for audience segmentation, enabling brands to deliver tailored messages to specific demographics. For instance, an educational technology company might target parents with young children through Facebook ads while running LinkedIn campaigns aimed at school administrators. Paid campaigns are particularly effective for product launches, limited-time offers, or expanding into new markets. However, it is crucial to maintain consistency between paid and organic content to ensure a cohesive brand presence.

Analytics and performance measurement are indispensable components of any social media strategy. Metrics such as engagement rates, follower growth, website traffic, and conversions provide insights into what resonates with the audience and what doesn't. A high number of likes on a post may indicate strong content, but deeper metrics like click-through rates and time spent on linked pages reveal whether the content is driving meaningful actions. Regularly analysing these metrics allows marketers to refine their strategies, optimise content, and allocate resources effectively.

Community engagement is equally important. Social media is not a one-way communication channel; it thrives on interaction. Responding to comments, acknowledging feedback, and participating in discussions demonstrate that the brand values its followers. This interaction extends to managing criticism constructively. Addressing negative feedback transparently and professionally can turn potentially damaging situations into opportunities to showcase the brand's integrity and responsiveness.

Finally, staying adaptable is crucial. Social media platforms are constantly evolving, introducing new features, algorithms, and user behaviours. What works today might not be as effective tomorrow. A successful CMO fosters a culture of experimentation, encouraging the team to test new formats, embrace emerging platforms, and adjust tactics based on results. For example, a brand that once relied heavily on Facebook might shift its focus to TikTok if data indicates that its target audience is more active on the latter.

In conclusion, a strong **social media strategy** is built on understanding the audience, creating authentic and diverse content, leveraging paid opportunities, and continuously analysing performance. By fostering genuine connections and staying adaptable in a rapidly changing digital environment, brands can use social media to achieve sustained engagement and growth. For CMOs, social media represents not just a marketing channel but a vital space for building relationships that drive long-term success.

4.4- -Content Marketing: Creating Value for Customers

Content marketing has emerged as one of the most powerful strategies for building meaningful relationships with customers in today's digital age. Rather than focusing on direct sales, content marketing is about offering valuable, relevant, and consistent information that addresses customer needs, solves their problems, or enriches their lives. For a **Chief Marketing Officer (CMO)**, the ability to craft and execute a content strategy that creates value is not just an optional add-on; it is a critical component of sustainable brand growth.

The core philosophy of content marketing is centred around **value creation**. This means that the content produced must serve a purpose beyond promoting a product or service. Whether it's educational blog posts, engaging videos, or interactive tools, the content should be designed to inform, inspire, or entertain. For example, a financial services company might publish articles on managing personal budgets or investing for beginners. These resources provide immediate value to readers, establishing the company as a trusted authority in its field. Over time, this trust can translate into customer loyalty and business growth.

Understanding the **target audience** is the foundation of effective content marketing. Before creating content, marketers must identify the needs, interests, and pain points of their audience. This requires thorough research, which may involve analysing customer feedback, conducting surveys, and studying market trends. For instance, a technology brand targeting small businesses might discover that its audience struggles with selecting cost-effective software. Armed with this insight, the brand can create content such as comparison guides, tutorials, or case studies to address these challenges.

Once the audience is well-defined, the next step is crafting **high-quality, relevant content**. The focus should be on addressing the audience's concerns in a manner that aligns with the brand's expertise and values. High-quality content is characterised by clarity, accuracy, and originality. It should be well-researched, engagingly written, and free of errors. Additionally, it should reflect the brand's voice and personality. A playful fashion brand, for example, might use a conversational tone and vibrant visuals, whereas a healthcare provider would adopt a more professional and empathetic approach.

The **format of content** is another critical consideration. Different audiences prefer consuming content in different ways, so offering a mix of formats can increase engagement. Blog articles, videos, infographics, podcasts, webinars, and downloadable eBooks all serve different purposes and appeal to various preferences. For instance, a fitness brand might use Instagram Stories for quick workout tips, YouTube for detailed exercise tutorials, and its blog for in-depth discussions on nutrition. This multi-format approach ensures that the content reaches as wide an audience as possible.

Consistency is key to maintaining audience interest and trust. Sporadic content production can result in disengagement, as followers may lose interest if they do not hear from the brand regularly. Establishing a content calendar helps ensure that content is published consistently. This calendar should include details such as the type of content, the platform it will be shared on, and the intended audience segment. Regular posting also improves search engine rankings, as consistent updates signal to search algorithms that the site is active and relevant.

To maximise the impact of content marketing, it is essential to focus on **distribution and promotion**. Even the most valuable content will fail to achieve its goals if it does not reach the intended audience. Social media, email marketing, search engine optimisation (SEO), and paid promotions are all effective ways to amplify content visibility. For example, a travel agency that creates a destination guide can promote it via its social media channels, send it to subscribers through email, and optimise it with keywords to attract organic traffic.

Measuring the success of content marketing efforts is equally important. Metrics such as **engagement rates**, **website traffic**, **time spent on a page**, and **conversion rates** provide insights into how well the content resonates with the audience. Analysing these metrics helps marketers refine their strategies, identifying which types of content perform best and which areas need improvement. For instance, if a series of blog posts generates significant traffic but few conversions, the brand may need to reevaluate its calls to action or optimise landing pages.

One of the most powerful aspects of content marketing is its ability to foster **long-term relationships** with customers. Unlike traditional advertising, which often seeks immediate results, content marketing builds trust and loyalty over time. By consistently offering value, brands position themselves as reliable partners in their customers' journeys. This trust not only leads to repeat business but also encourages word-of-mouth recommendations, expanding the brand's reach organically.

However, content marketing is not without its challenges. In a crowded digital space, standing out requires creativity and originality. Producing content that is merely adequate will not suffice when audiences are bombarded with information daily. Marketers must strive to deliver unique perspectives, compelling storytelling, and visually appealing designs to capture attention. Additionally, maintaining authenticity is crucial. Audiences can quickly detect when content feels insincere or overly promotional, which can damage the brand's credibility.

In conclusion, **content marketing** is a vital strategy for creating value, building trust, and driving long-term growth. By focusing on understanding the audience, delivering high-quality and relevant content, and ensuring consistent distribution, brands can foster meaningful connections that go beyond transactions. For CMOs, content marketing represents an opportunity to position their brand as a thought leader, a trusted resource, and a valued partner in the lives of their customers. When done well, it transforms marketing from a cost centre into a growth engine capable of delivering measurable and sustainable returns.

4.5- -Leveraging Data for Personalised Campaigns

In today's digital age, **leveraging data for personalised campaigns** has become a cornerstone of effective marketing. Consumers expect brands to deliver experiences tailored to their preferences, behaviours, and needs, and they are more likely to engage with companies that make them feel seen and understood. For a **Chief Marketing Officer (CMO)**, mastering the art of data-driven personalisation is both an opportunity and a challenge, requiring a delicate balance between using insights to enhance customer experiences and respecting privacy and ethical considerations.

At the heart of personalised campaigns lies the **collection and analysis of customer data**. Data comes in many forms, ranging from demographic information (age, location, income level) to behavioural insights (browsing habits, purchase history, time spent on specific pages). For example, a fashion retailer might track which categories a customer frequently explores, such as casual wear or formal attire, and then recommend products that align with these preferences. By connecting seemingly disparate pieces of information, brands can create a complete picture of their customers and anticipate their needs.

Personalisation begins with **segmentation**, the process of dividing a broad audience into smaller, more specific groups. This segmentation can be based on various criteria, such as demographics, interests, or buying patterns. A fitness brand, for instance, might create segments for beginners, intermediate users, and advanced athletes, tailoring its messaging accordingly. Beginners could receive workout guides, intermediates might be targeted with product bundles to elevate their routine, and advanced users could be invited to exclusive challenges or workshops. These targeted approaches increase the likelihood of engagement because they speak directly to the customer's experience and goals.

Timing is another critical factor in personalised campaigns. A well-timed message can make all the difference in whether a customer takes action. Analysing data allows marketers to identify patterns in customer behaviour, such as when they are most likely to open emails or make purchases. For instance, an online grocery service might notice that a particular customer frequently places orders on Sunday afternoons. Using this insight, the brand could send a personalised discount or reminder email just before the customer's typical ordering time, increasing the chances of conversion.

Automation plays a key role in scaling personalised campaigns. **Customer relationship management (CRM) systems** and marketing automation tools can track individual interactions and trigger tailored communications at the right moment. For example, an e-commerce platform might use automation to send abandoned cart emails with personalised product suggestions, reminding customers of items they left behind. This kind of follow-up not only recaptures potential revenue but also shows the customer that the brand pays attention to their journey.

However, personalisation must always prioritise **value creation** over intrusion. Consumers are becoming increasingly aware of how their data is used and are quick to reject experiences that feel overly invasive or irrelevant. Transparency is essential; brands should clearly communicate why they are collecting certain data and how it benefits the customer. For instance, an airline offering a personalised travel itinerary could explain that the recommendations are based on the customer's previous bookings and preferences, assuring them that the data serves a meaningful purpose.

The effectiveness of personalised campaigns also depends on the **quality of the data** being used. Inaccurate or outdated information can lead to missteps, such as recommending a product a customer has already purchased or addressing them with incorrect details. Investing in data hygiene and regularly updating, verifying, and cleaning customer records is essential for maintaining trust and delivering accurate recommendations.

Beyond transactional benefits, personalisation fosters **emotional connections** with customers. When people feel that a brand understands their unique needs, they are more likely to develop loyalty and advocate for the brand. A streaming service like Spotify, for example, uses personalisation to create highly engaging campaigns like Spotify Wrapped, which provides users with insights into their listening habits. This initiative not only delights customers but also generates substantial social media buzz as users share their personalised summaries online.

Despite its advantages, data-driven personalisation comes with its own set of challenges. One major concern is ensuring compliance with **data protection regulations** such as the General Data Protection Regulation (GDPR) in Europe. These laws mandate that consumers have control over their data, requiring brands to obtain explicit consent for collection and use. Failing to comply can result in hefty fines and reputational damage. As such, CMOs must work closely with legal and compliance teams to ensure that personalisation efforts adhere to all relevant regulations.

Ethical considerations also come into play. Brands must avoid using data in ways that could exploit or manipulate customers. For instance, targeting individuals based on vulnerabilities, such as financial hardship, is not only unethical but also risks severe backlash. Maintaining integrity in how data is used ensures that personalisation efforts enhance, rather than undermine, the brand's reputation.

In conclusion, **leveraging data for personalised campaigns** is about striking the right balance between technology, strategy, and empathy. By using data responsibly, segmenting audiences effectively, and delivering timely and relevant experiences, brands can foster stronger relationships and drive better results. For CMOs, personalisation is no longer just a competitive advantage; it is an expectation. However, to succeed in this space, marketers must remain vigilant about data accuracy, compliance, and ethical practices, ensuring that every interaction builds trust and creates genuine value for the customer.

4.6 - Influencer Marketing: Opportunities and Pitfalls

Influencer marketing has grown into a vital component of modern digital strategies, providing brands with a way to connect with audiences through trusted voices in specific niches. For a **Chief Marketing Officer (CMO)**, influencer marketing offers an opportunity to leverage the credibility, reach, and engagement of individuals who have built loyal followings. However, as promising as it may be, influencer marketing is not without its challenges, requiring careful planning and execution to maximise opportunities and mitigate potential pitfalls.

At its core, influencer marketing is about **authentic advocacy**. Influencers have cultivated trust with their audience by consistently delivering valuable, relatable, or entertaining content. When they endorse a product or service, their followers perceive it as a personal recommendation rather than a traditional advertisement. This authenticity gives influencer marketing an edge over other forms of advertising, especially among younger consumers who often value peer endorsements more than corporate messaging. For instance, a skincare brand might partner with a beauty influencer who shares their personal experience using the brand's products, creating a story that resonates with followers and drives interest.

One of the key opportunities in influencer marketing is the ability to **target niche audiences** effectively. Unlike broad digital campaigns, influencer partnerships allow brands to reach specific demographics that align with their product or service. For example, a sustainable fashion brand might collaborate with influencers known for promoting eco-conscious lifestyles, ensuring the message reaches an audience already interested in sustainability. This precision targeting not only increases relevance but also improves ROI by focusing efforts on a well-defined segment.

Content creation is another major advantage. Influencers are skilled at creating high-quality, engaging content that aligns with their personal brand and resonates with their audience. By collaborating with influencers, brands gain access to this content, which can be repurposed across various channels, such as social media, email marketing, or even websites. This saves time and resources while ensuring the content remains authentic and engaging. For instance, a travel company could work with a travel influencer to produce stunning visuals and compelling narratives about a destination, which can then be shared across both the influencer's and the brand's platforms.

Despite its advantages, influencer marketing comes with **significant challenges** that must be navigated carefully. One major pitfall is **inauthentic partnerships**. If an influencer promotes a product that does not align with their values or interests, their followers may perceive the endorsement as disingenuous, damaging both the influencer's credibility and the brand's reputation. For example, a fitness influencer endorsing unhealthy snacks or a vegan influencer promoting non-vegan products would likely face backlash. To avoid such scenarios, brands must thoroughly vet potential influencers, ensuring that their values, audience, and content style align with the brand's identity.

Another challenge is **measuring ROI**. Unlike traditional advertising, where metrics like clicks and conversions are easily tracked, influencer campaigns often focus on softer metrics like engagement, awareness, and sentiment. While these are valuable indicators, tying them directly to revenue can be difficult. To address this, brands can use unique tracking links, discount codes, or post-campaign surveys to quantify the impact of influencer partnerships. For instance, a fitness brand might provide an influencer with a unique code for their followers, enabling the brand to track purchases generated by the campaign.

Regulatory compliance is also a critical consideration. Many regions now require influencers to disclose sponsored content clearly to protect consumers from misleading endorsements. Failing to comply with these regulations can result in legal consequences and reputational damage. Brands must ensure that influencers follow disclosure guidelines, such as using hashtags like #ad or #sponsored in their posts. Educating influencers on these requirements and incorporating them into contracts helps maintain transparency and avoids potential pitfalls.

The cost of influencer marketing can be another hurdle. While micro-influencers with smaller followings may charge less, partnering with top-tier influencers can be expensive, especially for smaller brands. However, bigger does not always mean better. **Micro-influencers**, with audiences ranging from 10,000 to 100,000 followers, often deliver higher engagement rates and more authentic interactions. Their smaller, more niche communities tend to trust their recommendations more than those of mega-influencers. For example, a local craft beer company might achieve better results working with several micro-influencers in the food and drink niche than with a single celebrity chef.

Crisis management is another potential risk in influencer marketing. An influencer's behaviour outside their brand collaborations can impact the brands they endorse. Scandals, controversies, or public backlash against an influencer can spill over onto the brand, tarnishing its image. To mitigate this risk, brands should conduct thorough background checks before entering partnerships and include clauses in contracts that allow for disengagement in the event of damaging behaviour.

To succeed in influencer marketing, CMOs must prioritise **relationship building**. Treating influencers as partners rather than just marketing tools fosters trust and encourages genuine advocacy. Engaging with influencers regularly, involving them in campaign planning, and providing creative freedom ensures that their content feels natural and aligned with their personal brand. This collaborative approach often yields better results than imposing rigid guidelines.

In conclusion, **influencer marketing** offers significant opportunities for brands to reach new audiences, build trust, and create engaging content. However, it is not without its challenges, from managing authenticity and compliance to measuring ROI and navigating costs. For CMOs, the key to success lies in careful planning, thoughtful execution, and a focus on building authentic, long-term relationships with influencers. By addressing the pitfalls head-on and embracing the potential of this dynamic strategy, brands can unlock powerful connections that drive both awareness and loyalty.

4.7 - The Role of AI and Automation in Digital Marketing

In the ever-evolving landscape of digital marketing, **artificial intelligence (AI)** and **automation** have become indispensable tools, transforming how brands connect with audiences and optimise campaigns. For a **Chief Marketing Officer (CMO)**, these technologies offer unparalleled opportunities to scale operations, improve efficiency, and deliver personalised customer experiences. However, leveraging AI and automation effectively requires a clear strategy, ethical considerations, and a focus on maintaining the human touch that fosters authentic connections.

One of the most significant contributions of AI to digital marketing is its ability to analyse vast amounts of **data** in real time. Modern AI tools can process customer behaviours, preferences, and trends far faster than any human team. For instance, AI-driven analytics platforms can identify patterns in consumer purchasing habits, enabling marketers to predict future behaviours and tailor campaigns accordingly. A retailer, for example, might use AI to track which products are frequently purchased together and then create targeted bundle promotions, increasing average order value while enhancing the customer experience.

Automation, on the other hand, simplifies repetitive tasks, allowing marketers to focus on strategy and creativity. Automated systems can manage everything from email campaigns and social media scheduling to real-time ad placement. For instance, an e-commerce brand could use automated email workflows to re-engage customers who abandon their shopping carts, sending timely reminders and personalised discounts to encourage completion. By streamlining such tasks, automation not only saves time but also ensures consistency across channels.

One area where AI and automation excel is **personalisation at scale**. AI-powered tools can segment audiences into granular groups based on behaviours, demographics, or preferences and deliver tailored content to each segment. For example, a travel agency could use AI to send personalised travel recommendations to customers based on their past bookings and browsing history. Automation ensures these messages are delivered at the right time, such as just before a long weekend or holiday season, maximising the likelihood of engagement.

Chatbots and virtual assistants are another prominent application of AI in digital marketing. These tools allow brands to offer **real-time customer support** without requiring human intervention for every query. For example, a telecom company might use an AI chatbot to handle routine inquiries, such as billing or service troubleshooting, freeing up human agents to focus on complex issues. When implemented well, chatbots can enhance customer satisfaction by providing immediate responses and seamless problem resolution.

Dynamic advertising is another area revolutionised by AI. Platforms like Google Ads and Facebook Ads use machine learning algorithms to optimise ad placements and bidding strategies in real time. These systems analyse performance data to determine which ads resonate most with specific audience segments, ensuring that marketing budgets are allocated efficiently. For instance, a fashion brand might launch multiple ad variations showcasing different products and styles. AI analyses the performance of each variation and automatically prioritises the ones generating the highest engagement and conversions.

Despite these advantages, the adoption of AI and automation in digital marketing comes with its own set of challenges. One significant concern is maintaining the **human element**. While AI can efficiently handle data analysis and task execution, it lacks the emotional intelligence and creativity needed to craft compelling narratives or address nuanced customer concerns. For example, while a chatbot may handle basic queries, a frustrated customer is more likely to value a human response that demonstrates empathy and understanding. To overcome this limitation, marketers must strike a balance by using AI for efficiency while ensuring human oversight for emotionally sensitive interactions.

Another challenge is ensuring **data privacy and security**. AI and automation rely heavily on customer data to function effectively, but mishandling this data can lead to breaches of trust and legal repercussions. Regulations such as the General Data Protection Regulation (GDPR) in Europe and the California Consumer Privacy Act (CCPA) in the United States mandate strict guidelines for data collection and use. Brands must ensure that their AI systems operate transparently, allowing customers to understand how their data is being used and offering them control over their information.

Ethical concerns also arise with the use of AI in digital marketing. For instance, predictive algorithms may inadvertently reinforce biases present in the data they are trained on, leading to discriminatory practices in ad targeting or customer segmentation. A CMO must prioritise fairness and inclusivity by auditing AI systems regularly and implementing safeguards to mitigate potential biases.

Measuring the success of AI and automation initiatives is critical to ensuring they deliver value. Key performance indicators (KPIs) such as **conversion rates**, **cost per acquisition (CPA)**, and **customer retention rates** provide insights into the effectiveness of these tools. Regularly evaluating these metrics helps marketers identify areas for improvement and fine-tune their strategies. For example, if an automated email campaign shows low engagement, the messaging or timing may need adjustment.

Looking ahead, the potential of AI and automation in digital marketing continues to expand. Emerging technologies such as **predictive analytics**, **natural language processing (NLP)**, and **computer vision** are unlocking new possibilities for hyper-personalisation and customer engagement. For instance, NLP-powered tools can analyse customer sentiment in real-time, enabling brands to respond proactively to both positive and negative feedback. Similarly, computer vision technologies can enhance visual content strategies, such as creating shoppable images or tailoring product recommendations based on uploaded photos.

In conclusion, **AI and automation** are transformative forces in digital marketing, offering unparalleled efficiency, scalability, and personalisation. However, their successful implementation requires a strategic approach that balances technological capabilities with human creativity and ethical responsibility. For CMOs, embracing these tools is not just about staying competitive; it is about redefining how brands connect with customers in a rapidly evolving digital landscape. By leveraging AI and automation thoughtfully, marketers can create campaigns that are both data-driven and deeply human, fostering trust and loyalty in an increasingly automated world.

4.8 - Evaluating Digital Campaign Performance

Evaluating the performance of a **digital marketing campaign** is essential for understanding its effectiveness, refining future strategies, and maximising return on investment (ROI). For a **Chief Marketing Officer (CMO)**, campaign evaluation is not merely an end-stage activity but an ongoing process that provides actionable insights throughout a campaign's lifecycle. A robust evaluation framework ensures that resources are used efficiently and that marketing efforts resonate with the target audience.

A successful evaluation begins with **clear objectives**. Every campaign must have specific, measurable, achievable, relevant, and time-bound (SMART) goals, such as increasing website traffic by 20% over three months or generating 1,000 new leads during a product launch. These goals form the benchmark against which performance is measured. Without clear objectives, assessing success or failure becomes subjective and inconsistent.

Key performance indicators (KPIs) are the metrics used to measure progress towards these objectives. The choice of KPIs depends on the campaign's goals. For instance:

- **Awareness campaigns** might prioritise metrics such as impressions, reach, and brand mentions.
- **Engagement-focused campaigns** would track likes, shares, comments, and time spent on content.
- **Conversion-driven campaigns** would focus on sales, sign-ups, or downloads.

The next step in evaluating performance is **data collection and analysis**. Digital marketing platforms such as Google Analytics, Facebook Ads Manager, and HubSpot provide detailed metrics on campaign performance. These tools track user behaviour across channels, offering insights into what works and what doesn't. For example, if a pay-per-click (PPC) campaign drives traffic to a landing page but fails to generate conversions, the problem could lie in the page's design, messaging, or user experience. Identifying such gaps allows marketers to make targeted improvements.

Attribution modelling is another critical aspect of campaign evaluation. In today's multi-channel landscape, customers often interact with a brand several times before converting. A user might first see a social media ad, later visit the website via an email link, and finally make a purchase after a retargeting campaign. Attribution modelling assigns value to each touchpoint, helping marketers understand which channels contribute most to conversions. Models range from **last-click attribution** (crediting the final interaction) to more advanced methods like **multi-touch attribution**, which evaluates the cumulative impact of all touchpoints.

One of the most important yet often overlooked aspects of evaluation is **qualitative feedback**. While quantitative data provides a broad overview, qualitative insights add depth and context. Customer reviews, social media comments, and direct feedback from surveys can reveal how audiences perceive the campaign. For example, a new product launch campaign might generate significant traffic and sales, but qualitative feedback could highlight confusion about product usage, suggesting a need for clearer communication.

Campaign evaluation also requires monitoring **real-time performance**. Unlike traditional marketing efforts, digital campaigns can be adjusted mid-course based on performance data. For instance, if an email campaign's open rate is low, subject lines can be tested and refined to improve engagement. Similarly, if a PPC campaign's cost-per-click (CPC) exceeds expectations, targeting parameters can be adjusted to focus on more cost-effective audience segments.

Despite the wealth of data available, campaign evaluation faces challenges. **Data fragmentation** is a common issue, with insights scattered across multiple platforms. Integrating these data sources into a unified dashboard simplifies analysis and ensures consistency. Additionally, **metric overload** can be counterproductive. Not all metrics are equally relevant; focusing on those that align with campaign objectives prevents unnecessary complexity.

Another challenge lies in distinguishing **leading indicators** from **lagging indicators**. Leading indicators, such as click-through rates (CTR) or engagement, provide early signs of performance, while lagging indicators, such as sales or ROI, measure final outcomes. Both are important, but over-reliance on one at the expense of the other can lead to skewed evaluations. For example, a campaign with high CTR but low conversions might indicate a misalignment between ad messaging and landing page content.

Once the campaign concludes, a **comprehensive post-mortem analysis** should be conducted. This involves comparing results against the initial objectives, identifying successes, and uncovering areas for improvement. A well-documented post-mortem serves as a learning tool, ensuring that future campaigns benefit from past experiences. For instance, a campaign that struggled with low engagement might reveal that the target audience was too broad, prompting a more segmented approach next time.

Finally, it is crucial to communicate the results to stakeholders effectively. A detailed report that combines data visualisation (charts, graphs) with clear narratives ensures that insights are understood across teams. Highlighting both successes and lessons learned fosters transparency and collaboration, aligning the organisation around a shared understanding of performance.

In conclusion, **evaluating digital campaign performance** is a critical process that goes beyond merely tracking metrics. It involves setting clear objectives, choosing relevant KPIs, analysing data in real time, and incorporating both quantitative and qualitative insights. By approaching evaluation as an integral part of the campaign lifecycle, CMOs can refine strategies, optimise resource allocation, and achieve more impactful results. A commitment to thorough and transparent evaluation not only improves individual campaigns but also drives long-term growth and innovation across the organisation.

4.9 - Ethical Considerations in Digital Advertising

As digital advertising continues to dominate the marketing landscape, **ethical considerations** have taken centre stage. Consumers are more informed and discerning than ever, scrutinising how brands communicate, collect data, and position their offerings. For a **Chief Marketing Officer (CMO)**, maintaining ethical standards in digital advertising is not only a moral obligation but also a strategic necessity. Ethical missteps can erode trust, damage reputations, and invite legal repercussions, while responsible advertising can enhance credibility and foster long-term customer loyalty.

One of the most critical aspects of ethical digital advertising is the **responsible use of customer data**. The personalisation and targeting capabilities of digital platforms rely heavily on collecting and analysing user data. However, the line between relevant advertising and invasive practices is thin. Many consumers are uncomfortable with the idea of being tracked online, especially when they do not understand how their data is being used. Ensuring **transparency** is paramount. Brands must clearly communicate what data they collect, why they collect it, and how it benefits the customer. For example, a retailer offering personalised product recommendations can explain that these suggestions are based on the customer's browsing history, reassuring them that the data serves a constructive purpose.

Compliance with **data protection regulations** is also essential. Laws such as the General Data Protection Regulation (GDPR) in Europe and the California Consumer Privacy Act (CCPA) in the United States require brands to obtain explicit consent for data collection and provide users with the option to access, modify, or delete their data. Failing to adhere to these standards can result in significant fines and reputational damage. Ethical marketers go beyond compliance by fostering a culture of respect for privacy, ensuring that customers feel safe and valued when interacting with their brand.

Another ethical challenge lies in the **accuracy and honesty** of digital advertising. Exaggerated claims, misleading visuals, or hidden terms can quickly alienate customers and lead to public backlash. For instance, an advert that promises "free" products but includes hidden shipping fees is likely to frustrate and anger consumers. Ethical advertising requires clarity and honesty, with brands delivering on their promises without resorting to deceptive tactics. This approach not only builds trust but also sets the brand apart in a marketplace often criticised for its lack of transparency.

Targeting practices also raise ethical concerns. While micro-targeting allows brands to deliver highly relevant messages, it can be problematic if used irresponsibly. Targeting vulnerable groups, such as children, the elderly, or individuals facing financial hardship, with potentially harmful products or services is unethical and often illegal. For example, advertising high-interest payday loans to individuals in financial distress could be seen as exploitative. To avoid these pitfalls, brands should establish guidelines that prioritise fairness and inclusivity, ensuring that their campaigns do not take advantage of vulnerable audiences.

Content placement is another area where ethical considerations come into play. Programmatic advertising, while efficient, can sometimes lead to adverts appearing alongside inappropriate or harmful content. For instance, an advert for a family-friendly product might inadvertently appear on a website promoting extremist views or misinformation. Such placements can tarnish a brand's image and alienate its audience. To mitigate this risk, marketers should use tools that allow for greater control over where their adverts are displayed and regularly monitor placements to ensure alignment with the brand's values.

The rise of **native advertising**, where promotional content is designed to blend seamlessly with editorial material, further complicates the ethical landscape. While native ads can be highly effective, they can also mislead consumers if not clearly labelled as sponsored content. Ethical marketers ensure that such adverts are transparently identified, using labels like "sponsored" or "advertisement" to avoid confusing or deceiving the audience.

Additionally, the **frequency and format** of digital advertising require careful consideration. Overloading consumers with intrusive pop-ups, autoplay videos, or excessive retargeting can create a negative user experience. While these tactics may generate short-term results, they often lead to long-term damage, such as higher ad blocker usage or negative brand perception. Striking a balance between visibility and respect for the user's online experience is crucial. Ethical advertisers prioritise quality over quantity, focusing on creating ads that add value rather than disrupt.

Social responsibility is another growing expectation for brands in the digital advertising space. Consumers increasingly demand that brands take a stand on societal and environmental issues. While this presents an opportunity for meaningful engagement, it also requires authenticity and action. Brands must ensure that their messaging aligns with their practices. For example, a fashion company promoting sustainability initiatives must back its claims with tangible efforts, such as reducing waste or sourcing ethically. Empty promises or "greenwashing" can backfire, eroding trust and inviting criticism.

Lastly, **inclusive advertising** is an essential ethical consideration. Representation matters, and digital adverts should reflect the diversity of their audience. This includes portraying individuals of different ethnicities, genders, ages, and abilities in a respectful and authentic manner. Inclusive advertising not only broadens a brand's appeal but also demonstrates a commitment to equality and respect.

In conclusion, **ethical considerations in digital advertising** are integral to building trust, maintaining credibility, and achieving sustainable success. By prioritising transparency, honesty, inclusivity, and social responsibility, brands can create advertising strategies that resonate with consumers while upholding their values. For CMOs, navigating this complex ethical landscape requires vigilance, foresight, and a steadfast commitment to doing what is right, not just what is profitable. Ethical advertising is not merely a compliance exercise; it is a reflection of a brand's character and its respect for the people it serves.

4.10 - Case Study: A Multi-Channel Digital Campaign

Multi-channel digital campaigns are one of the most effective ways for brands to engage their audiences by leveraging multiple platforms and touchpoints. A well-executed multi-channel campaign ensures that each platform complements the others, creating a unified message while tailoring content for specific audiences. For a **Chief Marketing Officer (CMO)**, this approach allows for broader reach, increased engagement, and deeper customer connections. To illustrate, let's explore a hypothetical case study of **EcoGlow**, a sustainable beauty brand, and its campaign, **"Illuminate Your Natural Beauty."**

Campaign Objectives

EcoGlow's primary objectives for the campaign were threefold:

1. **Increase brand awareness** among eco-conscious consumers aged 25–45.
2. **Boost online sales** of its new range of natural skincare products by 20% within three months.
3. **Educate the audience** on the benefits of sustainable beauty practices.

To achieve these goals, EcoGlow designed a multi-channel campaign that included social media, email marketing, influencer partnerships, paid advertising, and a content-rich website.

Social Media: The Heart of Engagement

Social media was the campaign's primary engagement channel, given its ability to foster interaction and reach specific demographics. EcoGlow used **Instagram** for visually appealing posts and videos showcasing its products' ingredients and their eco-friendly packaging. Short-form videos demonstrated simple skincare routines, while carousel posts explained the brand's sustainable sourcing practices.

On **TikTok**, the brand targeted younger audiences with light-hearted content, including challenges like "#GlowNaturally," where users shared their no-makeup skincare results using EcoGlow products. This strategy encouraged user-generated content (UGC) and expanded reach organically.

Meanwhile, **Pinterest** was used to create visually appealing boards featuring beauty tips and eco-friendly lifestyle ideas. Each pin linked back to EcoGlow's website, driving traffic while reinforcing the brand's image as a sustainability leader.

Key results:

- Instagram Stories with polls and swipe-up links achieved a **45% engagement rate**.
- The TikTok challenge generated **500,000 user submissions**, significantly boosting visibility.
- Pinterest boards drove **15% of total campaign website traffic**.

Email Marketing: Personalised Outreach

EcoGlow leveraged its existing email subscriber base for direct, personalised communication. The campaign began with a **teaser email** introducing the new product line, followed by a series of emails sharing product benefits, testimonials, and exclusive discounts. Each email was tailored to different audience segments, such as first-time buyers and repeat customers.

To add value, the brand included educational content, such as downloadable skincare guides and sustainability tips, making the emails feel less promotional. For instance, one email provided a quiz to help users identify their skin type, followed by product recommendations based on the quiz results.

Key results:

- A **38% open rate**, well above industry standards.
- A **25% increase in email-driven sales** during the first month.

Influencer Partnerships: Building Credibility

EcoGlow partnered with **micro-influencers** in the sustainable beauty niche, ensuring authenticity and relatability. Each influencer created personalised content, such as skincare routine videos and "unboxing" posts, highlighting their genuine enthusiasm for the products. Additionally, EcoGlow collaborated with a few mid-tier influencers to extend its reach, carefully selecting creators whose audiences aligned with the brand's values.

To track performance, each influencer was given a unique discount code for their followers. This tactic not only measured ROI but also encouraged immediate purchases.

Key results:

- Influencer-generated content accounted for **30% of total sales** during the campaign.
- User sentiment analysis showed a **90% positive response** to the content, reinforcing the brand's credibility.

Paid Advertising: Amplifying Reach

Paid advertising complemented the organic efforts, focusing on **Google Ads** and **social media promotions**. Google Ads targeted high-intent keywords like "natural skincare" and "eco-friendly beauty products," driving traffic to product-specific landing pages. Retargeting ads reminded users who had visited the website or added items to their carts to complete their purchases.

On social media, paid promotions boosted visibility for high-performing posts, particularly TikTok videos and Instagram Stories. These ads were strategically timed to coincide with peak user activity, such as evenings and weekends.

Key results:

- Google Ads achieved a **20% conversion rate**, outperforming benchmarks.
- Retargeting ads led to a **40% reduction in cart abandonment rates**.

Website: The Campaign Hub

EcoGlow's website served as the central hub for the campaign, housing detailed product information, sustainability certifications, and a blog with educational content. The website's landing pages were optimised for mobile users and designed to guide visitors seamlessly from exploration to purchase.

The blog featured articles on sustainable skincare practices, interviews with the brand's founders, and in-depth product guides. These resources not only boosted SEO rankings but also reinforced EcoGlow's authority in the sustainable beauty space.

Key results:

- Website traffic increased by **50%** during the campaign.
- Blog engagement rates (time spent on page and social shares) increased by **30%**.

Key Takeaways

The **"Illuminate Your Natural Beauty"** campaign achieved remarkable success by integrating multiple channels into a cohesive strategy. By tailoring content to platform-specific strengths and maintaining a consistent brand message, EcoGlow delivered a memorable experience that resonated with its audience. The campaign's key achievements included:

- A **25% increase in sales**, surpassing the original goal.
- A **60% boost in social media followers**, broadening the brand's reach.
- Strengthened customer trust and loyalty through authentic storytelling and transparent practices.

Lessons for CMOs

For CMOs planning multi-channel campaigns, EcoGlow's example highlights several best practices:

1. **Align goals across channels:** Ensure every platform contributes to the campaign's overarching objectives.
2. **Leverage platform strengths:** Tailor content to suit the unique characteristics of each channel.
3. **Monitor and adapt in real time:** Use performance data to refine strategies and optimise results mid-campaign.

4. **Prioritise authenticity:** Build partnerships and content that genuinely reflect the brand's values.

5. **Measure comprehensively:** Combine quantitative metrics (e.g., sales, traffic) with qualitative insights (e.g., sentiment analysis) for a complete evaluation.

In conclusion, multi-channel campaigns are a powerful way to engage diverse audiences, drive measurable results, and reinforce brand identity. By integrating creativity, data, and customer-centricity, CMOs can orchestrate campaigns that not only achieve their goals but also leave a lasting impact.

Chapter 5

Customer-Centric Marketing

> "Customer loyalty is not a given; it's earned through consistency, transparency, and a relentless focus on delivering value."
>
> **Robert N. Jacobs**

In an era where customer expectations are constantly evolving, businesses must place the customer at the heart of their marketing strategies to thrive. Customer-centric marketing is not merely a tactic but a comprehensive approach to understanding, engaging, and building lasting relationships with customers.

This chapter explores the pivotal elements of creating exceptional customer experiences, from mapping dynamic customer journeys to leveraging data-driven insights, building detailed buyer personas, and fostering retention through tailored strategies. By emphasising empathy, personalisation, and continuous improvement, marketers can transform interactions into meaningful engagements, ensuring loyalty and advocacy in an increasingly competitive marketplace.

Understanding the Customer Journey

The **customer journey** is the blueprint of a customer's interaction with a brand, encompassing every stage, from initial awareness to becoming a loyal advocate. For a **Chief Marketing Officer (CMO)**, mapping and optimising this journey is essential for ensuring that each interaction aligns with customer needs and expectations, ultimately driving satisfaction and loyalty.

Modern customer journeys are no longer linear. Traditionally, marketers envisioned the journey as a straightforward funnel: **awareness**, **consideration**, **decision**, and **purchase**. Today, however, customers frequently jump between stages, revisit earlier decisions, and interact with brands across multiple channels. A customer might discover a product on Instagram, research reviews on Google, visit a store to see it in person and finally make a purchase online. This complexity demands a more nuanced understanding of how customers navigate their decision-making process. Key stages of the customer journey are:

- **Awareness**: The customer becomes aware of a product or service, often through advertising, word-of-mouth, or content marketing.
- **Consideration**: The customer evaluates options, compares competitors, and seeks validation through reviews or recommendations.
- **Decision**: A purchase decision is made, influenced by factors like pricing, trust in the brand, and convenience.
- **Post-Purchase**: The customer assesses their satisfaction and decides whether to continue engaging with the brand.
- **Advocacy**: A loyal customer becomes an ambassador, sharing their positive experiences and driving word-of-mouth referrals.

Each stage presents opportunities and challenges. For example, during the **awareness phase**, a clothing retailer might focus on creating visually appealing social media campaigns to capture attention. However, during the **post-purchase stage**, the focus shifts to providing exceptional support and fostering loyalty, such as by offering a hassle-free return process or personalised thank-you messages.

Mapping the customer journey involves identifying key **touchpoints** and evaluating their effectiveness. These touchpoints include:

- **Digital interactions**, such as website visits, social media engagement, and email marketing.
- **In-person experiences**, like store visits or event participation.
- **Customer service interactions**, such as live chat or phone support.

For instance, an e-commerce brand might use **website analytics** to identify a high bounce rate on its checkout page. This insight highlights a potential pain point; perhaps the process is too complex, or shipping costs are unclear. Addressing this issue by simplifying the checkout flow or offering upfront shipping estimates can significantly improve conversion rates.

Empathy is crucial in understanding the journey. Beyond tracking behaviours, brands must explore the **emotions** that influence customer decisions. For example, a customer shopping for health insurance might feel anxious about making the right choice. A brand that simplifies the decision-making process through easy-to-understand content and empathetic customer support can build trust and reduce stress.

Modern tools help brands refine the journey and enhance touchpoints:

- **AI-driven analytics** identify patterns and predict behaviours, allowing brands to anticipate customer needs.
- **Heatmaps** reveal how users interact with web pages, enabling improvements in design and usability.
- **CRM systems** consolidate customer data, providing a 360-degree view that supports personalisation.

For example, a fitness app might use CRM data to send tailored workout reminders based on a user's activity patterns, reinforcing engagement and satisfaction.

The journey doesn't end at the point of purchase. Post-purchase interactions are vital for building loyalty and encouraging repeat business. Examples include:

- Sending personalised thank-you emails with recommendations for complementary products.
- Offering loyalty rewards or discounts on future purchases.
- Following up with surveys to gather feedback and demonstrate that the brand values the customer's opinion.

These efforts reinforce positive experiences and foster long-term relationships.

Customer journeys are dynamic, evolving alongside consumer expectations and technological advancements. Regularly reviewing and updating journey maps ensures that strategies remain relevant. For instance, the rise of voice search and smart assistants has introduced new touchpoints that brands must integrate into their strategies.

In conclusion, understanding the **customer journey** is about more than identifying touchpoints, it's about creating seamless, meaningful interactions that align with customer needs and emotions. By empathising with their experiences, optimising key stages, and leveraging technology, CMOs can build trust, foster loyalty, and drive advocacy in a competitive market.

Building Buyer Personas

Buyer personas are a critical tool for designing customer-centric marketing strategies. These **semi-fictional profiles** represent ideal customers based on **real data and insights**, enabling brands to understand and address the needs, motivations, and behaviours of their target audience. For a **Chief Marketing Officer (CMO)**, developing comprehensive buyer personas is essential for crafting effective messaging and delivering personalised customer experiences.

A well-crafted **buyer persona** goes beyond basic **demographics** such as age, gender, and income level. It includes **psychographic data**, such as values, interests, and pain points, providing a holistic view of the customer. For example, a luxury skincare brand might create a persona named **Sophia**, a 38-year-old professional who prioritises high-quality, eco-friendly products and is willing to pay a premium for them. In contrast, a budget-conscious fitness brand could focus on **Mark**, a 29-year-old urban resident seeking affordable, space-saving workout solutions for his apartment. These profiles guide marketing strategies, ensuring relevance and impact.

The process of building personas begins with data collection. Key sources include:

- **Customer surveys**: Offering direct insights into preferences, challenges, and buying behaviours.

- **Social media analytics**: Highlighting trends, interests, and engagement patterns across platforms.

- **Purchase histories**: Providing a clear picture of product preferences and buying frequency.

- **Customer support feedback**: Revealing common complaints, questions, and areas of dissatisfaction. For instance, a travel agency might discover through surveys and purchase data that many of its customers are professionals aged 30–45 who prefer short, adventure-focused holidays. This information forms the foundation for a persona tailored to this audience's specific needs and interests.

Once data is collected, brands must look for patterns to group customers into meaningful segments. These **segments** may be based on shared demographics, values, or behaviours. For example, a fitness equipment company might develop three distinct personas:

1. **Beginner Bella**, a first-time gym-goer seeking simple and affordable equipment.

2. **Weekend Warrior Will** is a casual exerciser who values versatility and convenience.

3. **Athletic Alex**, a performance-driven athlete looking for advanced features and durability.

Empathy plays a critical role in building effective personas. Beyond analysing data, marketers must consider the **emotional factors** influencing customer decisions. For instance, a family-focused car buyer might prioritise safety and spaciousness out of concern for their loved ones, while a persona for an eco-conscious coffee brand could emphasise the customer's desire to make sustainable choices. Addressing these emotional triggers in **messaging**, **product design**, and **content marketing** fosters stronger connections and loyalty.

Buyer personas are not static. They should evolve as customer preferences, market conditions, and external factors change. For example, a technology company initially targeting millennials might notice that its audience is ageing and shift its messaging to include family-friendly features or sustainability. Regularly updating personas ensures that marketing strategies remain relevant and effective.

Using **buyer personas** effectively involves integrating them into all aspects of marketing. They guide **content creation**, **campaign targeting**, and **product development**, ensuring alignment with customer expectations. For example, a persona like **Eco-Minded Emma** might inspire a sustainable fashion retailer to emphasise ethically sourced materials and minimalist designs in its advertising. Similarly, a persona focused on convenience could drive a grocery delivery service to highlight its time-saving app features.

In conclusion, **buyer personas** are a strategic tool for understanding customers on a deeper level and tailoring marketing efforts to meet their needs. By grounding personas in **real data** and enriching them with **empathy**, brands can deliver personalised, impactful experiences that foster loyalty and trust. For CMOs, investing in well-crafted personas is not just a tactic; it's a vital step in achieving long-term success in a customer-centric marketplace.

Data-Driven Customer Insights

In today's competitive landscape, **data-driven customer insights** have become indispensable for creating effective marketing strategies. These insights allow brands to understand their customers deeply, anticipate their needs, and deliver personalised experiences. For a **Chief Marketing Officer (CMO)**, leveraging data is not just a tactical advantage; it is a strategic necessity for fostering loyalty and driving growth.

Customer data comes from numerous sources, offering a rich pool of information. **Website analytics**, for example, track browsing patterns, helping brands identify popular products or pages with high bounce rates. **Social media platforms** reveal trends, engagement levels, and audience sentiment, while **purchase histories** offer clues about buying habits and product preferences. **Surveys and feedback forms** provide qualitative data, capturing customer opinions and emotions. Together, these sources create a comprehensive picture of customer behaviour and expectations.

The value of **data-driven insights** lies in their ability to inform decision-making. For instance, a subscription-based streaming service might analyse user behaviour to identify the most-watched genres, enabling it to recommend relevant content. Similarly, a retail brand might notice that customers frequently abandon their carts due to high shipping costs. Addressing this issue, perhaps by offering free shipping thresholds, can improve the shopping experience and boost conversions.

Segmentation is one of the most powerful applications of customer data. By dividing customers into distinct groups based on shared characteristics, brands can deliver tailored messages and offers. For example, an online bookstore could segment its audience into fiction enthusiasts, academic readers, and self-help seekers. Each group would receive personalised recommendations that align with their interests, increasing the likelihood of engagement and purchase.

Predictive analytics takes data-driven insights to the next level by forecasting future customer behaviour. This allows brands to anticipate needs and act proactively. For example, a fitness app might use predictive models to identify users at risk of abandoning their workout routines. Sending motivational messages or offering personalised workout plans could help retain these customers and reinforce their commitment to the app.

Personalisation is another critical benefit of data-driven insights. Customers increasingly expect tailored experiences that align with their preferences. For instance, a beauty retailer might use purchase history to recommend complementary products or offer discounts on frequently purchased items. Such personalised interactions demonstrate that the brand values its customers, strengthening emotional connections and loyalty.

While the advantages of **data-driven strategies** are clear, they come with challenges. One significant concern is **data quality**. Outdated or incomplete data can lead to incorrect conclusions and wasted resources. Ensuring accuracy requires regular cleansing and validation. **Data silos**, where information is stored in disconnected systems, can also hinder effective analysis. Integrating data sources into a unified platform, such as a **Customer Relationship Management (CRM)** system, ensures consistency and accessibility.

Ethical considerations are equally important. Customers are increasingly aware of how their data is used, and mishandling it can damage trust. Brands must comply with regulations like **GDPR** and prioritise transparency, explaining how data will be used and ensuring it benefits the customer. For instance, a grocery delivery service might inform users that their data is used to suggest items they frequently buy, making the shopping process quicker and more convenient.

Measuring the effectiveness of **data-driven strategies** is essential for continuous improvement. Metrics like **conversion rates**, **customer lifetime value (CLV)**, and **engagement levels** reveal whether insights are driving desired outcomes. For example, an email campaign informed by segmentation might track open rates and purchases, providing a clear picture of its success.

In conclusion, **data-driven customer insights** empower brands to make informed, impactful decisions. By collecting, analysing, and acting on data responsibly, CMOs can anticipate customer needs, personalise experiences, and create lasting loyalty. In a market where customer expectations are constantly evolving, harnessing the power of data is not just a strategy; it is a cornerstone of sustainable success.

Developing a Customer Retention Strategy

While acquiring new customers is an essential focus for any business, **customer retention** is often more cost-effective and impactful in driving long-term profitability. Retaining existing customers not only reduces acquisition costs but also fosters loyalty, increases repeat purchases, and builds strong advocacy. For a **Chief Marketing Officer (CMO)**, crafting a robust **customer retention strategy** is a critical element of a customer-centric approach.

Customer retention begins with delivering consistent value. Customers return to brands that meet or exceed their expectations, whether through high-quality products, exceptional service, or unique experiences. For instance, a subscription box service offering carefully curated products tailored to a customer's preferences ensures they feel valued and understood. Consistency in delivering on promises is the foundation for building trust, which is the bedrock of loyalty.

Customer-Centric Marketing

Personalisation is key to successful retention. Customers expect interactions that reflect their unique preferences and behaviours. A robust **Customer Relationship Management (CRM)** system can help track purchase histories, browsing patterns, and engagement metrics, enabling personalised recommendations and targeted communication. For example, a fashion retailer might email a customer with suggestions for accessories that complement a recent clothing purchase or offer a discount on their favourite brands. These personalised touches show the customer they are more than just a number.

A well-designed **loyalty programme** is a powerful tool for encouraging repeat business. Offering incentives such as points, rewards, or exclusive benefits reinforces positive behaviour and strengthens emotional connections. For instance, a coffee shop might implement a rewards card, allowing customers to earn a free beverage after a set number of purchases. Alternatively, a travel company might offer tiered loyalty levels, granting frequent travellers access to priority check-ins, upgrades, or discounted fares. The key to an effective loyalty programme is ensuring the rewards are meaningful and align with customer values.

Proactive **customer engagement** is equally critical for retention. Brands must consistently stay connected with their audience, even outside of transactional moments. This can be achieved through thoughtful email campaigns, newsletters, or social media interactions. For example, a fitness app could send motivational messages, progress updates, or tips for staying on track, fostering a sense of ongoing support and partnership.

Exceptional customer service is a non-negotiable aspect of retention. A positive resolution to an issue can turn a dissatisfied customer into a loyal advocate. For example, if an airline responds swiftly to a lost luggage complaint, offering updates, a quick resolution, and compensation, the customer is more likely to remember the brand's care than the initial inconvenience. Empathy, efficiency, and responsiveness are critical qualities for support teams handling customer concerns.

Feedback loops play an important role in retention strategies. Gathering insights from surveys, reviews, and direct customer interactions allows brands to identify and address pain points. For instance, an e-commerce company might notice through customer surveys that unclear return policies are a recurring complaint. Simplifying the return process and clearly communicating it can enhance the overall experience and reduce friction, encouraging customers to continue shopping with the brand.

Metrics are essential for evaluating the success of retention efforts. Key indicators include **customer lifetime value (CLV)**, **churn rate**, **repeat purchase rate**, and **Net Promoter Score (NPS)**. These metrics provide insights into customer loyalty and satisfaction. For example, a streaming service tracking churn rates might notice that cancellations spike after free trials end. Addressing this with targeted retention campaigns, such as offering discounts or highlighting premium features, can reduce attrition and increase loyalty.

Transparency and ethical practices also contribute to retention. Customers are more likely to remain loyal to brands they trust. Honesty about pricing, policies, and product performance builds credibility. For instance, a skincare brand being upfront about the potential side effects of its products while offering detailed usage instructions shows care for the customer's well-being.

In conclusion, **developing a customer retention strategy** involves more than keeping customers engaged; it is about fostering lasting relationships built on trust, value, and consistent care. By focusing on personalisation, loyalty programmes, proactive engagement, and exceptional service, CMOs can create a customer-centric approach that drives long-term growth. Retention is not just about reducing churn; it is about building advocates who actively promote the brand and ensure its success in a competitive marketplace.

Feedback Loops: Listening to Your Audience

Feedback loops are a cornerstone of customer-centric marketing. They provide a mechanism for brands to collect, analyse, and act on customer insights, ensuring continuous improvement in products, services, and overall customer experience. For a **Chief Marketing Officer (CMO)**, establishing robust feedback loops is essential not only for addressing customer concerns but also for fostering trust and loyalty by showing customers that their voices matter.

The first step in creating an effective **feedback loop** is collecting customer input. Feedback can come from multiple sources, including surveys, online reviews, social media comments, and customer service interactions. For instance, an e-commerce retailer might send post-purchase surveys asking customers to rate their shopping experience, delivery efficiency, and product satisfaction. Social media monitoring can also provide unfiltered feedback, revealing both praise and complaints in real-time. Together, these sources offer a comprehensive view of customer sentiment.

Active listening is key to making feedback loops effective. Customers want to feel heard and valued, and ignoring or mishandling their input can erode trust. Brands should acknowledge all feedback, both positive and negative, and express gratitude for the customer's time and insights. For example, a software company might respond to a user's complaint about bugs with a message such as, "Thank you for sharing your concerns. We're addressing this issue and will keep you updated on the fix." This response demonstrates accountability and empathy, strengthening the relationship even in challenging situations.

Closing the loop is a critical yet often overlooked aspect of feedback management. Once customer feedback has been acted upon, it is important to communicate the changes made. For instance, if a restaurant receives multiple complaints about slow service, improving staff training or hiring additional team members addresses the root issue. Following up with customers, such as through a social media post explaining the improvements, shows that the brand takes feedback seriously and is committed to growth.

Customer-Centric Marketing

Recurring themes in customer feedback often highlight systemic issues or opportunities for innovation. Analysing patterns across multiple channels can reveal insights that individual comments might not. For example, a travel company noticing frequent complaints about confusing booking processes might redesign its website to offer clearer navigation and upfront pricing. Addressing such recurring issues improves customer experience and reduces friction across touchpoints.

Negative feedback, while uncomfortable, is one of the most valuable tools for improvement. Brands that embrace criticism as an opportunity rather than a threat can transform detractors into loyal advocates. For example, a fitness brand that receives complaints about the durability of its equipment might not only improve product materials but also offer replacements or refunds to affected customers. These actions demonstrate a commitment to quality and customer satisfaction.

Transparency is essential in managing feedback. Customers appreciate honesty, even when problems cannot be resolved immediately. For instance, a clothing retailer experiencing supply chain delays should proactively inform customers and provide updates rather than waiting for complaints to escalate. This approach builds trust, as it shows the brand values the customer's time and experience.

Feedback loops are also a powerful driver of **innovation**. Many successful products and features are born from customer suggestions. For example, a smartphone manufacturer noticing repeated requests for longer battery life might prioritise this feature in its next model. Engaging customers in the development process, such as by conducting beta testing or focus groups, further strengthens their loyalty and sense of ownership.

Measuring the effectiveness of feedback loops requires tracking key metrics, such as **Net Promoter Score (NPS)**, **Customer Satisfaction Score (CSAT)**, and resolution times for complaints. These indicators provide insights into how well the brand is addressing customer concerns and maintaining satisfaction. For instance, a rising NPS score suggests that customers are not only satisfied but also willing to recommend the brand to others.

In conclusion, **feedback loops** are a vital tool for listening to your audience, addressing their needs, and continuously improving their experience. By collecting input, responding with empathy, and taking meaningful action, brands can build stronger relationships and demonstrate their commitment to customers. For CMOs, mastering feedback loops is not just about solving problems; it is about fostering trust, loyalty, and advocacy in an ever-evolving marketplace.

Nurturing Customer Relationships Through CRM

In the era of personalisation and customer-centric marketing, **Customer Relationship Management (CRM)** systems are indispensable for fostering meaningful and long-lasting relationships. For a **Chief Marketing Officer (CMO)**, leveraging CRM effectively is key to understanding customer behaviour, delivering personalised experiences, and maximising lifetime value. A robust CRM system doesn't just store customer data; it provides actionable insights that help brands engage with customers on a deeper level.

At its core, a **CRM system** acts as a centralised hub for managing customer interactions across all touchpoints. It consolidates data from multiple channels, such as website visits, email campaigns, purchase histories, and customer service interactions, into a unified profile for each customer. This holistic view allows brands to track a customer's journey, anticipate their needs, and tailor communications accordingly.

Personalisation is one of the most powerful outcomes of a well-implemented CRM system. Customers today expect brands to understand their preferences and provide relevant, meaningful experiences. For example, a fitness subscription service might use CRM data to identify customers who haven't engaged recently and send them tailored workout reminders or personalised offers. This not only re-engages dormant users but also demonstrates that the brand values their involvement.

CRM systems also enable effective **segmentation**. By grouping customers based on shared characteristics or behaviours, brands can deliver highly targeted messages. For instance, an online bookstore might segment its audience into avid fiction readers, academic researchers, and self-help enthusiasts. Each group would receive customised recommendations, such as new releases in their preferred genre or discounts on relevant titles. Such tailored communications enhance engagement and increase the likelihood of repeat purchases.

Another critical function of CRM is its ability to facilitate automation. Automated workflows allow brands to maintain consistent communication without overwhelming their teams. Examples include:

- **Welcome emails** sent to new subscribers with tips or introductory offers.
- **Abandoned cart reminders**, encouraging customers to complete their purchases.
- **Milestone acknowledgements**, such as birthday discounts or loyalty anniversaries.

For example, a travel company might use CRM automation to send pre-trip checklists, destination guides, and post-trip feedback requests. These touchpoints create a seamless experience while strengthening the customer's relationship with the brand.

A well-integrated CRM system also improves **customer service**. When support teams have access to detailed customer profiles, they can provide faster, more informed assistance. For instance, if a customer contacts a telecom provider about a billing issue, the representative can view their history to resolve the problem efficiently. This reduces frustration and leaves a positive impression.

Transparency and ethical data usage are critical when using CRM systems. Customers are increasingly aware of how their data is collected and utilised, and mishandling it can damage trust. Brands must clearly communicate how they use customer data to improve services. For example, a food delivery app might inform users that their order history is used to suggest relevant dishes or customise promotions. Maintaining this transparency ensures that CRM efforts align with customer expectations and legal requirements like GDPR.

Measuring the success of CRM strategies is essential for optimisation. Key metrics include:

- **Customer retention rates**, indicating how well the brand maintains relationships over time.

- **Customer lifetime value (CLV)**, which measures the total revenue a customer generates during their relationship with the brand.

- **Engagement metrics**, such as email open rates, click-through rates, and campaign conversions.

For instance, an online clothing retailer using CRM might notice that customers with high engagement in loyalty programmes tend to have higher CLV. This insight could guide the brand to expand its loyalty offerings, further boosting retention and revenue.

Finally, CRM systems foster **cross-functional alignment**. By providing a unified view of customer data, CRM ensures that marketing, sales, and customer support teams work cohesively. For example, if the marketing team launches a campaign targeting frequent shoppers, the sales team can anticipate increased inquiries, while the support team is prepared to address potential questions about promotions.

In conclusion, **nurturing customer relationships through CRM** is about more than managing data; it's about using insights to create meaningful, personalised experiences. By understanding customer behaviour, automating thoughtful touchpoints, and aligning internal teams, brands can build trust and loyalty that drive long-term growth. For CMOs, investing in a strong CRM strategy is a cornerstone of successful, customer-centric marketing in an increasingly competitive landscape.

The Role of Customer Experience in Marketing

In today's competitive market, **customer experience (CX)** has become a defining factor for brand success. It encompasses every interaction a customer has with a brand, from the first point of contact to post-purchase engagement. For a **Chief Marketing Officer (CMO)**, creating and managing a seamless, positive **customer experience** is not just about meeting customer expectations; it is about exceeding them, fostering loyalty, and driving advocacy.

At its core, **CX** is about perception. How a customer feels about their interactions with a brand directly influences their behaviour. A customer who encounters smooth navigation on a website, prompt support for a query, or a personalised thank-you message is far more likely to return than one who experiences frustration or indifference. This is why **CX** plays a pivotal role in shaping brand perception and driving long-term success.

One key aspect of **customer experience** is **personalisation**. Customers today expect brands to understand their preferences and deliver relevant, tailored experiences. For instance, a streaming platform that recommends movies based on a user's viewing history provides a personalised experience that not only adds value but also deepens the emotional connection with the brand. Similarly, an e-commerce site that remembers past purchases and offers targeted discounts shows customers that they are valued as individuals.

Consistency is another critical factor in creating exceptional **CX**. Customers interact with brands across multiple channels, websites, apps, social media, physical stores, and more. Ensuring a cohesive experience across all touchpoints is essential for building trust and credibility. For example, a customer who starts a transaction online and completes it in-store should experience the same level of service and professionalism. This consistency reinforces the brand's reliability and fosters loyalty.

Technology plays a significant role in enhancing **CX**. Tools like **AI**, **chatbots**, and **data analytics** enable brands to offer faster, more accurate responses to customer needs. For example, a chatbot on a retail website can handle basic inquiries 24/7, reducing wait times and improving satisfaction. Similarly, **predictive analytics** can anticipate customer needs, such as reminding a customer to reorder a product they regularly purchase, creating a sense of convenience and care.

Transparency and trust are fundamental to **CX**. Customers are increasingly conscious of how brands handle their data and the ethical implications of their operations. A transparent brand that openly communicates its policies, pricing, and values builds stronger relationships. For instance, a cosmetics company highlighting its cruelty-free practices not only aligns with customer values but also strengthens emotional connections.

Feedback is a vital component of improving **CX**. Actively listening to customers through surveys, reviews, and social media comments provides valuable insights into what is working and what needs improvement. For example, a hospitality brand that receives consistent feedback about slow check-in processes might implement self-check-in kiosks to enhance the experience. Closing the feedback loop by informing customers about changes made based on their input further reinforces trust and loyalty.

Emotional connections are another layer of impactful **CX**. Brands that resonate with customers on an emotional level create lasting impressions. For example, a luxury hotel that surprises a guest with a personalised gift for a special occasion demonstrates thoughtfulness and care, turning a simple stay into a memorable experience. Similarly, brands that share compelling stories about their mission or impact can inspire deeper loyalty.

Measuring the success of **CX** initiatives requires a combination of quantitative and qualitative metrics. **Net Promoter Score (NPS)**, **Customer Satisfaction Score (CSAT)**, and **Customer Effort Score (CES)** are widely used to gauge customer sentiment. For example, a high **CES** score indicates that customers find interactions with the brand easy and convenient, which is a strong predictor of loyalty.

In conclusion, **customer experience** is the cornerstone of modern marketing, influencing how customers perceive, engage with, and advocate for a brand. By focusing on personalisation, consistency, transparency, and emotional connection, CMOs can create experiences that delight customers and foster loyalty. In a marketplace where customers have more choices than ever, investing in exceptional **CX** is not just a competitive advantage; it is a necessity for long-term success.

Managing Negative Feedback and Reviews

In the digital age, **negative feedback and reviews** are an inevitable aspect of any brand's interaction with its audience. While no company is immune to criticism, how a brand handles it can significantly impact its reputation, customer relationships, and long-term success. For a **Chief Marketing Officer (CMO)**, managing negative feedback effectively is a critical component of maintaining trust, addressing concerns, and fostering loyalty.

Negative feedback often feels daunting, but it is a valuable opportunity to learn and improve. Customers who share complaints are providing insights into pain points, unmet expectations, or potential flaws in a product or service. A proactive approach to managing feedback demonstrates accountability and a commitment to growth, turning what could be a reputational challenge into a chance to build trust.

Acknowledgement and empathy are the first steps in addressing negative feedback. Customers want to feel heard and understood. Ignoring or dismissing criticism can escalate dissatisfaction and alienate customers further. For example, if a customer leaves a review about delayed shipping, a brand's response might read: *"We're truly sorry for the inconvenience caused by the delay. We understand how frustrating this must be and are taking steps to ensure this doesn't happen again."* This type of empathetic response not only validates the customer's experience but also demonstrates that the brand values their feedback.

Transparency is crucial in managing negative reviews. If the issue is widespread, such as a product defect or service disruption, acknowledging it publicly and explaining the steps being taken to resolve it can prevent further backlash. For instance, a telecom company experiencing a network outage might issue a public statement detailing the problem and providing an estimated resolution time. This level of honesty builds credibility and reassures customers that the brand is committed to resolving the issue.

Offering solutions is an effective way to turn a negative experience into a positive one. Customers are often looking for resolutions rather than just apologies. Depending on the situation, this might involve refunds, replacements, discounts, or additional support. For example, an online retailer facing complaints about incorrect orders might offer free expedited shipping on a corrected order. This not only resolves the immediate issue but also demonstrates the brand's dedication to customer satisfaction.

Handling feedback on public platforms, such as social media and review websites, requires a careful balance of professionalism and authenticity. These platforms amplify the visibility of criticism, but they also provide an opportunity to showcase responsiveness and care. For instance, a restaurant receiving a negative Yelp review about poor service could respond with a message like: *"We're sorry your experience didn't meet our usual standards. We'd love the chance to make it right; please contact us so we can address your concerns personally."* This approach shows a willingness to engage and rectify the issue.

Brands must also differentiate between constructive criticism and **malicious or false claims**. While constructive feedback should be addressed with empathy and solutions, malicious comments aimed at damaging a brand's reputation may require a different strategy. Platforms often have guidelines for reporting or flagging inappropriate content, but responding professionally and presenting factual corrections can also mitigate the impact of false claims.

Learning from feedback is equally important. Recurring complaints often highlight systemic issues that need attention. For example, if customers frequently complain about confusing instructions for assembling a product, the brand should revise its user manual or provide additional resources, such as video tutorials. Acting on this feedback not only improves the product or service but also prevents similar complaints in the future.

Real-time monitoring tools are invaluable for managing negative feedback effectively. Social listening platforms such as Hootsuite or Brandwatch enable brands to track mentions, reviews, and sentiment across channels. This allows CMOs to identify issues as they arise and address them promptly before they escalate. For instance, a travel company noticing multiple tweets about delayed flights can respond quickly with updates and support, minimising frustration and demonstrating accountability.

Lastly, turning negative feedback into a positive experience creates loyal advocates. Customers appreciate brands that go the extra mile to resolve their concerns. For example, a customer frustrated with a delayed order might become a lifelong advocate after receiving a personalised apology and a discount on their next purchase. These moments of redemption can strengthen relationships and humanise the brand.

In conclusion, **managing negative feedback and reviews** is about more than damage control; it's about demonstrating care, accountability, and a commitment to improvement. By acknowledging concerns, offering solutions, and learning from criticism, CMOs can transform challenges into opportunities for building trust and loyalty. In an age where transparency and responsiveness are paramount, a brand's ability to handle negative feedback effectively is a defining factor in its reputation and success.

Creating Memorable Customer Touchpoints

In the world of customer-centric marketing, **touchpoints** represent every interaction a customer has with a brand, whether online, offline, or through communication channels. These moments collectively shape the customer's perception of the brand and influence their decisions. For a **Chief Marketing Officer (CMO)**, the challenge is to ensure that these touchpoints are not only seamless but also memorable, leaving a lasting positive impression.

Creating **memorable customer touchpoints** begins with understanding the **customer journey**. Each stage of this journey, **awareness**, **consideration**, **decision**, **purchase**, and **post-purchase**, offers opportunities to delight customers. For example, during the awareness phase, a visually engaging social media campaign with authentic storytelling can capture attention and spark curiosity. In contrast, the post-purchase stage focuses on maintaining satisfaction and encouraging loyalty, such as sending personalised thank-you emails or offering exclusive rewards for repeat purchases.

Personalisation plays a central role in creating impactful touchpoints. Customers are far more likely to remember interactions that feel tailored to their preferences, needs, or past behaviour. For example, an online clothing retailer can use data from purchase history to recommend complementary items or notify customers when their favourite brand launches a new collection. Such personalised touches demonstrate that the brand values the individual customer and understands their preferences, fostering a deeper emotional connection.

Consistency across all channels is equally important. In today's omnichannel world, customers interact with brands through multiple touchpoints, such as websites, apps, social media, and physical stores. A cohesive experience ensures that customers receive the same level of quality, attention, and messaging, regardless of where or how they engage. For instance, a customer who starts browsing products on a mobile app and completes their purchase in-store should encounter consistent pricing, promotions, and branding throughout.

Digital touchpoints often form the foundation of customer experiences in the modern age. A fast-loading, intuitive website with clear navigation ensures that customers can find what they need without frustration. Interactive features, such as augmented reality (AR) tools or virtual try-ons, add an element of excitement and engagement. For example, a furniture brand offering an AR feature that allows customers to visualise how a sofa will look in their living room creates a memorable and practical experience that stands out.

Equally significant are **in-person touchpoints**, where small, thoughtful gestures can leave lasting impressions. A coffee shop that remembers a regular customer's favourite order, greets them warmly, and offers a loyalty reward creates a sense of belonging that encourages repeat visits. These seemingly minor details differentiate the brand from competitors and ensure that customers feel valued.

Emotional connections are at the heart of memorable touchpoints. A brand that goes the extra mile to surprise or delight customers can create positive associations that endure. For instance, a subscription box service might include a handwritten thank-you note or an unexpected free gift in its deliveries. These personalised gestures exceed expectations and build goodwill, turning a simple transaction into an unforgettable experience.

Customer service interactions are another critical touchpoint. When customers seek help, their experience with the support team can make or break their perception of the brand. Quick, empathetic resolutions to issues demonstrate care and competence, strengthening trust. For example, an airline that swiftly rebooks a missed flight and provides compensation for the inconvenience leaves a more lasting positive impression than one that offers no proactive solutions.

To ensure touchpoints remain impactful, brands must actively seek **customer feedback** and refine their strategies. Surveys, reviews, and analytics provide valuable insights into what works and what needs improvement. For example, an e-commerce platform noticing frequent complaints about its return process might streamline it by offering prepaid labels and automated refunds. These enhancements reduce friction and improve the overall experience.

In conclusion, **creating memorable customer touchpoints** is about delivering value, evoking emotions, and building trust at every stage of the customer journey. By prioritising personalisation, ensuring consistency, and exceeding expectations, CMOs can craft experiences that not only delight customers but also foster loyalty and advocacy. In a competitive marketplace, memorable touchpoints are the key to standing out and creating lasting relationships with customers.

Case Study: Transforming Customer Experience

To demonstrate the power of a customer-centric approach, let us examine the case of **HomeStyle Solutions**, a mid-sized furniture retailer that transformed its **customer experience (CX)** strategy to address critical challenges and emerge as a leader in its industry. For a **Chief Marketing Officer (CMO)**, this example highlights the importance of listening to customers, adapting to their needs, and fostering loyalty through meaningful interactions.

The Challenge

HomeStyle Solutions faced significant hurdles in delivering a seamless customer experience. Common customer complaints included:

- **A confusing website interface**, which made it difficult for users to navigate and purchase items.
- **Inconsistent in-store service**, with staff failing to provide personalised recommendations or assistance.
- **Delayed deliveries**, leaving customers frustrated and leading to negative reviews.
- **Limited post-purchase engagement**, resulting in low customer retention and reduced lifetime value.

These issues were eroding customer trust and loyalty, causing HomeStyle to lose market share to competitors who prioritised CX. Recognising the urgency of the situation, the company decided to embark on a comprehensive transformation of its **customer experience strategy**.

The Transformation

HomeStyle's CMO spearheaded a company-wide initiative to address these pain points and redefine the brand's relationship with its customers. The transformation focused on three critical areas: **digital experience**, **in-store service**, and **post-purchase engagement**.

Enhancing the Digital Experience

The first step was overhauling HomeStyle's website to make it more intuitive and user-friendly. Key changes included:

- **Simplified navigation**, enabling customers to find products easily through improved categorisation and search functionality.

- The addition of an **augmented reality (AR) feature**, allowing customers to visualise how furniture would look in their homes before purchasing.

- **Real-time inventory updates** so customers can check product availability at nearby stores or online.

- A streamlined **checkout process**, reducing cart abandonment by offering multiple payment options and upfront shipping costs.

These changes significantly improved the digital journey, making it easier and more enjoyable for customers to shop online.

Improving In-Store Service

HomeStyle trained its in-store staff to deliver a personalised and engaging shopping experience. Initiatives included:

- Equipping staff with **tablet-based CRM systems**, enabling them to access customer profiles and provide tailored recommendations.

- Implementing a **one-on-one consultation programme** where customers could schedule appointments with interior design experts.

- Ensuring **consistent branding and messaging** so the in-store experience aligned seamlessly with the online journey.

These enhancements not only boosted customer satisfaction but also increased in-store sales by 20% within six months.

Fostering Post-Purchase Engagement

To build lasting relationships, HomeStyle focused on proactive communication and value-added services after the sale. Efforts included:

- Sending **personalised thank-you emails** with care instructions and styling tips for purchased items.

- Introducing a **loyalty programme** that rewarded repeat purchases with discounts, exclusive previews, and free design consultations.

- Actively monitoring **customer feedback** through surveys and online reviews, using insights to refine their products and services.

These post-purchase efforts strengthened customer loyalty, with repeat purchase rates rising by 30%.

The Results

HomeStyle's CX transformation yielded impressive outcomes:

- **Customer satisfaction scores increased by 45%**, reflecting the improvements in both online and in-store experiences.

- **Revenue grew by 25%** in the first year, driven by increased repeat purchases and new customer acquisition through positive word-of-mouth.

- **Net Promoter Score (NPS)** improved significantly, with customers praising the brand's personalisation efforts and streamlined processes.

- The new **AR feature** on the website became a standout success, with 60% of online shoppers using it during their purchasing journey.

Lessons for CMOs

The HomeStyle Solutions case study offers valuable lessons for CMOs seeking to prioritise customer experience:

- **Customer feedback is invaluable**: Listening to customers and addressing their concerns is the first step toward meaningful improvement.

- **Consistency is key**: Aligning online and offline experiences creates trust and reduces friction.

- **Personalisation drives loyalty**: Leveraging CRM tools and data insights allows brands to tailor interactions and foster stronger relationships.

- **Proactive engagement matters**: Staying connected with customers post-purchase builds long-term loyalty and advocacy.

Conclusion

The transformation of **HomeStyle Solutions** illustrates how a focus on **customer experience** can turn challenges into opportunities. By addressing customer pain points, leveraging technology, and fostering meaningful engagement, the company not only resolved its immediate issues but also positioned itself as a leader in its market. For CMOs, this case study reinforces the importance of a customer-first approach in creating sustainable growth and competitive advantage.

Chapter 6

Leading High-Performing Marketing Teams

> "Great marketing teams are not built on talent alone; they thrive where vision ignites purpose, collaboration fuels creativity, and every member feels empowered to transform challenges into opportunities for success."
>
> **Robert N. Jacobs**

In the dynamic landscape of modern marketing, the effectiveness of a team often determines the success of an organization's broader objectives. Chapter 6 delves into the art and science of building and leading high-performing marketing teams, a core responsibility for any Chief Marketing Officer (CMO). This chapter emphasises the importance of cultivating a cohesive, innovative, and results-driven team capable of navigating the challenges and opportunities in today's marketing environment.

From assembling the right mix of talent and fostering creativity to ensuring cultural alignment and promoting collaboration, the insights in this chapter provide a comprehensive roadmap for leadership excellence. Drawing on practical strategies, real-world examples, and actionable advice, it equips CMOs to inspire their teams, drive exceptional performance, and align individual contributions with organisational goals. By mastering these principles, marketing leaders can not only achieve impactful results but also create an environment where their teams thrive professionally and personally.

6.1 - Building and Scaling a Marketing Team

Building and scaling a **marketing team** is one of the most critical responsibilities of a **Chief Marketing Officer (CMO)**. A well-structured and effective team forms the backbone of all marketing strategies, ensuring that the company's goals are met with innovation, precision, and efficiency. Whether a company is a startup building a team from scratch or an established organisation looking to scale operations, success depends on assembling the right mix of talent and creating an environment where they can thrive.

The first step in building a marketing team is understanding the organisation's current needs and long-term objectives. A startup launching its first product will require a lean, versatile team capable of wearing multiple hats, while a larger enterprise may prioritise specialists to handle different functions like **content marketing**, **social media management**, or **SEO optimisation**. Defining these needs helps clarify the roles required and the skill sets to seek during recruitmentScaling a marketing team involves balancing the needs of today with the demands of tomorrow. A common mistake is over-hiring without a clear roadmap for integration. For example, rapidly adding team members without first establishing workflows or tools for collaboration can lead to inefficiency and frustration. To avoid this, a CMO must ensure that the infrastructure, such as project management tools, communication platforms, and reporting systems, is robust enough to support team growth.

Team structure is another vital consideration. Will the team operate as a centralised unit, or will it be divided into specialised departments? For instance, a global organisation might choose to have regional marketing teams tailored to local markets, while a smaller company might centralise operations for efficiency. Both approaches have their advantages, but the key is aligning structure with strategy.

Recruiting the right people is only part of the equation. Retaining talent is equally crucial, particularly in competitive industries. Offering professional development opportunities, promoting a positive workplace culture, and recognising individual contributions go a long way in keeping employees engaged. For example, a company that provides access to training programmes or certifications not only helps its team grow but also signals a commitment to its long-term success.

As the team scales, fostering communication becomes increasingly important. With more people involved, there is a greater risk of silos forming, where departments or individuals work in isolation rather than collaboratively. Regular meetings, open communication channels, and cross-functional projects can help break down these silos. For example, pairing content marketers with product managers on a campaign can ensure that messaging aligns with the product's features and benefits.

Lastly, scaling a marketing team also requires managing resources wisely. Budget constraints are often a concern, and CMOs must prioritise hiring roles that deliver the highest impact. For instance, investing in a **data analyst** early on can provide valuable insights that inform the entire team's strategy.

In conclusion, **building and scaling a marketing team** is not simply about filling positions, it's about creating a cohesive unit aligned with the company's goals and values. By focusing on strategic hiring, fostering collaboration, and providing the right tools for success, CMOs can ensure their team is prepared to drive growth and innovation at every stage of the company's journey.

6.2 - Hiring for Skills and Cultural Fit

Hiring for **skills** and **cultural fit** is an essential aspect of building a high-performing marketing team. For a **Chief Marketing Officer (CMO)**, the challenge is to identify candidates who not only possess the technical expertise to excel in their roles but also align with the company's values and mission. The right balance of these elements ensures that each hire contributes to the team's success while fostering a positive and collaborative work environment.

The hiring process begins with a clear understanding of the role and its requirements. A job description that accurately outlines the **skills**, **experience**, and **responsibilities** is crucial for attracting the right talent. For example, when hiring a **content marketing specialist**, the description should specify essential skills such as strong writing ability, SEO knowledge, and proficiency in analytics tools like Google Analytics. However, it should also highlight desirable traits, such as creativity and an ability to work collaboratively with cross-functional teams.

Technical skills are undeniably important, particularly as marketing becomes increasingly data-driven and reliant on technology. Roles such as **digital marketing managers**, **SEO specialists**, or **data analysts** require specific technical competencies, such as familiarity with platforms like HubSpot or Tableau. During the hiring process, assessing technical skills can involve practical tests, portfolio reviews, or situational interviews where candidates demonstrate their expertise.

However, hiring based solely on skills can be a mistake. **Cultural fit** is equally important, as it ensures that new team members align with the organisation's values, work ethic, and collaboration style. For instance, a company that prioritises innovation and flexibility may look for candidates who are comfortable taking risks and adapting to change. In contrast, a more traditional organisation might value discipline and adherence to established processes.

Assessing cultural fit involves understanding the candidate's approach to work, their values, and their interpersonal style. Behavioural interview questions can be particularly effective for this purpose. For example, asking candidates to describe how they handled a conflict within a team or how they adapted to a major change in a past role provides insights into their compatibility with the company's culture.

One common pitfall when hiring for cultural fit is inadvertently creating a team that lacks diversity. While it's important for team members to align with the organisation's values, hiring only those who think or act alike can stifle creativity and innovation. A CMO must strike a balance, ensuring that cultural fit does not become a barrier to diverse perspectives. For instance, a marketing team that includes professionals from different industries, backgrounds, and geographic regions is likely to approach problems with more creativity and generate more robust solutions.

Another critical factor is evaluating a candidate's **growth potential**. Skills can often be taught, but attitudes like curiosity, adaptability, and a willingness to learn are harder to instil. For example, a candidate for a social media manager position may lack experience with a particular platform but demonstrate a strong aptitude for learning and applying new tools. Hiring for potential, especially in fast-evolving industries like marketing, ensures the team remains agile and adaptable.

The onboarding process also plays a significant role in ensuring new hires integrate successfully into the team. Even the most skilled and culturally aligned candidates can struggle if they're not given the tools, resources, and support they need to succeed. A structured onboarding programme should include:

- A clear introduction to the company's mission, values, and culture.
- Training sessions tailored to the role.

- Opportunities to shadow colleagues or participate in team projects.

Finally, retaining top talent is just as important as hiring them. Recognising and rewarding achievements, offering professional development opportunities, and maintaining an inclusive work environment are key to keeping employees engaged and motivated.

In conclusion, **hiring for skills and cultural fit** is a nuanced process that requires a thoughtful approach. By identifying candidates with the right technical expertise and alignment with company values while also fostering diversity and growth potential, CMOs can build a marketing team that is not only highly skilled but also cohesive and resilient. This balance sets the stage for long-term success and a thriving workplace culture.

6.3 - Fostering Creativity and Collaboration

Creativity and collaboration are the lifeblood of a successful marketing team. In a landscape defined by constant innovation and rapid change, these qualities enable teams to develop groundbreaking campaigns, adapt to evolving trends, and deliver results that resonate with audiences. For a **Chief Marketing Officer (CMO)**, fostering an environment that encourages creative thinking while promoting seamless collaboration is essential to building a high-performing team.

Creativity thrives in environments that value experimentation and open-mindedness. To nurture creativity, leaders must encourage their teams to take risks and explore unconventional ideas without fear of failure. For example, a content marketing team brainstorming a new campaign might be urged to suggest bold, even outlandish, concepts during an ideation session. While not every idea will make it to execution, this process often uncovers fresh perspectives that lead to innovative solutions.

Providing time and space for creativity is equally important. Overloaded schedules and constant deadlines can stifle imagination, leading to formulaic or uninspired work. A practical solution is to allocate dedicated time for **creative exercises**, such as brainstorming sessions, workshops, or hackathons. For instance, a team could spend a day developing a campaign around a fictional product as a way to sharpen their creative skills and step outside the constraints of their usual projects.

Collaboration, on the other hand, ensures that creativity is harnessed effectively. A marketing team is typically composed of individuals with diverse expertise, writers, designers, analysts, and strategists. For these talents to work in harmony, the CMO must create a culture of mutual respect and open communication. This begins with breaking down silos between departments. For example, a product launch campaign might involve input from marketing, sales, and customer service teams. By ensuring these groups work together from the outset, the campaign benefits from a holistic approach that considers all aspects of the customer journey.

One powerful tool for fostering collaboration is cross-functional projects. These initiatives encourage team members from different disciplines to share their perspectives and skills. For example, pairing a data analyst with a creative director can lead to campaigns that are both visually compelling and data-driven. Such collaborations often result in solutions that neither party could have achieved alone.

Technology plays a vital role in facilitating collaboration. Tools like **Slack**, **Asana**, or **Trello** allow teams to communicate effectively, track progress, and stay aligned on goals. For remote or hybrid teams, video conferencing platforms and cloud-based document sharing ensure that everyone remains connected and productive, regardless of location. However, technology should enhance, not replace, human interaction. In-person or virtual team-building activities can strengthen bonds and improve trust among team members.

Encouraging a feedback culture is another crucial element. Constructive feedback helps refine ideas and improves overall output. For example, during the development of a digital ad campaign, designers and writers might exchange critiques to ensure the visuals and messaging align seamlessly. Regular feedback sessions not only enhance the quality of work but also foster a sense of shared ownership and accountability.

Leadership also plays a significant role in setting the tone for **creativity and collaboration**. A CMO who models openness, curiosity, and inclusivity inspires their team to follow suit. For example, a leader who actively participates in brainstorming sessions or seeks input from junior team members demonstrates that every voice matters. This inclusivity encourages team members to share their ideas freely, knowing that their contributions are valued.

Recognition and celebration of creative efforts further reinforce these behaviours. Highlighting successful campaigns during team meetings, sharing positive client feedback, or organising award ceremonies for standout contributions motivates team members to continue pushing boundaries. For instance, recognising a team for their innovative use of social media in a campaign not only boosts morale but also sets a benchmark for future projects.

Finally, collaboration must also address challenges constructively. Differences in opinion are inevitable, but they can lead to stronger ideas when handled with respect and professionalism. For example, if two team members disagree on a campaign direction, a leader can facilitate a discussion that explores both perspectives and seeks common ground. This approach ensures that conflicts do not hinder progress but instead contribute to more robust solutions.

In conclusion, **fostering creativity and collaboration** requires deliberate effort and a supportive environment. By encouraging risk-taking, promoting cross-functional teamwork, leveraging technology, and recognising contributions, CMOs can unlock the full potential of their marketing teams. Creativity generates ideas, while collaboration turns them into impactful results; together, they are the driving forces behind any successful marketing strategy.

6.4 - Setting Goals and Accountability Metrics

Setting clear goals and accountability metrics is crucial for the success of any marketing team. Without well-defined objectives and a system to measure progress, efforts can become misaligned, inefficient, or even counterproductive. For a **Chief Marketing Officer (CMO)**, establishing these frameworks ensures that team members have a clear understanding of their priorities and responsibilities while enabling the organisation to track performance and adapt strategies as needed.

Goals provide direction and focus. They serve as a roadmap for the marketing team, outlining what needs to be achieved within a given timeframe. However, goals must be more than just aspirational; they need to be specific, measurable, and actionable. This is where the **SMART framework, Specific, Measurable, Achievable, Relevant, Time-bound**, becomes invaluable. For example, rather than setting a vague objective like "increase website traffic," a SMART goal would be: *"Increase website traffic by 20% over the next quarter through improved SEO and targeted ad campaigns."* This approach provides clarity and makes it easier to evaluate success.

In addition to being SMART, goals should align with the company's broader objectives. For instance, if the organisation is focusing on launching a new product, the marketing team's goals might include generating buzz through a robust social media campaign, achieving a specific number of pre-orders, or securing media coverage in key publications. This alignment ensures that every marketing effort contributes to the company's overall vision and strategy.

While goals outline what needs to be achieved, accountability metrics define how progress is measured. These metrics serve as indicators of success, providing a clear picture of whether the team is on track to meet its objectives. Common marketing metrics include:

- **Lead generation**: The number of new leads acquired through campaigns or other efforts.
- **Conversion rates**: The percentage of leads that progress to customers.
- **Engagement metrics**: Likes, shares, comments, and other interactions on social media platforms.
- **Return on investment (ROI)**: The revenue generated compared to the cost of a campaign.
- **Customer retention rates**: The percentage of existing customers who continue to engage with the brand.

For example, a digital marketing team working on a content strategy might track metrics like website traffic, average session duration, and bounce rates to determine the effectiveness of their blog posts. By analysing these metrics, the team can identify which topics or formats resonate most with their audience and adjust their strategy accordingly.

Transparency is essential when setting goals and metrics. Team members must understand how their individual contributions align with the broader objectives. Tools like **OKRs (Objectives and Key Results)** can be highly effective in maintaining this alignment. For example, a content marketer's objective might be to "boost brand awareness," with key results such as "publishing 10 high-quality blog posts in a quarter" and "achieving a 15% increase in social media shares." OKRs provide a clear link between individual efforts and organisational goals, fostering accountability and motivation.

Regular progress reviews are also critical. Weekly or monthly check-ins allow the team to evaluate their performance, address roadblocks, and celebrate achievements. For example, a team running a paid advertising campaign might review metrics like click-through rates (CTR) and cost-per-click (CPC) during bi-weekly meetings. If the data indicates underperformance, the team can pivot by tweaking ad copy or targeting parameters to improve results.

Accountability is not about blame; it's about fostering ownership and ensuring that every team member understands their role in achieving success. When issues arise, leaders should focus on solutions rather than assigning fault. For instance, if a campaign falls short of its goals, a constructive discussion about what went wrong and how to improve can lead to valuable insights and stronger future efforts.

Technology can play a significant role in tracking goals and metrics. Tools like **Google Analytics**, **HubSpot**, and **Tableau** enable teams to monitor performance in real time and generate detailed reports. These tools provide a clear view of what's working and what needs adjustment, empowering teams to make data-driven decisions.

Celebrating milestones and achievements is an important part of maintaining morale and motivation. Recognising team members for meeting or exceeding goals fosters a sense of accomplishment and reinforces the value of their contributions. For instance, a social media team that achieves record engagement rates during a campaign could be recognised with a shoutout during a team meeting or a small celebration. These moments of recognition create a positive feedback loop, encouraging continued high performance.

In conclusion, **setting goals and accountability metrics** is essential for driving focus, alignment, and results in a marketing team. By defining clear objectives, tracking progress through meaningful metrics, and fostering a culture of ownership and celebration, CMOs can ensure their teams remain motivated and effective. In a fast-paced and results-driven industry, these practices provide the foundation for sustained success.

6.5 - Coaching and Mentoring Team Members

Coaching and mentoring are pivotal components of effective leadership within any marketing team. For a **Chief Marketing Officer (CMO)**, the ability to guide and support team members not only enhances individual performance but also fosters a culture of growth and collaboration. By investing in the professional and personal development of their team, CMOs can build a stronger, more engaged workforce capable of driving long-term success.

At its core, **coaching** involves helping team members enhance their skills, overcome challenges, and achieve their goals. Unlike traditional management, which often focuses on assigning tasks and monitoring outcomes, coaching emphasises empowering individuals to think critically, solve problems, and take ownership of their work. For example, a CMO coaching a junior marketer struggling with campaign analytics might ask thought-provoking questions like, *"What do you think the data is telling us?"* or *"How could we test your hypothesis further?"* This approach encourages the individual to develop analytical thinking skills and gain confidence in their abilities.

Mentoring, on the other hand, focuses on broader career development. A mentor serves as a trusted advisor, offering insights, guidance, and support based on their own experiences. For instance, a CMO mentoring a mid-level manager might share lessons learned from navigating challenges in their career, such as managing high-pressure campaigns or fostering cross-functional collaboration. This relationship builds trust and provides mentees with a roadmap for advancing their careers.

Both coaching and mentoring require a foundation of **trust and open communication**. Team members must feel comfortable sharing their struggles and aspirations without fear of judgment. This begins with creating a safe and supportive environment where feedback is welcomed and valued. For example, a CMO could establish regular one-on-one meetings with team members to discuss their goals, challenges, and progress. These conversations should be framed as collaborative discussions rather than performance evaluations, ensuring that the focus remains on growth and development.

Tailoring the approach to each individual is essential. Every team member has unique strengths, weaknesses, and career aspirations, and a one-size-fits-all strategy rarely works. For instance, an experienced marketer looking to move into a leadership role might benefit from mentorship in strategic thinking and decision-making, while a new hire could require hands-on coaching in mastering marketing tools or understanding company processes. Recognising and addressing these individual needs demonstrates a commitment to the success of each team member.

Feedback is a cornerstone of effective coaching and mentoring. Constructive feedback helps individuals identify areas for improvement while reinforcing their strengths. However, delivering feedback requires tact and empathy. Instead of focusing solely on mistakes, a CMO should highlight specific actions that can be improved and provide actionable advice. For example, instead of saying, *"Your campaign missed the mark,"* a more constructive approach might be, *"The campaign didn't resonate as strongly as we'd hoped. What do you think we could adjust in the messaging to better align with our audience?"* This type of feedback encourages reflection and problem-solving without diminishing confidence.

Role modelling is another powerful aspect of mentoring. A CMO who consistently demonstrates qualities like integrity, adaptability, and a strong work ethic inspires their team to emulate these behaviours. For example, if a CMO openly acknowledges their own mistakes and shares how they've learned from them, it sends a message that failure is a natural part of growth and innovation.

Providing opportunities for growth is equally important. This might include offering training programmes, workshops, or access to industry conferences. For instance, a team member interested in content marketing could be encouraged to attend a workshop on storytelling techniques, while a data-driven marketer might benefit from a certification in advanced analytics. Encouraging team members to pursue professional development not only enhances their skills but also shows that the organisation values their growth.

Recognition plays a vital role in mentoring and coaching. Celebrating achievements, whether big or small, reinforces positive behaviours and motivates individuals to continue striving for excellence. For example, recognising a team member for their innovative approach to a campaign during a team meeting or providing a personalised note of appreciation demonstrates that their contributions are noticed and valued.

Finally, coaching and mentoring are not one-time activities; they require ongoing effort and adaptation. Regularly revisiting goals, reassessing development needs, and refining strategies ensure that the support provided remains relevant and impactful. For example, a team member who initially struggled with presenting to clients might, after targeted coaching, develop this skill and require guidance on another aspect of their role, such as managing a project team.

In conclusion, **coaching and mentoring team members** is about empowering individuals to reach their full potential while fostering a culture of learning and collaboration. By building trust, providing tailored guidance, and celebrating progress, CMOs can inspire their teams to grow both personally and professionally. These practices not only strengthen the team but also contribute to the overall success and resilience of the organisation.

6.6 - Managing Remote and Global Teams

Managing **remote and global teams** has become a central responsibility for many marketing leaders, particularly as organisations expand their reach and adapt to the rise of flexible work environments. For a **Chief Marketing Officer (CMO)**, ensuring that remote and geographically dispersed teams function cohesively, effectively, and efficiently requires a combination of strong leadership, clear communication, and cultural sensitivity.

The first challenge of managing remote and global teams is addressing communication barriers. Team members working in different time zones or cultural contexts often face difficulties coordinating efforts and maintaining real-time communication. To overcome this, CMOs must implement clear and consistent communication strategies. This might include:

- Establishing **core working hours** where all team members overlap and can engage in real-time discussions.

- Leveraging collaboration tools like **Slack**, **Microsoft Teams**, or **Zoom** for instant messaging and video conferencing.

- Using project management platforms such as **Asana**, **Trello**, or **Monday.com** to track tasks, deadlines, and responsibilities transparently.

For instance, a global marketing team coordinating a product launch across North America, Europe, and Asia could hold weekly virtual meetings at a time that accommodates all time zones, supplemented by detailed follow-up emails outlining the next steps.

Cultural differences are another important consideration. Team members from diverse backgrounds bring unique perspectives, which can enrich creativity and innovation. However, these differences can also lead to misunderstandings or conflicts if not managed thoughtfully. CMOs should prioritise cultural sensitivity by fostering an environment of respect and inclusivity. For example:

- Encourage team members to share insights about their local markets, helping others understand different customer behaviours and preferences.

- Provide diversity training to raise awareness of cultural nuances and prevent unintentional biases.

- Adapt communication styles to suit regional preferences; for instance, some cultures value direct feedback, while others prefer a more indirect approach.

Trust is a cornerstone of managing remote teams. In a virtual environment, micromanagement can erode trust and hinder productivity. Instead, CMOs should focus on setting clear expectations and empowering team members to work independently. For example, a content manager in a remote team might be given ownership of an entire campaign, from ideation to execution, with periodic check-ins to provide guidance and feedback. This autonomy fosters accountability and confidence while reducing the need for constant oversight.

Technology plays a vital role in enabling remote and global teams to collaborate effectively. Tools that facilitate seamless communication, document sharing, and workflow management are essential. However, technology should also be used to create a sense of connection and team spirit. For instance:

- Host virtual team-building activities, such as trivia games or coffee chats, to strengthen relationships.
- Celebrate milestones and achievements through virtual celebrations, ensuring remote employees feel included in company culture.

Managing productivity in remote and global teams requires a shift from focusing on hours worked to evaluating outcomes. **Key performance indicators (KPIs)** should be clearly defined, enabling team members to understand how their contributions align with organisational goals. For example, a social media strategist might be measured by metrics like engagement rates, follower growth, or campaign conversions rather than the hours they spend on tasks.

Regular feedback is essential to maintaining alignment and motivation. CMOs should schedule one-on-one meetings with team members to discuss progress, address challenges, and provide coaching. These sessions not only ensure accountability but also demonstrate that the organisation values individual contributions. For instance, a remote employee managing influencer partnerships might use these meetings to share updates, seek advice, and discuss future strategies.

One of the biggest challenges in managing global teams is ensuring **consistency** while accommodating regional differences. A campaign that resonates in one market may fall flat in another due to cultural or economic factors. CMOs must strike a balance between creating unified brand messaging and empowering local teams to adapt strategies to their markets. For example, a global beauty brand might provide centralised guidelines for a product launch while allowing regional teams to tailor the messaging and visuals to suit local tastes.

Mental health and work-life balance are critical considerations in remote teams, where the boundaries between work and personal life can blur. CMOs should encourage practices that promote well-being, such as flexible scheduling and regular breaks. For instance, a remote team member in a different time zone should not feel pressured to attend late-night meetings or respond to emails outside their working hours.

Lastly, fostering a sense of belonging is crucial for remote and global teams. Employees who feel connected to the organisation are more likely to stay engaged and motivated. CMOs can achieve this by:

- Regularly sharing company updates to ensure everyone feels informed and included.
- Highlighting the contributions of remote team members in meetings or newsletters.
- Creating opportunities for in-person interactions, such as annual retreats or regional meet-ups, when possible.

In conclusion, **managing remote and global teams** requires a combination of strategic communication, cultural sensitivity, and trust-building. By leveraging technology, promoting inclusivity, and focusing on outcomes, CMOs can create a cohesive and high-performing team, regardless of geographical boundaries. As the future of work continues to evolve, these practices will be essential for maintaining productivity and fostering a strong organisational culture.

6.7 - Addressing Team Conflict Constructively

Team conflict is an inevitable part of any workplace, and in high-performing marketing teams, where creativity and collaboration are central, **conflicts** can arise due to differences in opinions, work styles, or priorities. For a **Chief Marketing Officer (CMO)**, addressing these conflicts constructively is not only critical to maintaining team harmony but also an opportunity to strengthen relationships and foster innovation.

Conflict in marketing teams often stems from misunderstandings, misaligned goals, or competing priorities. For example, a creative director may prioritise bold, unconventional ideas, while a data analyst might focus on measurable outcomes and adherence to performance metrics.

These differing perspectives can lead to disagreements during campaign development. However, rather than viewing such situations as purely negative, CMOs can approach them as opportunities to harness diverse viewpoints and drive better results.

The first step in resolving conflict constructively is to **recognise and acknowledge it**. Ignoring disputes can lead to resentment and a toxic work environment, while addressing them head-on demonstrates leadership and a commitment to the team's well-being. For example, if two team members frequently clash over resource allocation, a CMO should intervene early to understand the root cause and facilitate a resolution before the tension escalates.

Creating an environment of **open communication** is key. Team members should feel comfortable expressing their concerns without fear of retaliation or judgment. One effective approach is to establish ground rules for communication, such as ensuring that discussions remain respectful and focused on resolving the issue rather than assigning blame. For instance, during a team meeting where conflict arises, the CMO might step in to redirect the conversation, saying, *"Let's focus on finding a solution that works for everyone rather than dwelling on what went wrong."*

Active listening is another crucial skill in managing conflict. Often, team members feel frustrated because they believe their voices aren't being heard. A CMO can play a neutral role by listening to all parties involved and summarising their concerns to ensure everyone feels understood. For example, in a disagreement between a social media manager and a content strategist over campaign timelines, the CMO might say, *"I hear that you're concerned about meeting the launch deadline while you're worried about compromising content quality. Let's explore how we can balance both priorities."*

Facilitating **collaborative problem-solving** is the next step. Rather than imposing solutions, CMOs should encourage team members to work together to find common ground. This might involve brainstorming sessions, where everyone contributes ideas to address the issue. For example, a marketing team debating over budget allocation for digital ads versus event sponsorships could be encouraged to explore scenarios where resources are shared or priorities adjusted based on data insights.

In some cases, conflict may stem from deeper issues, such as unclear roles or expectations. Addressing these underlying factors is essential for preventing future disputes. For example, if two team members frequently overlap in their responsibilities, redefining their roles and ensuring clarity in task delegation can eliminate confusion and friction.

Empathy is a powerful tool in conflict resolution. Understanding the emotions and motivations behind a team member's actions can help diffuse tension and foster a more collaborative atmosphere. For instance, if a junior designer feels undervalued because their ideas are frequently dismissed, acknowledging their contributions and providing constructive feedback can rebuild confidence and trust.

While most conflicts can be resolved within the team, some situations may require mediation from an external party. In such cases, bringing in an HR representative or a neutral facilitator ensures that discussions remain impartial and focused on finding solutions. For example, a prolonged conflict between two senior team members over leadership style might benefit from an unbiased mediator to guide the conversation toward resolution.

Proactive measures can also help minimise conflict. Regular team-building activities and workshops on communication and collaboration skills create stronger bonds among team members, reducing the likelihood of disputes. Additionally, fostering a culture of recognition, where individuals are acknowledged for their contributions, helps mitigate feelings of competition or resentment.

Reflecting on conflicts after they are resolved is an opportunity for growth. CMOs can hold debrief sessions to discuss what went wrong, what was learned, and how similar situations can be handled in the future. For instance, after resolving a conflict over campaign deadlines, a team might agree to improve planning processes or establish clearer checkpoints to avoid miscommunication.

In conclusion, **addressing team conflict constructively** is an essential skill for any CMO leading a high-performing marketing team. By fostering open communication, practising active listening, and encouraging collaborative problem-solving, conflicts can be turned into opportunities for growth and innovation. In a fast-paced, creative environment, effectively managing disagreements ensures a cohesive and motivated team capable of delivering outstanding results.

6.8 - Measuring Team Performance and Productivity

Measuring **team performance and productivity** is a critical responsibility for any leader, especially a **Chief Marketing Officer (CMO)** managing a dynamic and results-driven marketing team. While creativity and innovation are key aspects of marketing, they must be balanced with clear metrics and tangible outcomes. Establishing effective methods to evaluate performance not only helps track progress toward goals but also identifies areas for improvement, recognises achievements, and drives overall team success.

The first step in measuring team performance is setting **clear goals and expectations**. Without well-defined objectives, it becomes difficult to evaluate whether the team is succeeding. Goals should be aligned with the organisation's broader strategy and broken down into individual or team-specific targets. For instance, a social media team might have a goal to increase engagement by 25% over the next quarter, while a content team might aim to publish 15 high-quality blog posts in the same period. These objectives provide a benchmark for assessing performance and ensure everyone understands their role in achieving success.

To measure progress effectively, key performance indicators (KPIs) must be established. KPIs vary depending on the team's focus areas and goals but typically include:

- **Lead generation metrics**: Number of new leads acquired through campaigns.
- **Conversion rates**: Percentage of leads or website visitors who become customers.
- **Engagement rates**: Likes, shares, and comments on social media platforms.
- **Campaign ROI**: Revenue generated relative to the cost of marketing efforts.
- **Content performance**: Views, shares, and time spent on blog posts or videos.

For example, a team running a paid advertising campaign might track click-through rates (CTR), cost per acquisition (CPA), and return on ad spend (ROAS) to determine the campaign's effectiveness. By reviewing these metrics regularly, CMOs can identify what's working, pinpoint challenges, and adjust strategies in real-time.

Qualitative assessments complement quantitative metrics by providing deeper insights into team performance. For instance, evaluating the quality of creative output, the effectiveness of communication within the team, or the alignment of messaging with the brand's voice often requires subjective analysis. Regular feedback from stakeholders, including sales teams, clients, or senior management, can provide valuable perspectives on the team's impact.

Productivity should also be assessed on an individual and team level. However, it's essential to avoid equating productivity with hours worked. Instead, focus on outcomes and efficiency. For example, a team member who completes a complex campaign ahead of schedule without compromising quality demonstrates high productivity, regardless of the time spent.

Technology plays a significant role in tracking and measuring performance. Tools like **Google Analytics**, **HubSpot**, and **Salesforce** provide detailed data on campaign results, while project management platforms such as **Asana**, **Trello**, or **Monday.com** allow CMOs to monitor task progress and team workload. These tools not only streamline reporting but also make it easier to identify bottlenecks or inefficiencies in workflows.

Regular performance reviews are crucial for maintaining accountability and fostering improvement. These reviews should be constructive, focusing on achievements as well as areas for growth. For instance, if a digital marketing specialist falls short of their KPI for email open rates, the CMO might discuss strategies for improving subject lines or timing. Conversely, if a content creator exceeds their goals for audience engagement, recognising their efforts can boost morale and motivation.

Team collaboration is another important factor in evaluating performance. Even the most talented individuals cannot achieve their best results without strong teamwork. CMOs should assess how well team members communicate, share ideas, and support one another. For example, a campaign that succeeds because of seamless collaboration between designers, copywriters, and analysts reflects not just individual skill but also collective effort.

Recognising achievements is just as important as identifying areas for improvement. Celebrating milestones, such as completing a successful campaign or exceeding quarterly goals, fosters a sense of accomplishment and motivates the team to maintain high performance. For example, a CMO might organise a team lunch or send personalised thank-you notes to acknowledge their hard work.

Finally, measuring performance should always include an opportunity for reflection and learning. After each major project or campaign, conducting a **post-mortem analysis** allows the team to review what worked, what didn't, and how processes can be improved. For instance, if a product launch campaign fell short of expectations, the team might identify that insufficient market research led to poor targeting, and adjustments can be made for future efforts.

In conclusion, **measuring team performance and productivity** is about striking a balance between quantitative metrics and qualitative insights. By setting clear goals, leveraging technology, fostering collaboration, and encouraging reflection, CMOs can ensure their teams remain focused, efficient, and motivated. Ultimately, these practices drive better results, foster continuous improvement, and create a high-performing marketing organisation.

6.9 - Celebrating Wins and Learning from Losses

Celebrating wins and learning from losses are equally important practices for maintaining a high-performing and motivated marketing team. For a **Chief Marketing Officer (CMO)**, these activities foster a culture of resilience, accountability, and continuous improvement, ensuring that every success is recognised and every setback becomes a stepping stone toward future growth.

Celebrating wins is about acknowledging achievements, both big and small. Recognising successes boosts morale, reinforces positive behaviours, and reminds the team of their collective capabilities. Whether it's launching a major campaign, surpassing key performance indicators (KPIs), or solving a challenging problem, celebrating accomplishments builds confidence and encourages the team to strive for excellence. For instance, if a team's social media campaign goes viral, increasing engagement by 50%, a CMO might acknowledge the effort during a team meeting, highlight the individuals who contributed, and even organise a small celebration to mark the achievement.

The way wins are celebrated should be meaningful and aligned with the company culture. Options range from informal gestures, like a public shoutout in a Slack channel, to more formal rewards, such as bonuses or team outings. For example:

- Sending personalised thank-you notes to team members after a successful product launch shows appreciation on an individual level.
- Hosting a team lunch or happy hour after meeting quarterly goals provides an opportunity for the team to bond and relax.

- Recognising standout achievements during company-wide meetings or newsletters demonstrates the team's impact on the broader organisation.

These moments of celebration not only boost team morale but also create a sense of camaraderie and belonging. They serve as a reminder that hard work is valued and that individual contributions matter in achieving collective success.

While celebrating wins is crucial, **learning from losses** is equally important. Marketing is a dynamic field where not every campaign or strategy will yield the desired results. Rather than ignoring failures or assigning blame, a forward-thinking CMO views setbacks as opportunities for growth and innovation.

The first step in learning from losses is conducting a **post-mortem analysis**. After a project or campaign falls short, the team should come together to discuss what went wrong, what could have been done differently, and what lessons can be applied moving forward. For example, if a product launch campaign failed to generate sufficient interest, the team might identify that market research was insufficient or that messaging didn't resonate with the target audience. These insights can guide future efforts and prevent similar mistakes.

Creating a **blame-free environment** is critical during these discussions. Team members must feel comfortable sharing their perspectives and acknowledging their own mistakes without fear of judgment. A CMO can set the tone by framing the conversation as a collaborative effort to learn and improve. For instance, they might say, *"This campaign didn't perform as well as* *we'd hoped. Let's figure out why together so we can do better next time."*

Documenting lessons learned ensures that insights from failures are captured and shared across the team. For example, maintaining a centralised repository of post-mortem reports can help teams identify patterns or recurring issues. If multiple campaigns experience low engagement rates due to unclear calls to action, this insight can inform a team-wide initiative to improve copywriting and design practices.

Balancing accountability with encouragement is key to learning from losses. While it's important to address areas for improvement, recognising effort and potential keeps the conversation constructive. For example, if a paid advertising campaign underperformed, the CMO might acknowledge the team's creativity in crafting compelling visuals while suggesting ways to refine targeting strategies.

Losses can also be an opportunity to innovate. Many breakthroughs occur when teams are pushed to rethink their approaches and experiment with new ideas. For instance, if a traditional email marketing campaign fails to generate leads, the team might pivot to exploring interactive content or gamified experiences. Encouraging a mindset of experimentation helps teams embrace risk and view setbacks as part of the creative process.

Finally, combining celebrations and lessons ensures that both successes and failures contribute to the team's growth. After a major campaign, for example, a CMO might organise a debrief session that highlights what went well and what could be improved. This balanced approach ensures that wins are celebrated without complacency and that losses are analysed without negativity.

In conclusion, **celebrating wins and learning from losses** are vital practices for building a resilient and motivated marketing team. By recognising achievements, fostering a culture of continuous learning, and approaching setbacks constructively, CMOs can inspire their teams to embrace challenges and strive for excellence. These practices not only drive individual and collective growth but also create a supportive environment where success is shared, and every experience contributes to the team's long-term success.

6.10 - Case Study: Turning Around a Struggling Team

Transforming a struggling marketing team into a high-performing one is a daunting yet rewarding challenge for any **Chief Marketing Officer (CMO)**. It requires a combination of strong leadership, strategic planning, and an ability to inspire and motivate individuals to achieve their potential. This case study examines how a mid-sized software company, **TechAdvantage**, successfully turned around its underperforming marketing team and built a foundation for long-term success.

The Challenge

When the new CMO joined TechAdvantage, the marketing team faced several critical issues:

- **Lack of clear goals and direction**: Team members were unsure of their priorities, leading to wasted effort and missed opportunities.
- **Low morale**: A high turnover rate and lack of recognition left the remaining employees disengaged and frustrated.
- **Inefficient processes**: Campaigns were frequently delayed due to poor planning and unclear communication.
- **Underutilised talent**: Team members felt their skills were overlooked or underappreciated.
- **Declining performance**: Lead generation and brand awareness metrics were consistently below expectations.

The CMO recognised that these issues stemmed from systemic problems rather than individual failings. To address them, they devised a comprehensive plan to rebuild the team's confidence, processes, and performance.

The Strategy

1. Setting Clear Goals and Metrics

The first step was to establish clarity around the team's objectives. The CMO worked with leadership to align marketing goals with the company's overall strategy. These goals were broken down into measurable targets for each team member, ensuring accountability and focus. For example:

- The content marketing team was tasked with increasing blog traffic by 30% over six months.

- The paid advertising team aimed to reduce cost-per-click (CPC) by 20% while maintaining lead quality.

This clarity helped team members understand their roles and how their efforts contributed to the company's success.

2. Addressing Morale and Motivation

To rebuild morale, the CMO prioritised recognition and communication. Regular team meetings were introduced to celebrate achievements, both big and small. For instance, when the email marketing specialist achieved a record open rate for a campaign, their work was highlighted during a company-wide meeting. Additionally, one-on-one sessions allowed team members to share their concerns and aspirations, fostering a sense of trust and openness.

The CMO also introduced a professional development programme, offering access to workshops, certifications, and conferences. This investment in employee growth demonstrated the company's commitment to its people and helped reignite their enthusiasm.

3. Streamlining Processes

Inefficiencies in campaign planning and execution were addressed by implementing project management tools such as **Asana** and introducing clear workflows. Each campaign was assigned a project lead responsible for timelines, deliverables, and coordination across teams. Weekly check-ins ensured accountability and allowed for quick resolution of any issues.

For example, during the launch of a new product, the project lead worked closely with the content, design, and digital advertising teams to ensure all assets were ready on time. This streamlined approach reduced delays and improved overall efficiency.

4. Leveraging Individual Strengths

The CMO recognised that team members were often assigned tasks that didn't align with their strengths. By conducting a skills audit, they identified each individual's expertise and reassigned responsibilities accordingly. For instance:

- A designer with a passion for storytelling was moved to video production, where they created compelling brand videos that increased engagement on social media.
- A data analyst who had been working on campaign reporting was tasked with leading market research initiatives, providing valuable insights for strategy development.

This realignment not only improved performance but also boosted job satisfaction as team members felt their talents were being utilised effectively.

5. Fostering Collaboration

Collaboration was encouraged through cross-functional projects and open communication channels. Teams that had previously operated in silos were brought together to share ideas and align their efforts. For example, the SEO team collaborated with content writers to optimise blog posts for search engines, leading to a significant increase in organic traffic.

The Results

Over the course of a year, the transformation at TechAdvantage yielded remarkable results:

- **Improved performance**: Lead generation increased by 40%, and brand awareness metrics exceeded targets.
- **Higher morale**: Employee satisfaction surveys showed a 75% improvement in team sentiment.
- **Greater efficiency**: Campaign timelines were reduced by an average of 20%, enabling the team to execute more projects.
- **Stronger retention**: Turnover rates dropped significantly, with employees citing better recognition and opportunities for growth as key reasons for staying.
- **Enhanced creativity**: The team launched several innovative campaigns, including a viral video series that drove substantial engagement.

Lessons Learned

The turnaround at TechAdvantage offers several key lessons for CMOs facing similar challenges:

- **Clarity is key**: Setting clear goals and expectations aligns efforts and provides a sense of purpose.
- **People come first**: Investing in morale, recognition, and professional growth builds a motivated and loyal team.
- **Processes matter**: Streamlined workflows and efficient tools enable teams to work smarter, not harder.
- **Leverage strengths**: Aligning tasks with individual skills maximise potential and boosts job satisfaction.

- **Collaboration drives success**: Cross-functional teamwork generates innovative ideas and ensures alignment across the organisation.

Conclusion

Transforming a struggling marketing team requires vision, patience, and a commitment to continuous improvement. The CMO at TechAdvantage demonstrated that with the right strategies, even a team facing significant challenges can be revitalised to deliver exceptional results. For CMOs, this case study highlights the importance of combining strategic leadership with empathy and adaptability to create a team that thrives in any environment.

# Chapter 7

Advanced Analytics and ROI Measurement

> "Numbers may tell the story of the past, but the way you interpret them will write the story of your future."
> **Robert N. Jacobs**

In the fast-evolving landscape of modern marketing, data has emerged as a game-changing force. For a Chief Marketing Officer (CMO), mastering advanced analytics and ROI measurement is not merely a technical pursuit but a strategic imperative. With customers interacting across a myriad of touchpoints, from social media to email campaigns and in-store visits, the ability to collect, analyse, and act on data has become essential for delivering measurable results and driving business growth.

This chapter delves into the transformative power of advanced analytics, offering CMOs the tools to navigate complex customer journeys, optimise campaigns, and justify investments. By unpacking the nuances of key performance indicators (KPIs), attribution models, and predictive analytics, we will explore how marketing leaders can transition from reactive decision-making to proactive strategies. Through a combination of real-world examples, practical frameworks, and actionable insights, this chapter equips readers with the knowledge to unlock the full potential of data in crafting personalised, impactful, and ethical marketing initiatives.

7.1 - The Importance of Data in Modern Marketing

In today's digital age, **data** has become the backbone of effective marketing. For a **Chief Marketing Officer (CMO)**, understanding and leveraging data is essential for making informed decisions, optimising strategies, and delivering measurable results. Data empowers marketing teams to move beyond intuition, providing a foundation for evidence-based approaches that drive success in an increasingly competitive landscape.

The value of **data-driven marketing** lies in its ability to reveal customer behaviour, preferences, and trends; unlike traditional approaches that rely heavily on assumptions, modern marketing leverages real-time data to craft personalised experiences that resonate with specific audiences. For instance, an e-commerce brand can use behavioural data to identify a customer's purchasing patterns and recommend products that align with their interests. This targeted approach not only increases conversion rates but also strengthens customer loyalty. Data also plays a critical role in **campaign performance measurement**. Without clear metrics, it's impossible to determine whether a strategy is achieving its goals. For example, a paid advertising campaign might generate significant website traffic, but without analysing conversion data, the team cannot assess its actual impact on sales. By tracking key performance indicators (KPIs), CMOs can evaluate which efforts are delivering the desired results and adjust their strategies accordingly.

Advanced Analytics and ROI Measurement

One of the most transformative aspects of data is its role in **predictive insights**. Modern analytics tools enable marketers to anticipate future trends and customer behaviours. For instance, a subscription service analysing past purchase histories can predict when customers are likely to renew or cancel their memberships, allowing the brand to take proactive measures. These predictive capabilities help CMOs allocate resources more effectively and improve campaign timing.

However, the rise of data also brings challenges. One major concern is the sheer volume of information available. Without proper organisation and analysis, data can become overwhelming, leading to confusion rather than clarity. Additionally, ensuring **data quality** is critical. Inaccurate or incomplete data can lead to poor decisions and wasted resources. For example, a retail brand basing its inventory strategy on outdated sales data might overstock low-demand items, resulting in financial losses.

Ethical considerations are another crucial aspect of data usage. Customers are increasingly aware of how their data is collected and used, and mishandling this information can damage trust. CMOs must prioritise transparency and comply with regulations such as **GDPR**, ensuring that all data collection and analysis practices are ethical and customer-focused.

In conclusion, **data** is an indispensable tool for modern marketing, offering insights that drive personalisation, optimise campaigns, and predict future outcomes. For CMOs, mastering data usage is not just a technical skill; it's a strategic imperative.

By embracing a data-driven mindset, marketing leaders can deliver meaningful results while building trust and loyalty with their audiences.

7.2 - Key Metrics and KPIs for CMOs

For a **Chief Marketing Officer (CMO)**, the ability to define, track, and interpret **key performance indicators (KPIs)** is essential to measuring the success of marketing initiatives. KPIs provide a framework for evaluating the effectiveness of campaigns, team performance, and overall strategy, allowing CMOs to make data-driven decisions that align with organisational goals. Choosing the right metrics ensures that marketing efforts are not only creative but also deliver tangible business results.

The first step in identifying meaningful KPIs is understanding the organisation's broader objectives. Every KPI must tie back to a strategic goal, whether it's increasing revenue, improving brand awareness, or fostering customer loyalty. For instance, if a company's primary goal is growth, a CMO might focus on metrics such as **lead generation**, **customer acquisition cost (CAC)**, and **conversion rates**. Conversely, if the emphasis is on retention, metrics like **customer lifetime value (CLV)** and **churn rate** become more relevant.

In digital marketing, website performance metrics are foundational. These include:

- **Traffic volume**: The total number of visitors to a website, segmented by source (e.g., organic, paid, or social).

Advanced Analytics and ROI Measurement

- **Bounce rate**: The percentage of visitors who leave the site after viewing only one page, indicating potential issues with user experience or content relevance.
- **Conversion rate**: The proportion of visitors who complete a desired action, such as making a purchase or signing up for a newsletter.

For example, an e-commerce company might set a KPI of achieving a 5% increase in website conversions over a quarter. By monitoring this metric, the CMO can determine whether efforts like improving site design or launching targeted campaigns are yielding results.

Engagement metrics are equally critical, especially in content and social media marketing. These metrics track how audiences interact with a brand's content, providing insights into its resonance and effectiveness. Key engagement metrics include:

- **Likes, shares, and comments** on social media platforms.
- **Click-through rates (CTR)** for email marketing campaigns.
- **Time spent on content**, such as blog posts or videos.

For instance, a tech company launching a new product might track the number of shares and comments on its announcement video to gauge audience interest. High engagement indicates that the messaging resonates, while low engagement suggests the need for adjustments.

ROI metrics are perhaps the most critical for demonstrating the value of marketing efforts. These include:

Advanced Analytics and ROI Measurement

- **Marketing ROI**: The revenue generated relative to the cost of campaigns. For example, a CMO investing £10,000 in a digital ad campaign that generates £50,000 in sales has achieved a 400% ROI.
- **Customer acquisition cost (CAC)**: The cost of acquiring a new customer, calculated by dividing total marketing spend by the number of new customers gained.
- **Customer lifetime value (CLV)**: The total revenue a customer generates over their relationship with the brand.

Balancing these metrics is essential. While CAC focuses on the cost-efficiency of acquisition, CLV highlights the long-term value of retaining customers. For instance, reducing CAC may involve cutting back on premium acquisition channels, but if those channels attract high-value customers, the trade-off could negatively impact CLV.

Brand awareness and sentiment are also vital KPIs for CMOs looking to build and maintain a strong market presence. These metrics include:

- **Share of voice (SOV)**: The percentage of industry-related conversations that involve the brand compared to competitors.
- **Net Promoter Score (NPS)**: A measure of customer loyalty determined by how likely customers are to recommend the brand.
- **Sentiment analysis**: Evaluating the tone of mentions on social media or review sites to gauge public perception.

For example, a hospitality brand might monitor NPS to understand how customer experiences impact loyalty, using the insights to improve service quality and marketing strategies.

Selecting the right KPIs is not enough, **regular monitoring and reporting** are essential for ensuring that goals are met. Tools like **Google Analytics**, **HubSpot**, and **Tableau** provide real-time dashboards that enable CMOs to track progress and adjust strategies as needed. For instance, if a campaign targeting new customers underperforms, the CMO can quickly identify the issue, whether it's poor ad targeting, ineffective messaging, or a lack of reach, and implement corrective measures.

Finally, it's important to communicate KPIs effectively to stakeholders. Executives often require a high-level overview of marketing performance, while team members benefit from granular insights that guide their daily tasks. A CMO might create separate reports for these audiences, highlighting key takeaways for leadership and detailed performance data for the marketing team.

In conclusion, **key metrics and KPIs** provide a structured way for CMOs to evaluate and optimise marketing efforts. By selecting metrics that align with organisational goals, monitoring progress regularly, and communicating insights effectively, CMOs can demonstrate the value of marketing initiatives and ensure that strategies deliver meaningful results.

7.3 - Understanding Attribution Models

Advanced Analytics and ROI Measurement

Attribution models are a critical tool for understanding how various marketing efforts contribute to a customer's journey and eventual conversion. For a **Chief Marketing Officer (CMO)**, mastering attribution is essential to optimising campaigns, allocating budgets effectively, and demonstrating a clear return on investment (ROI). The modern customer journey is no longer linear; it spans multiple touchpoints, from digital ads and social media to emails and offline interactions. This complexity makes attribution models a vital part of measuring marketing success.

Attribution models assign credit to the touchpoints involved in a customer's journey, helping marketers understand which efforts are driving results. For instance, a customer may discover a product through an Instagram ad, visit the website for more information, and finally complete a purchase after receiving an email promotion. Attribution models help assign a percentage of credit to each of these interactions, providing insights into their relative importance.

Several types of attribution models exist, each with its advantages and limitations:

- **First-Touch Attribution:** Assigns all credit to the customer's first interaction with the brand, such as discovering a product through a social media ad. While this model highlights what initially attracts customers, it overlooks the importance of follow-up interactions.
- **Last-Touch Attribution:** Assigns all credit to the final interaction before conversion, such as an email campaign that leads directly to a purchase. This method is simple to

Advanced Analytics and ROI Measurement

implement but fails to account for earlier efforts that nurtured the customer.

- **Linear Attribution:** Distributes credit equally across all touchpoints in the journey, offering a balanced view of the customer's experience. However, this approach assumes all touchpoints are equally influential, which is rarely the case.

- **Data-Driven Attribution:** Uses machine learning and historical data to assign credit based on the actual impact of each interaction. While this model provides the most accurate insights, it requires robust analytics tools and large datasets, making it less accessible for smaller organisations.

Choosing the right attribution model depends on the organisation's goals, sales cycle, and available resources. For example:

- A company focused on **brand awareness** might prioritise first-touch attribution to understand which channels are driving initial customer interest.

- A company aiming to **maximise conversions** may benefit from a **time-decay model**, which gives more weight to interactions closer to the point of sale.

- Businesses with **longer and more complex sales cycles** often find that position-based attribution, assigning greater credit to the first and last touchpoints, provides actionable insights.

Attribution models also present challenges:

- **Data fragmentation**: Information may be spread across different tools and platforms, making it difficult to track the entire customer journey accurately. Integrating systems like **Google Analytics**, **Salesforce**, or **HubSpot** can help consolidate data.

- **Privacy regulations**: Laws like **GDPR** introduce limitations on data collection, requiring CMOs to balance the need for insights with legal and ethical considerations.

- **Cross-channel complexity**: Customers engage with multiple channels, often blurring the lines of direct influence.

Despite these challenges, effective attribution unlocks significant opportunities for optimisation. By understanding which touchpoints drive the most conversions, CMOs can allocate budgets more effectively, focusing resources on high-performing channels. For example, If data-driven attribution reveals that **retargeting ads** significantly influence customer decisions, a brand might increase investment in this area while reducing spending on less impactful channels.

Attribution insights also enable CMOs to refine the **customer experience**. For instance, if analysis shows that customers frequently drop off after visiting a product page, the team can investigate whether issues like slow page load times or unclear calls-to-action are deterring conversions.

In conclusion, **understanding attribution models** is essential for CMOs to navigate the complexities of modern marketing. By selecting the right model, addressing challenges such as data fragmentation, and leveraging insights to optimise campaigns, marketing leaders can gain valuable clarity into their efforts' effectiveness. Attribution not only measures success but also informs smarter decisions, enabling teams to deliver measurable outcomes.

7.4 - Advanced Tools for Marketing Analytics

In today's data-driven marketing landscape, **advanced analytics tools** are indispensable for understanding customer behaviour, optimising campaigns, and measuring ROI. For a **Chief Marketing Officer (CMO)**, choosing and utilising the right tools can unlock valuable insights that drive smarter decision-making and maximise impact. These tools help analyse vast amounts of data, providing actionable recommendations that enhance efficiency and improve results across marketing channels.

Advanced analytics tools fall into several categories, each addressing specific needs:

- **Customer Relationship Management (CRM) Systems**: Tools like **Salesforce**, **HubSpot**, and **Zoho CRM** allow marketers to track customer interactions, manage leads, and measure the effectiveness of campaigns. For example, a CRM can help identify which touchpoints are most effective at converting leads into customers, enabling the team to refine their approach.

- **Web Analytics Platforms**: **Google Analytics** and **Adobe Analytics** are among the most widely used tools for monitoring website traffic, user behaviour, and conversion rates. These platforms offer insights into how visitors interact with websites, such as the most popular pages, average session duration, and bounce rates. For instance, if a brand notices a high bounce rate on its pricing page, it

Advanced Analytics and ROI Measurement

might indicate that the pricing structure or presentation needs adjustment.

- **Social Media Analytics Tools**: Platforms like **Hootsuite**, **Sprout Social**, and **Buffer** provide in-depth metrics on engagement, follower growth, and campaign performance across social media channels. These tools enable marketers to identify trends, measure the impact of posts, and determine the ROI of paid social campaigns.

- **Business Intelligence (BI) Tools**: Tools like **Tableau**, **Power BI**, and **Looker** allow for advanced data visualisation and reporting. They enable teams to consolidate data from multiple sources, such as CRM systems, web analytics, and email platforms, into a single dashboard. This holistic view helps CMOs identify correlations and trends that might otherwise go unnoticed.

One of the most transformative developments in marketing analytics is the integration of artificial intelligence (AI) and machine learning (ML). These technologies enhance the capabilities of traditional tools by automating analysis, identifying patterns, and predicting future behaviours. For example:

- AI-powered tools like **Marketo Engage** and **Pardot** can segment audiences based on behaviour and deliver personalised content in real-time, improving engagement and conversion rates.

- ML models in platforms like **Google Ads** optimise campaign bidding strategies, ensuring maximum ROI by predicting which keywords or audiences are likely to drive conversions.

Advanced Analytics and ROI Measurement

Predictive analytics is another critical function of advanced tools. By analysing historical data, tools like **IBM SPSS** and **Alteryx** can forecast future trends, enabling CMOs to plan campaigns proactively. For instance, a retail brand might use predictive analytics to anticipate seasonal demand spikes and adjust inventory and marketing budgets accordingly.

In addition to capabilities, integration is a crucial consideration when selecting tools. A fragmented ecosystem of platforms can lead to data silos and inefficiencies. Choosing tools that seamlessly integrate with existing systems ensures a unified approach to data management. For example, connecting **Google Analytics** with **HubSpot** enables teams to link website performance with lead generation and sales outcomes.

Despite their advantages, advanced tools come with challenges. First, **cost** can be a barrier, particularly for smaller teams or organisations. High-end platforms like **Adobe Analytics** or **Tableau** require significant investment, making it essential to evaluate whether the potential ROI justifies the expense. Second, the complexity of these tools often requires specialised expertise. Training team members or hiring dedicated analysts ensure that the organisation can fully leverage the tools' capabilities.

Privacy and data security are also critical considerations. As regulations like **GDPR** and **CCPA** place stricter requirements on data handling, CMOs must ensure that their analytics tools comply with these laws. For instance, platforms that anonymise customer data or offer robust consent management features help maintain compliance while protecting customer trust.

Advanced Analytics and ROI Measurement

To maximise the benefits of advanced tools, CMOs should establish clear objectives and KPIs before implementation. For example:

- If the goal is to improve website performance, a tool like **Google Analytics** can track metrics such as load times, navigation paths, and drop-off rates.

- If the objective is to enhance customer retention, a CRM system like **Salesforce** can monitor customer lifecycle stages and trigger automated re-engagement campaigns.

Finally, reporting is an essential part of using advanced tools effectively. Tools with strong reporting capabilities enable CMOs to communicate insights to stakeholders clearly and concisely. For instance, a BI tool like **Tableau** can create interactive dashboards that showcase real-time campaign performance, allowing executives to monitor progress at a glance.

In conclusion, **advanced tools for marketing analytics** empower CMOs to make data-driven decisions, optimise campaigns, and demonstrate ROI with precision. By selecting tools that align with organisational goals, integrating them into a cohesive system, and ensuring compliance with data privacy regulations, marketing leaders can unlock the full potential of their analytics capabilities. In a competitive and fast-evolving landscape, these tools are not just an advantage; they are a necessity for achieving sustained success.

7.5 - Creating Dashboards for Executive Reporting

For a **Chief Marketing Officer (CMO)**, communicating marketing performance and insights to executives is a critical responsibility. While data-driven decision-making is a cornerstone of modern marketing, presenting data in a concise and actionable way is essential to gaining support and alignment from leadership. **Dashboards** designed for executive reporting are a powerful tool for this purpose, allowing CMOs to showcase key metrics, trends, and ROI at a glance.

An effective executive dashboard is more than a collection of charts and graphs; it's a storytelling tool that translates complex data into meaningful insights. Executives often focus on high-level outcomes, such as revenue growth, customer acquisition, and brand equity. Therefore, dashboards should be designed to highlight these areas while minimising technical jargon or unnecessary details. For instance, a dashboard showcasing the success of a recent product launch might include metrics like:

- **Total revenue generated**: The overall sales figures attributable to the campaign.
- **Customer acquisition cost (CAC)**: The average cost of acquiring new customers during the campaign.
- **Return on investment (ROI)**: The financial return relative to campaign expenses.

The first step in creating an effective dashboard is defining the key performance indicators (KPIs) that matter most to the organisation. These KPIs should align with the company's strategic goals. For example:

- If the organisation prioritises growth, the dashboard might focus on metrics such as lead generation, conversion rates, and market share.

- If customer retention is a key goal, metrics like churn rate, Net Promoter Score (NPS), and customer lifetime value (CLV) should take precedence.

The design of the dashboard is equally important. Executives value clarity and efficiency, so the layout should prioritise readability. Some best practices for dashboard design include:

- **Using visuals effectively:** Charts, graphs, and infographics help convey complex data in an easily digestible format. For example, a line graph showing monthly revenue growth provides a clear visual of upward trends.

- **Grouping related metrics**: Organising data into logical categories, such as acquisition, engagement, and ROI, makes it easier for viewers to navigate the dashboard.

- **Highlighting key insights:** Use colour coding, bold text, or icons to draw attention to important findings, such as a significant increase in customer acquisition or a drop in conversion rates.

The choice of tools also plays a crucial role in dashboard creation. Platforms like **Tableau**, **Power BI**, and **Google Data Studio** offer robust capabilities for designing interactive dashboards that can be customised to meet executive needs. These tools allow for real-time data updates, enabling executives to monitor performance as it unfolds. For instance, a retail brand using Google Data Studio might create a dashboard that tracks Black Friday sales metrics in real-time, allowing leadership to make immediate adjustments to marketing strategies.

Dashboards should not only display current performance but also provide **context and comparisons**. For example:

Advanced Analytics and ROI Measurement

- Showing **month-over-month growth** helps executives understand whether current metrics are improving or declining.
- Including **benchmarks** against industry standards or competitors highlights how the organisation is performing in the market.
- Adding **historical trends** illustrates the impact of past campaigns and informs future decision-making.

While dashboards are primarily used for reporting, they can also serve as a **collaborative tool**. CMOs can use dashboards during executive meetings to facilitate discussions about marketing performance and strategy. For example, if a dashboard reveals a dip in social media engagement, the team might explore whether this is due to content relevance, posting frequency, or platform algorithm changes. By presenting the data clearly, the dashboard becomes a starting point for action-oriented conversations.

Customisation is another important aspect of executive dashboards. Different stakeholders may have varying interests and priorities. For instance:

- The **CEO** may focus on high-level outcomes like revenue growth and market share.
- The **CFO** may prioritise metrics related to cost efficiency, such as ROI and CAC.
- The **COO** may look for operational insights, such as campaign timelines and resource allocation.

Creating tailored dashboards for each audience ensures that the information presented is relevant and actionable. For example, the CEO's dashboard might feature a simplified summary of overall marketing performance, while the CFO's version includes detailed cost breakdowns and budget utilisation.

Dashboards should evolve over time to reflect changing business goals and market conditions. Regular updates ensure that the data remains relevant and actionable. For instance, during a product launch, the dashboard might focus on metrics like pre-orders and media coverage. Once the launch is complete, the focus could shift to customer retention and post-purchase engagement metrics.

In conclusion, **creating dashboards for executive reporting** is a vital skill for CMOs seeking to align marketing efforts with organisational goals. By selecting the right KPIs, leveraging advanced tools, and designing dashboards that prioritise clarity and relevance, CMOs can effectively communicate marketing performance to leadership. Dashboards not only demonstrate the value of marketing initiatives but also foster collaboration and informed decision-making, ensuring long-term success.

7.6 - Balancing Short-Term Results with Long-Term ROI

For a **Chief Marketing Officer (CMO)**, achieving a balance between **short-term results** and **long-term return on investment (ROI)** is one of the most complex and critical challenges. While short-term metrics, such as sales spikes or lead generation, are essential for maintaining momentum and meeting immediate business needs, long-term ROI ensures sustained growth, customer loyalty, and brand equity. Successfully navigating this balance requires strategic planning, resource allocation, and a clear understanding of organisational priorities.

Short-term results often focus on campaigns designed to generate immediate impact. Examples include seasonal promotions, flash sales, or pay-per-click (PPC) advertising. These efforts typically rely on highly measurable metrics such as:

- **Conversion rates**: The percentage of customers completing a desired action, such as making a purchase or signing up for a newsletter.
- **Click-through rates (CTR)**: The effectiveness of digital ads in driving traffic to a landing page or website.
- **Revenue growth**: Short-term boosts in sales attributable to a specific campaign.

For instance, an online retailer launching a holiday campaign might use targeted PPC ads and email marketing to drive traffic and maximise sales during a peak shopping period. These short-term efforts are crucial for hitting quarterly revenue goals and meeting immediate cash flow requirements.

However, focusing solely on short-term outcomes can lead to **unsustainable growth**. Overemphasis on quick wins, such as aggressive discounting, may erode brand value or attract price-sensitive customers who lack long-term loyalty. Additionally, short-term tactics often fail to address broader goals like

Advanced Analytics and ROI Measurement

customer retention, brand awareness, or market share expansion.

Long-term ROI, on the other hand, prioritises strategies that deliver enduring value. These initiatives often require significant upfront investment but yield benefits over time. Examples include:

- **Brand-building campaigns**: Efforts to establish a strong brand identity and emotional connection with customers, such as storytelling-driven advertising or cause marketing.

- **Customer retention programmes**: Initiatives like loyalty schemes or personalised experiences that encourage repeat purchases and increase customer lifetime value (CLV).

- **Content marketing**: Producing valuable, evergreen content such as blogs, eBooks, or webinars that establish authority and attract organic traffic over months or years.

For example, a tech company investing in thought leadership by creating industry reports and hosting webinars may not see immediate revenue spikes but will build trust and credibility that pay dividends in the long run.

The key to balancing these approaches lies in **aligning marketing strategies with business objectives**. CMOs must collaborate with leadership to define short- and long-term goals and ensure that both are supported by appropriate marketing initiatives. A practical framework for this alignment might involve:

- Allocating **60-70% of the budget** to long-term strategies, such as brand-building and customer retention.
- Reserving **30-40%** for short-term campaigns that drive immediate results and support operational cash flow.

This balanced approach ensures that the organisation can meet immediate demands without sacrificing future growth.

Another critical component of achieving balance is **measuring success across multiple timeframes**. Short-term metrics like sales or CTR provide immediate feedback on campaign performance, while long-term indicators such as brand equity, CLV, and customer loyalty offer insights into sustained impact. For instance:

- Tracking **monthly sales growth** provides insight into the success of short-term campaigns.
- Monitoring **NPS scores** over a year reflects long-term customer satisfaction and advocacy.

Scenario planning is a valuable tool for managing the trade-offs between short- and long-term goals. By modelling potential outcomes, CMOs can anticipate the impact of prioritising one approach over the other. For example, if increasing ad spending to boost short-term sales would compromise the budget for a long-term brand-building initiative, scenario analysis helps determine whether the trade-off is justified.

Collaboration across departments is also essential for balancing these priorities. For instance, sales teams often focus on immediate revenue, while product teams may prioritise innovations that deliver long-term value. A CMO can act as a bridge, ensuring that marketing efforts align with both perspectives. For example, a short-term promotional campaign might be paired with a long-term product education initiative to ensure sustainable growth.

Finally, **flexibility and adaptability** are critical. Market conditions, consumer behaviours, and competitive landscapes can shift unexpectedly, requiring adjustments to the balance between short- and long-term efforts. For instance, during an economic downturn, a brand might temporarily shift resources toward short-term promotions to maintain cash flow while preserving its commitment to long-term initiatives.

In conclusion, **balancing short-term results with long-term ROI** is a strategic challenge that requires careful planning, measurement, and adaptability. By aligning efforts with organisational goals, monitoring outcomes across timeframes, and maintaining flexibility, CMOs can deliver immediate impact while laying the groundwork for sustained success. This dual focus ensures that marketing not only drives current performance but also builds a foundation for future growth and resilience.

7.7 - Overcoming Challenges in Data Interpretation

In the age of data-driven marketing, **data interpretation** is both a critical opportunity and a significant challenge. For a **Chief Marketing Officer (CMO)**, the ability to extract actionable insights from data can mean the difference between a successful campaign and wasted resources. However, the complexity, volume, and variability of data often lead to challenges that can hinder effective decision-making. Addressing these obstacles requires not only technical expertise but also a strategic and collaborative approach.

One of the most common challenges in data interpretation is dealing with **data overload**. Modern marketing tools generate massive amounts of information, from website traffic and email engagement to customer demographics and social media metrics. While this abundance is valuable, it can quickly become overwhelming without clear priorities. For example, a marketing team might receive dozens of metrics from a single campaign, but not all of them are equally important. To overcome this, CMOs must focus on **key performance indicators (KPIs)** that align with specific business goals. For instance:

- A campaign aimed at driving conversions might prioritise **click-through rates (CTR)** and **conversion rates** over broader metrics like impressions.

- A brand-building initiative might focus on **share of voice (SOV)** and **engagement rates** instead of immediate sales.

Data silos are another significant barrier to effective interpretation. In many organisations, different departments use separate tools and platforms to manage their data. For example, the sales team might rely on a CRM system, while the marketing team uses web analytics tools. These silos can lead to fragmented insights, making it difficult to gain a holistic view of the customer journey. Integrating data sources into a unified platform, such as **Tableau**, **Power BI**, or a CRM like **Salesforce**, is crucial. These tools consolidate data and provide cross-departmental visibility, enabling CMOs to connect the dots between marketing efforts and business outcomes.

Data quality issues further complicate interpretation. Inaccurate, incomplete, or outdated data can skew insights and lead to poor decisions. For example, relying on outdated customer preferences might result in irrelevant targeting, wasting marketing budget. Regular data audits, standardised data entry protocols, and automated validation processes can help maintain accuracy. For instance:

- Implementing real-time data updates ensures that marketing teams always work with the latest information.
- Using tools like **Google Data Studio** can highlight inconsistencies or anomalies in data, allowing teams to address issues promptly.

Another common challenge is **misinterpreting correlations as causations**. For instance, an increase in website traffic during a campaign might be attributed to digital ads, but deeper analysis could reveal that organic search or influencer marketing played a larger role. CMOs must encourage their teams to dig deeper into data, using attribution models and advanced analytics to identify the true drivers of performance. For example, tools like **Marketo** or **HubSpot** provide multi-touch attribution models that reveal how various touchpoints contribute to conversions.

Bias in data interpretation is another obstacle. Teams may unconsciously prioritise data that supports their assumptions while ignoring conflicting evidence. To combat this, CMOs should foster a culture of objectivity, encouraging team members to question findings and seek alternative explanations. For instance, presenting data in anonymised formats or using third-party validation can reduce the influence of biases.

Privacy regulations, such as GDPR and CCPA, also create challenges in data interpretation. These laws restrict data collection and usage, limiting the scope of available insights. While compliance is non-negotiable, CMOs can adapt by focusing on high-quality, consent-based data collection methods. For example:

- Building first-party data through direct customer interactions, such as surveys or loyalty programmes.
- Using anonymised or aggregated data to gain insights while respecting privacy requirements.

Visualisation tools play a critical role in overcoming interpretation challenges. Tools like **Looker**, **Tableau**, and **Google Data Studio** transform raw data into charts, graphs, and dashboards that make insights more accessible. For instance, a line graph showing month-over-month growth in engagement rates is far easier to interpret than a table of raw numbers. By presenting data visually, CMOs can communicate findings effectively to stakeholders and team members.

Training and upskilling are also essential for addressing gaps in data literacy. Many marketers lack the technical expertise to analyse and interpret complex datasets. Offering workshops, certifications, or access to online courses ensures that team members develop the skills needed to handle advanced tools and methodologies. For example:

- A digital marketing team could benefit from training in Google Analytics to better understand website performance metrics.
- Content marketers might learn to use SEO tools like **SEMRush** to analyse keyword trends and audience behaviour.

CMOs should embrace **predictive analytics** to anticipate future trends rather than merely analysing past performance. Predictive models use historical data to forecast customer behaviours, enabling proactive decision-making. For instance, a retail brand might predict seasonal demand for certain products and adjust its inventory and marketing strategies accordingly.

In conclusion, **overcoming challenges in data interpretation** requires a combination of clear priorities, robust tools, and a culture of objectivity and continuous learning. By addressing data overload, silos, and biases, CMOs can unlock the full potential of their data and translate it into actionable insights. In an increasingly data-driven world, mastering interpretation is essential for driving informed decisions, optimising campaigns, and achieving sustainable success.

7.8 - Predictive Analytics and Forecasting

In the rapidly evolving landscape of modern marketing, **predictive analytics** and **forecasting** have become indispensable tools for a **Chief Marketing Officer (CMO)**. These advanced techniques enable marketers to anticipate future trends, behaviours, and outcomes, allowing for proactive decision-making and improved allocation of resources. By leveraging historical data, machine learning algorithms, and statistical models, predictive analytics transforms raw information into actionable insights that drive long-term success.

At its core, **predictive analytics** involves analysing historical data to identify patterns and correlations that can predict future events. For example, an e-commerce company might use past purchase data to forecast which products are likely to be in high demand during a specific season. Similarly, a subscription-based business can predict customer churn by analysing behavioural patterns, such as declining engagement or skipped payments. These insights allow CMOs to develop targeted strategies that address potential challenges or capitalise on opportunities before they arise.

Forecasting, a related discipline, focuses on projecting future outcomes based on existing data and market trends. While predictive analytics often delves into specific customer behaviours, forecasting tends to provide a broader overview of metrics such as revenue, market share, or campaign performance. For instance, a CMO might use forecasting tools to estimate monthly revenue growth for the next quarter, enabling the team to set realistic goals and allocate budgets effectively.

One of the most powerful applications of predictive analytics is in customer segmentation and targeting. By analysing demographic, behavioural, and transactional data, marketers can identify high-value customer segments and tailor campaigns accordingly. For example:

- A retail brand might use predictive analytics to identify customers who are likely to make repeat purchases and target them with personalised loyalty offers.

- A streaming service could analyse viewing habits to recommend content that keeps users engaged and reduces churn.

Predictive analytics also enhances **lead scoring**, helping sales and marketing teams prioritise prospects based on their likelihood to convert. For instance, a B2B software company might use a predictive model to assign scores to leads based on factors such as industry, company size, and previous interactions with the brand. This ensures that resources are focused on the most promising opportunities, improving conversion rates and sales efficiency.

In **campaign optimisation**, predictive analytics provides valuable insights into what strategies are likely to deliver the best results. For example:

- A digital advertising team might use predictive models to determine the optimal budget allocation across platforms, ensuring maximum ROI.

- An email marketing team could forecast the best times to send campaigns based on historical open and click-through rates, increasing engagement.

Forecasting plays a critical role in long-term planning. By predicting trends in customer behaviour, market conditions, and competitive dynamics, CMOs can make informed decisions about resource allocation, product development, and market expansion. For instance, a fashion retailer might forecast rising demand for sustainable clothing and adjust its inventory and marketing strategies to align with this trend.

However, implementing predictive analytics and forecasting comes with challenges. One of the most significant is ensuring **data quality**. Inaccurate or incomplete data can lead to flawed predictions, resulting in poor decisions. To address this, CMOs must invest in robust data collection processes and tools, such as CRM systems and analytics platforms, that ensure accuracy and consistency.

Another challenge is the **interpretation of predictions**. Predictive models often present probabilities rather than certainties, which can be difficult for teams to act upon. For example, if a model predicts a 70% likelihood of customer churn, marketers must decide how aggressively to intervene. Training teams in data literacy and scenario planning helps bridge this gap, enabling them to use predictions effectively.

Ethical considerations are also crucial. Predictive analytics relies heavily on customer data, and mishandling this information can damage trust and violate privacy regulations such as **GDPR**. CMOs must prioritise transparency, ensuring that data collection and usage are ethical and compliant. For instance, using anonymised or aggregated data can provide insights while respecting individual privacy.

The tools used for predictive analytics and forecasting range from specialised platforms like **IBM SPSS**, **Alteryx**, and **RapidMiner** to integrated solutions in popular marketing software like **HubSpot**, **Salesforce Einstein**, and **Google Analytics 4**. These tools use machine learning algorithms to process vast datasets and generate actionable predictions. For example, a predictive analytics tool might analyse the performance of past campaigns to recommend optimal strategies for future initiatives.

Finally, **collaboration across teams** is essential for maximising the value of predictive analytics. Insights generated by these models often have implications beyond marketing, influencing sales, product development, and customer service. For instance, forecasting a spike in product demand might prompt the operations team to adjust inventory levels, ensuring that supply meets customer expectations.

In conclusion, **predictive analytics and forecasting** empower CMOs to stay ahead in an increasingly competitive and fast-paced market. By leveraging these techniques to anticipate customer needs, optimise campaigns, and plan for the future, marketing leaders can make proactive decisions that drive growth and innovation. While challenges such as data quality and ethical considerations must be addressed, the benefits of predictive analytics far outweigh the risks, making it an essential tool for modern marketing success.

7.9 - Avoiding Common Analytics Pitfalls

Advanced Analytics and ROI Measurement

In the age of data-driven marketing, the ability to interpret and act on insights is a cornerstone of effective decision-making. However, even the most advanced analytics systems can be undermined by common **pitfalls** that compromise accuracy, relevance, or usability. For a **Chief Marketing Officer (CMO)**, recognising and avoiding these pitfalls is essential for ensuring that analytics efforts deliver meaningful value and support strategic goals.

One of the most prevalent pitfalls is **focusing on vanity metrics**. These metrics, such as website visits, social media likes, or impressions, may look impressive, but often fail to provide actionable insights. For example, a campaign that generates a large number of likes on Instagram might appear successful, but if those likes do not translate into meaningful engagement, leads, or sales, the campaign's true impact is limited. To avoid this, CMOs should prioritise metrics that align with business objectives, such as **conversion rates**, **customer acquisition cost (CAC)**, or **return on investment (ROI)**. By focusing on these indicators, marketing teams can ensure their efforts contribute directly to organisational success.

Overlooking data quality is another critical issue. Inaccurate, incomplete, or outdated data can lead to flawed analyses and poor decision-making. For instance, using outdated customer profiles for a segmentation strategy might result in irrelevant messaging that alienates audiences. To mitigate this risk, CMOs must implement robust data validation processes and conduct regular audits to ensure data integrity. Tools like **Google Data Studio** or **Tableau** can help identify discrepancies or anomalies in datasets, enabling teams to address issues promptly.

Advanced Analytics and ROI Measurement

A related challenge is **data silos**, where information is stored in isolated systems across different departments. For example, the sales team may use a separate CRM platform from the marketing team, making it difficult to integrate insights and track the full customer journey. Breaking down these silos requires collaboration and the adoption of tools that facilitate data sharing, such as **HubSpot** or **Salesforce**. Unified systems allow CMOs to connect disparate datasets, providing a more comprehensive view of performance and customer behaviour.

Another common pitfall is **misinterpreting correlation as causation**. This occurs when a relationship between two variables is mistakenly assumed to imply a direct cause-and-effect link. For example, a spike in sales following a social media campaign might not necessarily mean the campaign drove the increase; it could be coincidental or influenced by other factors, such as seasonal trends or competitor activity. CMOs should encourage their teams to dig deeper, using methods like A/B testing or controlled experiments to validate hypotheses and confirm causation.

Over-reliance on a single metric can also lead to skewed perspectives. While KPIs are valuable for measuring success, focusing exclusively on one metric risks overlooking the bigger picture. For instance, prioritising customer acquisition metrics without considering retention could result in high churn rates and reduced customer lifetime value (CLV). A balanced approach that tracks multiple metrics ensures a more nuanced understanding of performance.

The complexity of **attribution models** is another area where marketers often falter. Choosing the wrong model can distort insights and misallocate credit among touchpoints. For example, a first-touch attribution model may overemphasise the role of initial interactions, while a last-touch model might undervalue the nurturing efforts that led to the final conversion. CMOs must carefully select attribution models that align with their goals and use tools like **Google Analytics 4** or **Marketo** to implement multi-touch attribution for a more accurate representation of campaign impact.

Neglecting context is a less obvious but equally damaging pitfall. Analytics without context can lead to misguided conclusions. For example, a drop in email open rates might seem alarming, but if it coincides with industry-wide trends or external factors like holiday seasons, it may not indicate a significant issue. Including benchmarks, historical data, and competitor analysis ensures that metrics are interpreted in the right context.

Bias in data interpretation is another challenge that CMOs must address. Confirmation bias, for instance, leads teams to focus on data that supports preconceived notions while ignoring conflicting evidence. To counteract this, CMOs should foster a culture of objectivity, encouraging teams to question assumptions and consider alternative explanations. Tools that anonymise data or present insights visually can also help reduce bias by emphasising facts over subjective interpretations.

Finally, **failing to act on insights** is a missed opportunity that undermines the value of analytics. Collecting data and generating reports is only the first step; the true impact comes from translating insights into action. For example, if analytics reveal a high bounce rate on a product page, the next step should involve investigating the issue, whether it's slow load times, unclear messaging, or poor design, and implementing solutions to improve user experience.

To avoid this pitfall, CMOs should ensure that every analytics initiative has a clear purpose and actionable outcomes. Regularly reviewing insights in team meetings, assigning responsibilities for follow-up actions, and tracking the results of changes made are all practices that reinforce a culture of accountability and continuous improvement.

In conclusion, **avoiding common analytics pitfalls** requires a proactive and strategic approach. By prioritising relevant metrics, ensuring data quality, maintaining objectivity, and acting on insights, CMOs can maximise the value of their analytics efforts. These practices not only enhance decision-making but also drive better outcomes, ensuring that marketing strategies are both effective and aligned with broader business goals.

7.10 - Case Study: Driving ROI Through Data

To illustrate the power of data-driven marketing, let us examine how a global skincare brand, **GlowPure**, transformed its approach to campaigns and achieved a remarkable **return on investment (ROI)** by leveraging advanced analytics and predictive insights. This case study highlights the importance of setting clear goals, using the right tools, and fostering a culture of data-informed decision-making.

Advanced Analytics and ROI Measurement

The Challenge

GlowPure had been investing heavily in digital marketing but struggled to demonstrate consistent ROI. Key challenges included:

- **Unclear attribution**: The team couldn't identify which channels were driving conversions, leading to inefficient budget allocation.
- **Low campaign engagement**: Despite significant ad spend, customer engagement on social media and email campaigns was underwhelming.
- **High churn rates**: Many customers made one-time purchases but didn't return, impacting customer lifetime value (CLV).
- **Fragmented data**: Insights were siloed across multiple platforms, making it difficult to get a holistic view of performance.

Recognising the need for a more strategic approach, GlowPure hired a new **Chief Marketing Officer (CMO)** to spearhead the transformation. The CMO's mandate was clear: use data to optimise marketing efforts, improve customer retention, and increase overall ROI.

The Solution

1. Establishing Clear Metrics and Goals

The first step was to define measurable objectives that aligned with GlowPure's business strategy. These goals included:

- Reducing customer acquisition cost (CAC) by 20%.

- Increasing CLV by 30% through improved retention.
- Identifying the top-performing marketing channels to optimise budget allocation.
- Achieving a 15% increase in engagement across key campaigns.

The team selected KPIs to track progress, such as **conversion rates**, **email open rates**, and **ROI by channel**.

2. Integrating Data Across Platforms

To address the issue of fragmented data, GlowPure implemented Google Analytics 4 and integrated it with their CRM system (HubSpot) and e-commerce platform. This created a unified data ecosystem, providing a complete view of the customer journey. For example:

- The team could now track how a customer moved from viewing a social media ad to purchasing a product online.
- Cross-platform tracking allowed for better attribution, helping the team understand the impact of each touchpoint.

3. Leveraging Predictive Analytics

GlowPure partnered with a predictive analytics provider to build models that forecasted customer behaviours. By analysing historical purchase data, the team identified patterns that indicated high churn risk, such as customers who didn't repurchase within 60 days. Based on these insights, the CMO launched a **retention campaign** targeting these customers with personalised discounts and product recommendations. This initiative reduced churn rates significantly and boosted repeat purchases.

4. Optimising Campaign Performance

With clear attribution data, the team discovered that email marketing was outperforming paid social ads in terms of ROI. They redirected 15% of the ad budget to email campaigns and focused on creating segmented, highly personalised content. For instance:

- New customers received welcome emails with tailored skincare routines.
- Long-time customers were offered loyalty discounts and exclusive early access to new products.

The team also used A/B testing to refine campaign elements, such as subject lines and call-to-action buttons, leading to a 25% increase in email open rates.

5. Implementing Real-Time Dashboards

To track performance, the CMO introduced real-time dashboards using **Tableau**. These dashboards provided insights into key metrics, such as daily sales, ROI by channel, and engagement trends. During weekly meetings, the team reviewed these dashboards to identify opportunities and address underperforming areas. For example, when the dashboards revealed low engagement with a social media campaign, the team quickly adjusted the ad creative and targeting, improving click-through rates within days.

The Results

Advanced Analytics and ROI Measurement

Within a year, GlowPure's data-driven approach delivered transformative results:

- **ROI improved by 35%**, driven by better budget allocation and more effective campaigns.

- **Customer lifetime value (CLV)** increased by 40%, thanks to targeted retention efforts.

- **Customer acquisition cost (CAC)** dropped by 25% as the team focused on high-performing channels.

- **Engagement rates rose by 20%**, particularly in email campaigns, which became a major revenue driver.

The insights gained from predictive analytics also helped GlowPure forecast inventory needs more accurately, reducing stockouts and improving customer satisfaction.

Lessons Learned

GlowPure's success offers several key takeaways for CMOs:

- **Unified data systems are essential**: Integrating platforms ensures a holistic view of the customer journey, enabling better attribution and decision-making.

- **Predictive analytics drives proactive strategies**: Anticipating customer behaviours allows for timely interventions that improve retention and ROI.

- **Personalisation boosts engagement**: Tailored messaging resonates more deeply with customers, leading to higher conversions and loyalty.

- **Real-time insights enable agility**: Dashboards that provide up-to-date metrics empower teams to pivot quickly and optimise campaigns.

Conclusion

The GlowPure case study demonstrates the transformative power of **data-driven marketing**. By leveraging advanced tools, predictive analytics, and real-time reporting, the company not only overcame its challenges but also achieved sustainable growth. For CMOs, this example underscores the importance of a strategic approach to data, one that combines technical expertise with a clear focus on business objectives. In a competitive landscape, using data to drive ROI is not just a best practice; it's a necessity for long-term success.

Chapter 8

Innovation and Growth Marketing

> "The most effective marketing strategy isn't just about reaching customers; it's about creating value so compelling they never want to leave."
>
> **Robert N. Jacobs**

In today's fast-evolving market landscape, innovation and growth marketing are not just tools; they are imperatives for driving sustainable success. For Chief Marketing Officers (CMOs), the challenge lies in navigating complex, ever-changing dynamics to deliver measurable results and long-term value. This chapter delves into the transformative strategies that redefine marketing as a catalyst for innovation and growth.

Chapter 8 explores the multidimensional aspects of growth marketing, including the art of leveraging experimentation, embracing customer-centricity, and fostering cross-functional collaboration. By combining creative ingenuity with data-driven insights, growth marketing moves beyond traditional approaches, ensuring scalability, agility, and impact. The insights and frameworks presented here are tailored to empower CMOs to innovate boldly, adapt swiftly, and stay ahead in an increasingly competitive environment.

8.1 - What is Growth Marketing?

Innovation and Growth Marketing

Growth marketing is a dynamic and data-driven approach to achieving scalable, sustainable business growth. It goes beyond traditional marketing by focusing on experimentation, customer retention, and iterative improvement. For a **Chief Marketing Officer (CMO)**, growth marketing is not just about acquiring new customers; it's about maximising the value of each customer throughout their lifecycle, from acquisition to retention and advocacy.

Unlike conventional marketing, which often emphasises broad campaigns aimed at building awareness, growth marketing hones in on measurable outcomes such as customer acquisition cost (CAC), customer lifetime value (CLV), and conversion rates. A defining characteristic of growth marketing is its emphasis on continuous experimentation. Marketers test hypotheses, refine strategies, and implement changes based on data insights. For example:

- An e-commerce brand might experiment with different email subject lines to determine which drives higher click-through rates.

- A subscription-based service might test various pricing tiers to optimise customer sign-ups and long-term retention. Another hallmark of growth marketing is its cross-functional nature. Growth marketers work closely with product teams, data analysts, and customer support to ensure that every aspect of the customer journey is optimised. For instance, a product team might introduce a new feature based on feedback gathered from marketing campaigns, while the customer support team provides insights into common pain points that marketing can address through targeted messaging.

Personalisation is a cornerstone of growth marketing. By tailoring campaigns to specific audience segments, growth marketers increase engagement and drive conversions. For example, a fitness app might send personalised workout recommendations based on user activity data, creating a more meaningful connection with its audience.

The iterative nature of growth marketing also requires a mindset shift. Instead of viewing failure as a setback, it's seen as an opportunity to learn and improve. A failed A/B test, for instance, provides valuable insights into what doesn't resonate with customers, guiding the next iteration of the campaign.

In summary, **growth marketing** is a holistic and agile approach that prioritises measurable results, continuous improvement, and customer-centricity. For CMOs, adopting a growth mindset means embracing change, fostering innovation, and relentlessly pursuing strategies that deliver long-term value.

8.2 - Identifying New Market Opportunities

For a **Chief Marketing Officer (CMO)**, the ability to identify and capitalise on **new market opportunities** is essential for driving sustainable growth. This process involves a combination of strategic foresight, deep customer understanding, and thorough market analysis. While established markets offer stability, venturing into untapped segments or addressing emerging customer needs can unlock significant potential for innovation and revenue expansion.

Identifying new opportunities begins with understanding market trends. Keeping a pulse on industry developments, consumer behaviours, and technological advancements is crucial. For example, the rise of eco-consciousness has created opportunities for brands to introduce sustainable products and services. A CMO in the retail industry might identify a growing demand for ethically sourced clothing and launch a new line to cater to this audience. By proactively analysing trends, CMOs can position their organisations ahead of competitors.

Customer insights are another vital resource. Listening to current customers and understanding their pain points often reveals unmet needs or underserved segments. Tools like surveys, focus groups, and social media monitoring provide valuable data on customer preferences and challenges. For instance, a tech company noticing frequent customer complaints about outdated software features might identify an opportunity to develop a new product that addresses these issues. Similarly, analysing patterns in customer behaviour, such as preferences for specific product categories, can guide marketing efforts towards emerging niches.

Competitor analysis plays a key role in identifying gaps in the market. By evaluating the strengths and weaknesses of competitors, CMOs can pinpoint areas where their organisation can differentiate itself. For example, a CMO in the hospitality industry might notice that competitors lack family-friendly amenities and use this insight to create a unique selling proposition (USP) that appeals to this demographic.

Expanding into **new geographic markets** is another avenue for growth. While entering international markets presents challenges, it can significantly boost revenue if executed correctly. For example, a food brand entering a new country might conduct market research to understand local tastes, preferences, and cultural nuances. This ensures that products are tailored to resonate with the target audience. Leveraging partnerships with local distributors or agencies can also ease entry into unfamiliar markets.

Emerging technologies often create new opportunities for businesses willing to innovate. For instance, the widespread adoption of augmented reality (AR) and virtual reality (VR) has opened doors for experiential marketing. A furniture brand might use AR to let customers visualise how a piece of furniture fits into their home, providing a competitive edge while addressing a common customer challenge. CMOs who embrace technology early often position their organisations as industry leaders.

Market segmentation is another valuable strategy. Instead of treating the customer base as a monolithic group, segmenting by demographics, psychographics, or behaviour allows organisations to uncover specific subgroups with unique needs. For instance, a skincare brand might identify a growing demand for products tailored to men, enabling it to develop a new product line targeting this underserved segment. Segmentation not only reveals new opportunities but also enhances marketing efficiency by delivering highly targeted campaigns.

Another avenue for opportunity lies in **partnerships and collaborations**. By aligning with complementary brands or organisations, CMOs can tap into new audiences and offer expanded value propositions. For example, a fitness brand partnering with a healthy food delivery service can create bundled offerings that attract health-conscious consumers while sharing marketing costs.

While identifying opportunities is exciting, CMOs must also evaluate their feasibility. **Market research** and **financial modelling** help determine whether pursuing a new opportunity aligns with the organisation's capabilities and goals. Factors such as market size, potential ROI, competitive landscape, and resource requirements should be thoroughly analysed. For instance, while entering a highly competitive market might seem appealing, it may require significant investment with uncertain returns, making it a less viable option than focusing on a smaller, untapped niche.

Timing is another critical factor. Launching a product or service too early, before the market is ready, can result in low adoption rates. Conversely, entering a saturated market too late may limit potential gains. CMOs must strike the right balance by monitoring market readiness and aligning launches with consumer demand.

Identifying new market opportunities requires a blend of creativity, data-driven insights, and strategic planning. By staying attuned to market trends, leveraging customer and competitor insights, and embracing innovation, CMOs can position their organisations to seize emerging opportunities and achieve sustainable growth. This proactive approach not only fuels expansion but also ensures that businesses remain relevant and competitive in a rapidly evolving landscape.

8.3 - Experimentation and A/B Testing

Experimentation and A/B testing are cornerstone practices in **growth marketing**, enabling organisations to refine strategies, improve customer engagement, and optimise outcomes through data-driven decision-making. For a **Chief Marketing Officer (CMO)**, these techniques represent a methodical approach to testing ideas, identifying what works, and scaling success while minimising risk.

A/B testing, at its simplest, involves comparing two or more variations of a marketing element to determine which performs better. It could be as straightforward as testing two email subject lines or as complex as comparing entirely different user journeys on a website. For example, a retail brand might test two versions of a homepage: one featuring a seasonal sale prominently and another highlighting new arrivals. By analysing metrics such as click-through rates (CTR) or conversion rates, the CMO can determine which version resonates more with the target audience.

The value of A/B testing lies in its ability to remove guesswork from decision-making. Instead of relying on intuition, marketing teams use empirical evidence to guide their strategies. This is particularly important in a competitive market where small improvements can have a significant impact on results. For instance:

- A 1% increase in email open rates, achieved by optimising subject lines through A/B testing, could lead to thousands of additional website visits.
- Testing different ad creatives for a social media campaign might reveal a design that generates higher engagement, allowing the team to maximise ROI.

Experimentation extends beyond A/B testing to include multivariate testing, pilot programmes, and exploratory campaigns. While A/B testing typically isolates a single variable (e.g., headline, call-to-action, or colour scheme), multivariate testing evaluates the impact of multiple variables simultaneously. For example, an e-commerce brand could test various combinations of product images, descriptions, and pricing formats to identify the optimal mix for driving sales.

One of the most important aspects of experimentation is hypothesis formation. Before launching a test, marketers must clearly define what they are testing and why. A good hypothesis is specific, measurable, and based on previous insights or observations. For example:

- Hypothesis: Adding customer testimonials to the product page will increase conversions by 15% because they build trust with new visitors.

Once the hypothesis is established, the test is conducted on a subset of the audience to minimise risk. Statistical significance is a critical consideration; marketers must ensure that results are not due to chance but represent a true preference or behaviour among the target audience. For instance, testing a pop-up promotion over a week with insufficient traffic may produce misleading results. Tools like **Google Optimize**, **Optimizely**, and **VWO** help manage experiments and calculate significance accurately.

Experimentation is particularly valuable for customer journey optimisation. By testing different touchpoints, such as landing pages, email campaigns, or checkout processes, CMOs can identify friction points and implement solutions. For example:

- If A/B testing reveals that a complex checkout process leads to cart abandonment, simplifying the steps could significantly boost conversions.
- Testing different retargeting ad sequences might reveal which frequency and messaging strategy drives the highest engagement without overwhelming customers.

Personalisation is another area where experimentation shines. Marketers can test personalised messaging against generic content to evaluate its impact. For instance, a streaming service could test email campaigns that recommend shows based on viewing history versus a generic "top picks" list. If personalised emails perform better, the team can scale this approach to maximise engagement.

While experimentation offers significant benefits, there are challenges to overcome. **Bias** is a common pitfall where preconceived notions influence how tests are designed or interpreted. CMOs must ensure that experiments are conducted objectively, with no agenda beyond uncovering the truth.

Additionally, **resource allocation** can be a concern. Running multiple experiments requires time, effort, and budget, so prioritising tests with the highest potential impact is essential.

Another consideration is **timing and audience segmentation**. Testing during an atypical period, such as a holiday season, may not produce results that are representative of normal conditions. Similarly, failing to segment audiences appropriately can lead to skewed insights. For example, a test targeting a diverse audience without accounting for demographic differences might obscure valuable insights specific to particular segments.

Scaling the insights from successful experiments is the final step. Once a variation proves effective, it should be implemented broadly and monitored to ensure that performance remains consistent. For example:

- If an A/B test shows that a new email format generates higher open rates, the template can be standardised across campaigns.
- If a pilot programme in one region delivers strong results, it can be expanded nationally or globally.

Experimentation and A/B testing empower CMOs to take a scientific approach to marketing. By testing hypotheses, analysing results, and scaling proven strategies, marketers can continually refine their efforts, maximise ROI, and stay ahead of the competition. These practices ensure that marketing decisions are not only informed but also effective, driving growth through a cycle of learning and improvement.

8.4 - Driving Product Innovation Through Marketing

Marketing has long been seen as the vehicle for promoting products, but for a **Chief Marketing Officer (CMO)**, it is also a driving force behind **product innovation**. In a competitive landscape where customer needs evolve rapidly, marketing plays a crucial role in shaping products that align with market demands, foster differentiation, and deliver value. By leveraging data, customer insights, and cross-functional collaboration, marketing can influence product development and ensure that innovation is not only creative but also commercially viable.

Understanding customer needs is the foundation of marketing-led product innovation. Through surveys, focus groups, and social listening, marketers gather insights into what customers want, what problems they face, and how they use existing products. For instance, a fitness equipment company may discover through social media monitoring that customers want compact, multi-functional equipment for small spaces. This insight could lead to the development of a product that addresses this need, providing a competitive advantage.

Data analytics further enhances this process by uncovering trends and patterns in customer behaviour. Tools like Google Analytics, HubSpot, and Power BI allow marketers to analyse how customers interact with products, revealing pain points and opportunities. For example:

- Heatmaps might show where users frequently click on an app interface, indicating features they find most useful.

- Sales data might reveal which product variations (e.g., colours, sizes, or configurations) are most popular, informing future offerings.

Armed with these insights, CMOs can advocate for product improvements or entirely new offerings. For instance, if data shows that customers frequently abandon their shopping carts because a product lacks a particular feature, marketing can bring this issue to the product team and suggest enhancements.

Collaborating with product development teams is essential for driving innovation. Marketing acts as the voice of the customer, ensuring that development efforts are customer-centric. For example, during the creation of a new tech gadget, marketers might provide feedback on desired features, user experience (UX) design, or pricing models based on customer research. This collaboration ensures that the product meets market expectations while staying aligned with the brand's overall strategy.

Marketing-led product innovation is also fuelled by competitor analysis. By studying the strengths and weaknesses of competitors' products, CMOs can identify gaps in the market that their organisation can fill. For example:

- If competitors in the skincare industry focus primarily on anti-ageing products, a brand might innovate by creating a line that targets stress-induced skin issues, a relatively untapped niche.
- Monitoring customer reviews of competing products can also highlight common complaints that the company's offerings can address.

Campaign testing and feedback loops are other critical components of marketing-driven innovation. Marketers often test concepts, packaging, or positioning through pilot campaigns before full-scale product launches. For example, a food brand introducing a new flavour might test it in select markets, using sales data and customer feedback to refine the product or decide whether to expand the rollout. These feedback loops ensure that products are fine-tuned based on real-world input, reducing the risk of failure.

Marketing also plays a pivotal role in **branding and positioning innovations**. Sometimes, the product itself may not change significantly, but rebranding or repositioning can reinvigorate its appeal. For instance, a beverage company might repackage an existing drink as a wellness product, targeting a new audience and tapping into trends like health-conscious living.

Emerging technologies provide additional avenues for innovation. For example:

- **Augmented reality (AR)** can enhance product demonstrations, allowing customers to visualise how a product will look or function in their environment.
- **AI-powered personalisation** can guide product recommendations based on individual customer preferences, creating a unique experience that fosters loyalty.

Sustainability is another driver of product innovation. With consumers increasingly valuing eco-friendly practices, CMOs can push for sustainable materials, packaging, or processes in product development. For example, a fashion brand might introduce a line of clothing made entirely from recycled fabrics, aligning with environmental trends while differentiating itself from competitors.

However, driving product innovation through marketing is not without challenges. Resistance to change within the organisation, limited budgets, or conflicting priorities between marketing and product teams can create obstacles. To overcome these barriers, CMOs must:

- Build strong cross-functional relationships to foster collaboration.
- Present clear, data-backed business cases for proposed innovations.
- Align innovation efforts with broader organisational goals to secure buy-in from leadership.

Innovation doesn't end with product development; it extends to **customer experience (CX)**. Marketing can influence how customers interact with the product post-purchase, ensuring that the experience is seamless and enjoyable. For example, a software company might develop onboarding tutorials or personalised training sessions based on customer feedback, enhancing satisfaction and retention.

Driving product innovation through marketing requires a customer-centric approach, data-driven insights, and collaboration across teams. By identifying unmet needs, advocating for improvements, and leveraging emerging trends, CMOs can ensure that their organisations remain competitive and relevant. Marketing-led innovation not only creates better products but also strengthens brand loyalty and drives sustainable growth.

8.5 - The Role of Partnerships and Collaborations

Partnerships and collaborations are a cornerstone of modern marketing strategies, offering opportunities to expand reach, enhance capabilities, and deliver greater value to customers. For a **Chief Marketing Officer (CMO)**, building strategic alliances with complementary organisations, influencers, or even competitors can be a powerful way to achieve growth and innovation. Partnerships not only amplify marketing efforts but also foster innovation by combining strengths and resources.

One of the most significant benefits of partnerships is the ability to **reach new audiences**. By collaborating with a brand that serves a similar but non-competing customer base, companies can tap into new markets without the high costs associated with traditional acquisition strategies. For example, a fitness brand partnering with a meal delivery service creates a mutually beneficial relationship, as both audiences are likely to share an interest in health and wellness. Joint campaigns, such as cross-promotions or bundled offers, allow each brand to leverage the other's audience and boost visibility.

Enhancing brand credibility is another advantage of strategic collaborations. When a brand aligns itself with a trusted partner, it gains credibility by association. For instance, a small tech startup partnering with an established hardware manufacturer can gain customer trust more quickly than if it operated independently. This strategy is particularly effective for new entrants to the market who need to build trust and authority.

Partnerships can also drive product innovation by combining the expertise and resources of both parties. Co-branding initiatives often result in unique offerings that neither brand could have developed on its own. For example:

- A fashion brand and a tech company might collaborate to create a line of smart clothing, combining style with functionality.
- An automotive manufacturer might partner with a leading AI company to develop advanced driver-assistance systems that appeal to tech-savvy consumers.

In the digital age, **influencer collaborations** have become a popular form of partnership. Influencers bring authenticity and relatability to marketing efforts, as their audiences trust their recommendations. For example, a skincare brand working with a well-known beauty influencer can generate awareness and drive sales more effectively than traditional advertising. However, successful influencer partnerships require careful vetting to ensure alignment with brand values and audience demographics.

Partnerships also play a critical role in content marketing. Collaborating with subject-matter experts, media outlets, or educational institutions can lead to the creation of high-quality, engaging content. For instance:

- A financial services company might partner with a university to produce a white paper on emerging investment trends, enhancing its thought leadership in the industry.

- A travel agency might collaborate with a popular travel blogger to create destination guides that inspire potential customers.

Shared resources are another key advantage of collaborations. By pooling budgets, tools, or personnel, partners can achieve economies of scale and reduce costs. For example, two startups with complementary products might co-host a virtual event, sharing the cost of promotion and production while reaching both of their audiences.

Despite the benefits, partnerships and collaborations come with challenges. **Misaligned objectives** can lead to conflicts or underwhelming results. For instance, if one brand prioritises short-term sales while the other focuses on long-term brand building, the partnership may struggle to deliver meaningful outcomes. To mitigate this, CMOs must establish clear, mutually agreed-upon goals and expectations from the outset. A detailed partnership agreement outlining responsibilities, timelines, and success metrics ensures alignment and accountability.

Another potential challenge is the **risk to brand reputation**. Aligning with the wrong partner can damage trust and credibility. For example, a brand that collaborates with a partner involved in a scandal risks being associated with negative perceptions. Conducting thorough due diligence and ongoing performance evaluations helps mitigate these risks.

Measuring success is a critical aspect of managing partnerships. CMOs should establish KPIs that reflect the partnership's objectives, such as increased sales, audience growth, or improved engagement metrics. For example:

- Tracking referral traffic from a partner's website can indicate the effectiveness of digital collaboration.
- Monitoring joint campaign performance, such as conversions from co-branded emails, provides insights into the partnership's ROI.

Partnerships can also be a vehicle for **corporate social responsibility (CSR)**. Collaborating with non-profits or advocacy groups allows brands to contribute to meaningful causes while enhancing their public image. For instance, a beverage company partnering with an environmental organisation to promote recycling initiatives demonstrates its commitment to sustainability, resonating with socially conscious consumers.

Successful partnerships require **ongoing communication and collaboration**. Regular check-ins, performance reviews, and open channels of communication ensure that both parties remain aligned and can adapt to changing circumstances. For example, if a co-marketing campaign underperforms, both brands can collaborate to adjust strategies in real-time, maximising impact.

Partnerships and collaborations offer significant opportunities for growth, innovation, and enhanced customer value. By carefully selecting partners, aligning objectives, and fostering open communication, CMOs can create mutually beneficial relationships that drive results. Whether through co-branding, influencer campaigns, or shared resources, partnerships have the potential to amplify marketing efforts and position organisations for long-term success.

8.6 - Scaling Campaigns: Challenges and Solutions

Scaling marketing campaigns is a critical skill for any **Chief Marketing Officer (CMO)**. A campaign that performs well on a small scale often has the potential to deliver even greater returns when expanded. However, scaling comes with its own set of challenges, from resource allocation and budget management to maintaining campaign quality and consistency. For CMOs, effectively navigating these challenges ensures that campaigns reach larger audiences while delivering measurable and sustainable results.

The first challenge in scaling campaigns is ensuring alignment with organisational goals. A campaign that works for a niche audience or local market might not align with the broader objectives of the company when expanded. For example, a regional product launch that generates strong engagement might require significant adaptation for national or international markets. CMOs must evaluate whether scaling aligns with the company's strategic priorities and assess its feasibility based on factors such as market readiness, brand perception, and competitive dynamics.

Another significant challenge is **maintaining consistency across channels and geographies.** As campaigns grow, they often involve more stakeholders, channels, and markets, increasing the complexity of execution. For example, a global campaign must balance local cultural nuances with overarching brand messaging. A CMO expanding a campaign internationally might ensure localisation of content while retaining a consistent brand voice. Collaborating with regional teams or agencies helps achieve this balance.

Resource allocation is another key consideration. Scaling requires additional budget, personnel, and tools, which can strain existing resources. For instance:

- A campaign that relies heavily on paid ads may need increased spending to reach new audiences.
- Expanding a video campaign may require additional production capacity, from creating more content to adapting it for different formats and platforms.

CMOs must ensure that scaling efforts are supported by adequate resources without compromising other initiatives. Prioritising high-performing channels and allocating budgets accordingly helps maximise ROI. For example, if data shows that email marketing delivers higher conversion rates than paid social, resources can be reallocated to prioritise email campaigns.

Campaign performance tracking becomes more challenging as campaigns scale. Metrics that were manageable on a smaller scale, such as conversion rates or engagement metrics, can become harder to monitor across multiple platforms and regions. CMOs must invest in robust analytics tools, such as **Google Analytics**, **Tableau**, or **HubSpot**, to maintain visibility into performance. Creating dashboards that consolidate data from all channels provides a centralised view, enabling real-time decision-making.

One of the most overlooked challenges in scaling campaigns is **audience fatigue.** Expanding the reach of a campaign increases the risk of overexposure, leading to diminishing returns. For example, running the same ad too frequently on social media can result in decreased engagement and even negative sentiment. To address this, CMOs must diversify content and refresh creative elements regularly. A campaign that relies on a mix of formats, such as video, carousel ads, and static images, can sustain interest while reaching broader audiences.

Technology and automation play a critical role in overcoming scalability challenges. Tools like **Marketo**, **Pardot**, or **Hootsuite** enable teams to automate repetitive tasks, such as email scheduling, ad placement, and performance reporting. For example, an e-commerce brand scaling its Black Friday campaign might use automation to manage inventory-based ads, ensuring that products are promoted dynamically as availability changes. Automation reduces manual workload, allowing teams to focus on strategy and creative innovation.

Testing and optimisation are equally important during scaling. A campaign that works well on a small scale may encounter unexpected issues when expanded, such as variations in audience preferences or competitive pressures in new markets. CMOs should continue A/B testing and monitor metrics closely to identify areas for improvement. For instance:

- Testing different ad creatives in larger markets can reveal preferences that were not apparent in smaller test audiences.
- Segmenting audiences more granularly ensures that messaging resonates across diverse customer groups.

Collaboration across teams and departments is essential for successful scaling. As campaigns grow, marketing teams often need support from sales, product, and customer service teams to ensure consistency and alignment. For example, a campaign promoting a new product feature might require training for customer service representatives to handle increased inquiries. Clear communication and coordination among all stakeholders ensure that scaling efforts run smoothly.

Budget management is another crucial aspect. Scaling campaigns can quickly become expensive, and without careful oversight, costs can spiral out of control. CMOs must continuously evaluate the ROI of scaled campaigns and adjust spending accordingly. For example, if a campaign expansion into a new market delivers lower-than-expected returns, resources can be redirected to higher-performing regions or initiatives.

CMOs must be prepared to **adapt to unforeseen challenges.** Scaling campaigns often involves navigating complexities such as changing market conditions, regulatory requirements, or unexpected competition. Agility and flexibility are key to overcoming these obstacles. For instance, if a regulatory change affects how ads can be targeted in a particular region, the team must quickly adjust strategies to comply while maintaining campaign effectiveness.

Scaling campaigns requires a strategic and resourceful approach. By aligning efforts with organisational goals, maintaining consistency, leveraging technology, and managing resources effectively, CMOs can expand their campaigns while sustaining quality and ROI. While scaling presents challenges, it also offers significant opportunities for growth, making it an essential skill for marketing leaders aiming to maximise their impact on a larger scale.

8.7 - Incorporating Sustainability into Growth Strategies

Incorporating **sustainability** into **growth strategies** has become an essential focus for modern businesses, and for a **Chief Marketing Officer (CMO)**, it is an opportunity to align marketing goals with environmental and social responsibility. As consumers increasingly prioritise eco-conscious and ethical practices, integrating sustainability into growth strategies not only enhances brand reputation but also drives long-term success by appealing to a values-driven audience.

At the heart of sustainable growth strategies is the principle of **balancing profitability with responsibility**. This means designing initiatives that contribute to business objectives while minimising environmental impact and fostering social good. For example, a clothing brand aiming to grow market share might launch a sustainable line of apparel made from recycled materials. Such initiatives demonstrate a commitment to sustainability while tapping into the growing demand for eco-friendly products.

One of the first steps in incorporating sustainability into growth strategies is conducting a **thorough audit** of current practices. CMOs need to evaluate the environmental impact of marketing activities, supply chains, and product life cycles. For instance, a CMO at a food and beverage company might assess the carbon footprint of packaging, transportation, and promotional materials. Insights from this audit can guide the development of targeted initiatives, such as switching to biodegradable packaging or reducing waste in promotional campaigns.

Customer insights also play a critical role in shaping sustainable strategies. Surveys, focus groups, and social media analysis can reveal what sustainability issues matter most to the target audience. For example:

- A cosmetics brand may discover that its audience values cruelty-free products and sustainable packaging, leading to initiatives that address both concerns.
- A technology company might learn that customers are interested in energy-efficient products and services, driving innovation in this area.

Sustainability efforts often involve **collaborations and partnerships**. Working with organisations that specialise in sustainability can enhance credibility and amplify impact. For instance, a retail brand might partner with an environmental organisation to plant trees for every purchase, combining growth initiatives with tangible contributions to environmental health. Partnerships with non-profits, certifications from organisations like **Fair Trade** or **LEED**, and collaborations with suppliers committed to sustainable practices further reinforce a brand's commitment.

Transparency and communication are crucial for gaining trust and support from customers. Consumers are increasingly sceptical of superficial sustainability claims, often referred to as "greenwashing." To avoid this, CMOs must ensure that all sustainability initiatives are backed by measurable results and clear reporting. For example:

- Sharing annual sustainability reports that outline reductions in carbon emissions or waste provides evidence of progress.

- Creating campaigns that educate consumers about the impact of their choices, such as the benefits of choosing a product made with renewable resources, helps build trust and engagement.

Incorporating sustainability into growth strategies often requires product innovation. Brands must rethink their offerings to align with sustainable principles without compromising quality or customer appeal. For instance:

- A beverage company might innovate by introducing refillable packaging options or transitioning to plant-based materials for bottles and caps.

- A home goods brand might explore circular economy models, encouraging customers to return used items for refurbishment or recycling.

- Marketing campaigns themselves can also be made more sustainable. For example:

- Digital campaigns reduce the environmental impact associated with printing and distributing physical materials.
- Events and activations can adopt greener practices, such as using energy-efficient lighting, compostable materials, and locally sourced catering.

One of the challenges in adopting sustainable growth strategies is balancing **short-term costs with long-term benefits**. Implementing eco-friendly practices often requires upfront investment, which can strain budgets. However, the long-term advantages, such as increased customer loyalty, reduced operational costs, and compliance with evolving regulations, often outweigh these initial expenses. CMOs must build a compelling business case for sustainability, demonstrating its alignment with both ethical values and financial goals.

Sustainability also provides a platform for storytelling and engagement. Sharing authentic stories about the brand's sustainability journey resonates with consumers on an emotional level. For example:

- Highlighting the people behind sustainable sourcing initiatives, such as farmers or artisans, can create a personal connection with the audience.
- Documenting the impact of initiatives, such as the number of plastic bottles saved through a refillable packaging programme, reinforces credibility and inspires action.

Metrics and KPIs are essential for tracking the success of sustainability-focused growth strategies. CMOs should establish clear goals, such as reducing carbon emissions by a specific percentage or achieving a set target for recycled materials in products. Regularly monitoring these metrics ensures accountability and helps refine strategies over time. For instance:

- Tracking customer adoption rates for eco-friendly product lines can indicate how well sustainability efforts align with consumer preferences.
- Measuring waste reduction in campaigns provides insights into the effectiveness of green marketing practices.

CMOs must view sustainability as a long-term commitment rather than a one-time initiative. As environmental and social challenges evolve, so too must the brand's strategies. For example, a company that initially focuses on reducing plastic waste might later expand its efforts to address energy use or water conservation. Staying proactive and adaptive ensures that sustainability remains a core part of the brand's identity.

Incorporating sustainability into growth strategies is both a responsibility and an opportunity for CMOs. By aligning business goals with environmental and social values, marketing leaders can create initiatives that resonate with modern consumers, build trust, and drive long-term success. Through transparency, collaboration, innovation, and measurable impact, sustainability becomes a powerful driver of growth in an increasingly conscientious marketplace.

8.8 - Staying Ahead of Industry Disruptions

For a **Chief Marketing Officer (CMO)**, staying ahead of **industry disruptions** is not just a strategic advantage but a necessity.

Rapid advancements in technology, shifting consumer behaviours, and unpredictable market conditions have made disruption a constant force in the business landscape. Successfully navigating these challenges requires foresight, agility, and the ability to turn uncertainty into opportunity.

Understanding the nature of disruptions is the first step in staying ahead. Disruptions often arise from technological innovation, regulatory changes, or new market entrants introducing unexpected competition. For example, the rise of streaming services disrupted the traditional television and film industries, forcing established players to adapt or risk obsolescence. Similarly, the adoption of artificial intelligence (AI) and automation has transformed marketing processes, enabling hyper-personalisation and predictive analytics while rendering some traditional methods less effective.

To anticipate disruptions, CMOs must prioritise **market intelligence**. Staying informed about industry trends, emerging technologies, and competitor activity is essential. Tools like **Trendwatching**, **CB Insights**, and **Statista** provide valuable insights into upcoming shifts and potential disruptors. For example, a CMO in the retail sector might monitor trends in augmented reality (AR) shopping experiences, identifying opportunities to integrate AR into their own strategies before competitors.

Customer insights also play a crucial role. By understanding evolving customer needs and preferences, CMOs can stay ahead of shifts in demand. For instance:

- Monitoring social media conversations can reveal emerging consumer values, such as sustainability or inclusivity, prompting brands to adjust their messaging or offerings.

- Analysing purchase patterns can indicate when customers are adopting new technologies or behaviours, such as an increased preference for subscription models.

Embracing technology is one of the most effective ways to stay ahead of disruption. From AI and machine learning to blockchain and virtual reality (VR), technology provides tools to innovate, optimise, and differentiate. For example:

- AI-powered tools like **Marketo Engage** or **HubSpot** enable advanced customer segmentation and personalised marketing at scale.

- Blockchain technology can enhance transparency and trust in supply chains, appealing to ethically conscious consumers.

While technology adoption is essential, it is equally important to **remain agile**. Agility enables organisations to pivot quickly in response to unexpected changes. For CMOs, this might mean rethinking campaign strategies in light of a sudden regulatory shift or reallocating budgets to focus on emerging channels. For example, when privacy regulations like **GDPR** limited traditional data collection methods, agile organisations quickly shifted to prioritising first-party data and consent-driven practices.

Scenario planning is another critical tool for staying ahead of disruptions. By modelling various potential futures, CMOs can prepare for a range of outcomes and develop contingency plans. For example:

- A global brand might simulate the impact of a recession on consumer spending and design campaigns that emphasise value and affordability.
- A tech company might explore scenarios where new competitors disrupt the market and identify ways to differentiate its products.

Collaboration and partnerships also help navigate disruptions. Partnering with startups, technology providers, or research institutions allows brands to stay at the forefront of innovation. For instance, a healthcare company might collaborate with a biotech startup to explore the potential of wearable health monitors, addressing an emerging consumer demand for personalised health data.

One of the biggest challenges in responding to disruption is overcoming **internal resistance to change**. Established organisations often face inertia, with teams reluctant to adopt new methods or abandon familiar practices. CMOs must lead by example, fostering a culture of innovation and continuous improvement. This includes encouraging experimentation, rewarding creative problem-solving, and providing training to ensure teams are equipped to handle new tools and processes.

Proactive communication with stakeholders is also essential during times of disruption. CMOs must articulate the rationale behind strategic shifts, ensuring alignment across departments and gaining support from leadership. For example, if a brand plans to invest heavily in metaverse marketing, a disruptive yet uncertain channel, the CMO should present a clear business case, highlighting potential benefits and risk mitigation strategies.

Measuring success in disruptive environments requires flexibility and adaptability. Traditional KPIs may not fully capture the impact of innovative strategies. CMOs should develop metrics that reflect both short-term results and long-term potential. For instance:

- Tracking brand sentiment during a disruptive campaign can provide insights into how customers perceive the brand's adaptability and relevance.
- Monitoring engagement with new technologies, such as AR or VR experiences, can indicate the effectiveness of experimental approaches.

Disruption also presents opportunities for **thought leadership**. By positioning the brand as a pioneer in addressing industry challenges, CMOs can enhance credibility and attract attention. For example, a financial services company might publish insights on how blockchain technology will reshape transactions, establishing itself as an authority in the field.

Staying ahead of industry disruptions requires a proactive, strategic approach. By monitoring trends, embracing technology, fostering agility, and encouraging innovation, CMOs can not only navigate change but also seize opportunities to lead. While disruptions can be challenging, they also provide a chance to differentiate, adapt, and thrive in an ever-evolving marketplace.

8.9 - Tools and Frameworks for Agile Marketing

For a **Chief Marketing Officer (CMO)**, the adoption of **agile marketing** is essential for maintaining relevance and competitiveness in an increasingly fast-paced and unpredictable marketplace. Agile marketing is rooted in flexibility, collaboration, and iterative processes that allow marketing teams to adapt quickly to shifting customer behaviours, market trends, and internal business priorities. To implement agile effectively, marketers must employ the right **tools** and **frameworks** that streamline workflows, enhance communication, and provide actionable insights.

One of the core components of agile marketing is **project management**. Tools like **Trello**, **Asana**, and **Monday.com** are indispensable for organising tasks, tracking progress, and fostering collaboration across teams. These platforms use visual boards to divide tasks into manageable segments, often referred to as "sprints." For instance, a content team might break down a campaign into stages such as brainstorming, drafting, editing, and publishing, assigning each task to specific team members. This approach ensures accountability and keeps the entire team aligned.

Data-driven decision-making is another critical element of agile marketing, and tools such as Google Analytics, HubSpot, and Tableau are invaluable. These platforms enable teams to monitor campaign performance in real-time, identify trends, and adjust strategies based on data. For example:

- **Google Analytics** can track customer behaviours such as click-through rates (CTR) or bounce rates, helping teams understand how users interact with a website.

- **HubSpot integrates CRM**, marketing automation, and analytics, offering a complete view of customer interactions and campaign outcomes.
- **Tableau** provides advanced data visualisation capabilities, creating interactive dashboards that consolidate metrics from multiple sources into actionable insights.

Another essential aspect of agile marketing is **team communication**. Real-time collaboration tools such as **Slack** and **Microsoft Teams** facilitate seamless interaction among team members, particularly in remote or distributed work environments. For example, a campaign team working across multiple time zones might use Slack to create dedicated channels for asset sharing, performance updates, and problem-solving discussions. This ensures that all team members remain informed and aligned, regardless of their location.

Automation tools are integral to agile workflows, allowing teams to streamline repetitive tasks and focus on strategy and innovation. Platforms like Marketo, Mailchimp, and Pardot automate processes such as email campaigns, social media scheduling, and lead nurturing. For example:

- A CMO scaling a holiday campaign might use Marketo to automate dynamic retargeting ads, ensuring that customers who viewed specific products are reminded to return and complete their purchase.
- Mailchimp's personalisation features can dynamically tailor email content based on customer preferences, increasing engagement while saving time.

The iterative nature of agile marketing relies on **experimentation and testing**. Tools such as **Google Optimize** and **Optimizely** empower teams to conduct A/B tests or multivariate experiments to refine campaigns. For instance, testing different versions of an email subject line can reveal which generates higher open rates, guiding future messaging decisions.

Frameworks like Scrum and Kanban provide the structure necessary for implementing agile marketing effectively. Scrum encourages teams to work in short sprints, with regular stand-up meetings to review progress, address obstacles, and plan the next steps. Kanban, on the other hand, focuses on visualising workflows and managing work-in-progress limits to ensure efficiency. For example:

- A Scrum-based approach might involve dedicating a two-week sprint to testing new ad creatives for a product launch.
- A Kanban board could track ongoing tasks like blog creation, social media management, and performance analysis, ensuring transparency and accountability.

While agile marketing offers significant benefits, challenges can arise, particularly in maintaining focus and managing resources. Over-reliance on frequent iterations can sometimes lead to inefficiency if priorities are not clearly defined. To address this, CMOs should:

- Establish a **prioritisation framework** that ensures teams focus on high-impact tasks.

- Use dashboards to consolidate metrics and monitor performance across channels.
- Regularly review and refine workflows to eliminate redundancies and bottlenecks.

Tools and frameworks for agile marketing are essential for enabling CMOs and their teams to adapt quickly, make informed decisions, and optimise marketing outcomes. By combining project management platforms, data analytics tools, automation solutions, and iterative frameworks, agile marketing drives innovation, collaboration, and sustained growth. The result is a marketing strategy that is both responsive and resilient, equipped to thrive in a constantly changing environment.

8.10 - Case Study: Launching a Growth Initiative

For a **Chief Marketing Officer (CMO)**, launching a growth initiative is a strategic undertaking that requires a balance of data-driven planning, creativity, and execution. This case study explores how a mid-sized direct-to-consumer (DTC) skincare brand, **Glowly**, successfully launched a growth initiative that increased customer acquisition by 40% and boosted customer lifetime value (CLV) through innovative marketing and cross-functional collaboration.

The Challenge

Glowly had reached a growth plateau. While its products were well-regarded within its niche, the brand struggled to expand beyond its existing audience. Several challenges hindered its progress:

- **Market saturation:** Competitors offering similar products made it difficult for Glowly to stand out.
- **Limited brand awareness:** The company's marketing efforts were focused on loyal customers, neglecting untapped markets.
- **Inefficient acquisition costs:** Customer acquisition cost (CAC) was rising due to ineffective targeting and reliance on traditional methods like paid social media ads.
- **Underutilised customer insights:** The company collected data but lacked a cohesive strategy for leveraging it.

Recognising the need for a comprehensive growth initiative, the CMO developed a strategic plan focused on **expanding Glowly's market reach, improving efficiency, and fostering long-term customer loyalty.**

The Strategy

1. Identifying a New Target Market

Glowly conducted extensive **market research** to uncover untapped opportunities. Using analytics tools like **Google Trends** and **Facebook Audience Insights**, the team identified a growing demand among men for skincare solutions tailored to their needs. Focus groups and surveys confirmed that many men felt underserved by existing brands and were seeking simple, effective products.

Armed with this insight, the team decided to launch a product line targeting this segment, emphasising minimalist routines and multi-functional products.

2. Leveraging Cross-Functional Collaboration

Glowly's growth initiative relied heavily on collaboration across marketing, product development, and customer experience teams. The product team developed a line of skincare products designed specifically for men, featuring neutral packaging and simple formulations. Marketing worked closely with the product team to ensure the new line aligned with customer expectations, and customer service trained representatives to address questions unique to this demographic.

3. Creating a Personalised Marketing Campaign

To connect with the new audience, the marketing team developed a highly **personalised campaign** using first-party data. They segmented audiences by demographic and behavioural data, creating tailored messaging that addressed specific concerns, such as acne, dry skin, or anti-ageing.

Key elements of the campaign included:

- **Social media ads** featuring relatable male influencers sharing their skincare routines.
- **Email marketing campaigns** that introduced customers to the benefits of a simplified skincare routine, with product recommendations based on their interests.
- A dedicated **landing page** for the new product line, optimised with A/B-tested headlines and calls-to-action to maximise conversions.

4. Building Partnerships

Glowly partnered with a popular fitness brand to co-promote the new product line. This partnership included bundled offers, such as a free travel-sized cleanser with the purchase of a gym membership. The collaboration gave Glowly access to a broader audience while aligning its brand with health-conscious consumers.

5. Incorporating Sustainability

To appeal to eco-conscious customers, Glowly introduced sustainable packaging for the new product line, made from recyclable materials. The brand also highlighted its commitment to cruelty-free testing and environmentally friendly sourcing, aligning with growing consumer demand for ethical practices.

The Results

Glowly's growth initiative yielded impressive results within six months:

- **40% increase in customer acquisition:** The men's product line attracted a new audience, contributing to a significant boost in first-time buyers.

- **20% improvement in CAC efficiency:** The personalised marketing approach reduced acquisition costs by targeting the right audience with tailored messaging.

- **25% increase in customer lifetime value (CLV):** Cross-promotions and loyalty incentives encouraged repeat purchases.

- **Enhanced brand awareness:** The partnership with the fitness brand and influencer collaborations generated substantial media coverage and social media engagement, increasing Glowly's visibility.

Lessons Learned

Glowly's success offers valuable lessons for CMOs launching growth initiatives:

- **Leverage customer insights:** Thorough market research can uncover untapped opportunities and guide product development.
- **Collaborate across teams:** Cross-functional alignment ensures that product, marketing, and customer experience efforts work cohesively.
- **Invest in personalisation:** Tailored messaging and offers resonate more deeply with audiences, improving acquisition and retention rates.
- **Prioritise sustainability:** Ethical practices and eco-friendly solutions not only appeal to modern consumers but also enhance brand reputation.
- **Build partnerships strategically:** Aligning with complementary brands amplifies reach and adds value to both audiences.

Conclusion

Launching a growth initiative requires a well-coordinated strategy that combines innovation, data-driven insights, and collaboration. Glowly's success in expanding its market share while maintaining cost efficiency demonstrates the power of targeted initiatives. For CMOs, this case study highlights the importance of being customer-centric, agile, and creative in designing strategies that foster sustainable growth.

Chapter 9

Managing Challenges as a CMO

> "The mark of a great CMO is not in avoiding challenges but in embracing them as stepping stones to innovation and growth."
> **Robert N. Jacobs**

Leadership in marketing is as rewarding as it is challenging. For Chief Marketing Officers (CMOs), navigating the complexities of modern business requires a dynamic blend of creativity, data-driven insights, and adaptive leadership. Whether it's managing relationships across departments, responding to market crises, or balancing competing priorities, the role of the CMO demands resilience, foresight, and a deep understanding of organisational dynamics.

Chapter 9 delves into the multifaceted challenges that CMOs encounter, providing actionable strategies to address them effectively. From fostering alignment with internal stakeholders and the C-suite to tackling resource constraints and technological advancements, this chapter offers a comprehensive guide to thriving in an ever-evolving landscape. As marketing leaders face mounting pressures to deliver both immediate results and long-term value, the lessons within these pages equip CMOs to lead with confidence, creativity, and strategic clarity.

9.1 - Navigating Internal Stakeholder Relationships

For a **Chief Marketing Officer (CMO)**, one of the most significant challenges is managing relationships with internal stakeholders. The CMO's role requires collaboration across departments, alignment with organisational objectives, and constant communication with diverse teams. Each stakeholder, whether from finance, operations, sales, or the executive suite, has unique priorities and expectations. The ability to navigate these relationships effectively is critical for achieving marketing success and fostering organisational harmony.

The foundation of effective stakeholder management lies in **understanding stakeholder priorities**. For example, the sales team may be focused on immediate lead generation, while the finance team prioritises cost efficiency and ROI. By recognising and respecting these different perspectives, CMOs can tailor their communication and strategies to address specific concerns. For instance, during a budget discussion, presenting data on how marketing efforts directly impact sales growth can bridge the gap between marketing and finance. **Building trust and credibility** is essential when working with stakeholders. Regular updates, transparent reporting, and consistent delivery of results help establish the CMO as a reliable leader. For example, a CMO might create a monthly performance report that includes key metrics such as campaign ROI, customer acquisition cost (CAC), and customer lifetime value (CLV). Sharing successes and addressing challenges candidly demonstrates accountability and builds confidence.

Collaboration is another key aspect of stakeholder management. Working closely with other department heads ensures that marketing initiatives align with broader organisational goals. For example, collaborating with the product team during a new launch helps ensure that marketing messages accurately reflect the product's features and benefits. Similarly, aligning with HR on internal branding initiatives strengthens company culture and employee engagement.

However, navigating stakeholder relationships is not without challenges. **Conflicting priorities** can create tension, particularly when resources are limited. For example, if the IT department prioritises infrastructure upgrades while marketing needs support for implementing a new analytics tool, the CMO must advocate for their team's needs while remaining sensitive to organisational constraints. Open communication and compromise are vital in these situations.

Another common challenge is managing **expectations**. Stakeholders often have high expectations for immediate results, particularly in high-pressure industries. Educating stakeholders about the timeline and impact of marketing efforts is crucial. For instance, explaining that brand-building campaigns require time to generate measurable results can help temper unrealistic demands.

CMOs can also leverage stakeholder mapping to identify key influencers within the organisation and prioritise their engagement. Stakeholder mapping involves categorising stakeholders based on their level of influence and interest in marketing initiatives. For example:

- **High-influence, high-interest stakeholders** (e.g., the CEO) require regular updates and close collaboration.
- **Low-influence, high-interest stakeholders** (e.g., junior sales staff) may benefit from periodic briefings to build alignment.

Ultimately, successful stakeholder management requires empathy, adaptability, and proactive communication. By understanding stakeholder needs, building trust, and fostering collaboration, CMOs can navigate complex relationships and ensure that marketing efforts contribute to organisational success.

9.2 - Managing Up: Communicating with the C-Suite

For a **Chief Marketing Officer (CMO)**, effectively **managing up** and maintaining strong communication with the **C-suite** is vital for securing buy-in, demonstrating the value of marketing, and ensuring alignment with broader organisational goals. The C-suite, including the CEO, CFO, and other executives, often has different priorities, perspectives, and expectations compared to the marketing team. The ability to bridge this gap is a defining characteristic of a successful CMO.

Understanding the C-suite's perspective is the foundation of effective communication. Executives are primarily focused on high-level business objectives, such as revenue growth, cost efficiency, market share, and shareholder value. Marketing activities, while essential, are often viewed through the lens of how they contribute to these overarching goals. A CMO must frame their communication in terms of outcomes that resonate with the C-suite. For instance:

- Instead of discussing campaign details, emphasise how a specific marketing initiative drove a 20% increase in revenue or reduced customer acquisition cost (CAC) by 15%.
- Highlight how a brand-building campaign enhanced customer loyalty, resulting in higher customer lifetime value (CLV).

Data and storytelling are powerful tools for managing up. CMOs must back their strategies and results with clear, actionable data while weaving it into a compelling narrative. For example, when presenting to the CFO, the CMO might share metrics like ROI, marketing efficiency ratios, and forecasted revenue impact, using visual aids like charts and dashboards for clarity. Pairing this data with real-world examples, such as how a recent campaign engaged a high-value customer segment, adds context and emotional resonance.

Regular and structured communication is essential. Scheduling consistent touchpoints, such as monthly updates or quarterly reviews, ensures that the C-suite remains informed about marketing efforts. These sessions should focus on key metrics, progress against goals, and any obstacles or opportunities that require executive input. For example, a quarterly presentation to the board might include:

- A summary of key marketing initiatives and their outcomes.

- Insights into market trends and customer behaviour that impact the organisation's strategy.
- Recommendations for budget adjustments or resource allocation based on data-driven forecasts.

One of the challenges in managing up is **addressing competing priorities** within the C-suite. For instance, the CFO may focus on cost control, while the CEO prioritises growth and innovation. The CMO must navigate these dynamics by demonstrating how marketing initiatives balance these goals. For example, showcasing how marketing automation tools can reduce operational costs while improving campaign efficiency aligns with both perspectives.

Another common challenge is **educating the C-suite on marketing's evolving role.** Traditional views of marketing as a cost centre rather than a growth driver can hinder progress. The CMO must advocate for modern marketing's impact on customer acquisition, retention, and brand equity. For example:

- Explaining how customer data platforms (CDPs) enable personalised experiences that increase retention rates.
- Demonstrating how content marketing drives organic traffic, reducing dependency on paid channels over time.

Proactively addressing challenges is another critical aspect of managing up. Executives appreciate transparency and solutions-oriented thinking. For example, if a major campaign underperforms, the CMO should present a candid assessment of what went wrong, lessons learned, and a plan for improvement.

This approach builds trust and credibility, showing the CMO's accountability and strategic mindset.

Tailoring communication style to each executive's preferences is equally important. Some may prefer high-level summaries, while others value detailed data. For example:

- The CEO might want a concise overview of how marketing supports strategic goals.
- The CFO might require in-depth financial metrics, such as ROI, budget utilisation, and cost-per-lead.

Finally, CMOs must position themselves as strategic partners within the C-suite. This means contributing to discussions beyond marketing, such as organisational growth, mergers and acquisitions, or technological investments. For instance, a CMO involved in the evaluation of a potential acquisition might provide insights into the target company's brand strength, market positioning, and customer loyalty.

In conclusion, **managing up and communicating with the C-suite** requires a combination of strategic thinking, data-driven insights, and tailored messaging. By understanding executive priorities, providing clear and impactful updates, and positioning marketing as a key driver of business success, CMOs can build strong relationships with the C-suite and secure the support needed to execute ambitious strategies.

9.3 - Balancing Marketing and Sales Alignment

For a **Chief Marketing Officer (CMO)**, ensuring strong **alignment between marketing and sales** is one of the most crucial and challenging aspects of driving business success. While marketing and sales teams often share the same ultimate goal, increasing revenue and fostering customer loyalty, their methods, priorities, and metrics can differ significantly. Achieving alignment requires collaboration, mutual understanding, and a commitment to shared objectives.

At the core of **marketing and sales alignment** is the principle of treating these departments as two halves of a unified revenue engine. Marketing is responsible for generating awareness and demand, while sales takes the baton to close deals and build long-term relationships. A well-aligned organisation creates a seamless journey for the customer, from initial contact to final purchase and beyond. For example, a lead nurtured by marketing through personalised email campaigns should transition smoothly to the sales team, which can then tailor its pitch based on the customer's previous interactions.

Establishing shared goals is critical for fostering collaboration. Both teams must agree on metrics that reflect their interdependence, such as lead conversion rates, customer acquisition cost (CAC), and revenue growth. For instance:

- Marketing's goal might include generating a specific number of qualified leads each quarter.
- Sales might aim to achieve a set percentage of conversions from those leads.

By linking these objectives, both teams are incentivised to work together rather than in silos.

Clear communication channels between marketing and sales are essential for maintaining alignment. Regular meetings, such as weekly or bi-weekly syncs, provide opportunities to share updates, address challenges, and celebrate successes. For example:

- Marketing can share insights on which campaigns are driving the most leads and adjust strategies based on sales feedback.

- Sales can provide information on common customer objections or pain points, which marketing can address through targeted content or revised messaging.

Defining and agreeing on lead qualifications is another vital step. One of the most common sources of friction between marketing and sales is the definition of a "qualified lead." Marketing might pass on leads that sales consider unready or irrelevant, leading to frustration and inefficiency. To resolve this, both teams should collaborate on creating clear criteria for lead scoring. For example:

- A marketing-qualified lead (MQL) might be defined as someone who downloads a white paper and visits the website's pricing page.

- A sales-qualified lead (SQL) could be an MQL who schedules a demo or explicitly requests a follow-up from a sales representative.

Implementing **lead scoring systems** within CRM platforms like **HubSpot**, **Salesforce**, or **Marketo** ensures that only high-quality leads are handed off to sales, increasing conversion rates and reducing wasted effort.

Technology also plays a pivotal role in aligning marketing and sales. **Integrated platforms** allow for seamless data sharing and visibility across both teams. For example:

- Marketing automation tools can track how a lead interacts with campaigns, such as opening emails or clicking ads, and pass this data to the sales team.
- Sales tools can feed data back into marketing systems, showing which messaging resonates most and informing future campaigns.

Despite the benefits, challenges in alignment persist. One common issue is **conflicting priorities**, such as sales focusing on immediate revenue while marketing invests in long-term brand building. To address this, CMOs must emphasise the value of both approaches and create a balanced strategy that supports short- and long-term goals. For instance, while marketing campaigns might focus on immediate lead generation, they can also include elements that enhance brand awareness and customer loyalty.

Another challenge is resolving **cultural differences** between the two teams. Marketing often operates on creativity, storytelling, and long-term planning, while sales thrive on urgency, numbers, and direct results. Bridging this gap requires fostering a culture of mutual respect and collaboration. For example:

- Hosting joint workshops or team-building activities can build rapport and encourage knowledge sharing.
- Creating a "win together" mindset by celebrating joint successes, such as hitting a revenue milestone, reinforces

the idea that both teams are working toward a shared purpose.

Feedback loops further enhance alignment. Sales should provide regular feedback on lead quality, while marketing should share insights on campaign performance and adjustments based on sales input. For instance, if a sales report that leads from a particular channel consistently underperforms, marketing can reallocate resources to higher-performing channels.

Finally, leadership plays a vital role in sustaining alignment. The CMO, alongside the Head of Sales or Chief Revenue Officer (CRO), must model collaboration and accountability. By demonstrating alignment at the leadership level, they set an example for their teams to follow.

In conclusion, **balancing marketing and sales alignment** is both an art and a science. By establishing shared goals, fostering clear communication, leveraging technology, and addressing cultural differences, CMOs can create a unified approach that drives revenue, improves customer experience, and strengthens organisational cohesion. When marketing and sales operate in harmony, the organisation as a whole becomes more effective, agile, and competitive.

9.4 - Handling Budget Cuts and Resource Constraints

One of the most challenging aspects of being a **Chief Marketing Officer (CMO)** is managing the impact of **budget cuts and resource constraints**. Whether triggered by economic downturns, shifting organisational priorities, or unexpected crises, reductions in budget and resources can place immense pressure on marketing teams to do more with less. Successfully navigating these challenges requires creativity, strategic prioritisation, and a focus on efficiency without compromising effectiveness.

The first step in addressing budget cuts is to **reassess priorities**. Not all marketing initiatives deliver equal value, and during times of constraint, it's essential to identify the campaigns and channels that drive the greatest return on investment (ROI). For example:

- Paid media campaigns might be paused in favour of lower-cost, high-impact tactics such as content marketing or email campaigns.
- Non-essential projects, such as experimental initiatives or rebranding efforts, may be deferred in favour of core campaigns that align closely with business objectives.

By focusing on activities that directly contribute to revenue, customer acquisition, or retention, CMOs can ensure that limited resources are used where they have the most impact.

Data and analytics play a crucial role in making these decisions. Tools like **Google Analytics**, **HubSpot**, and **Tableau** provide insights into campaign performance, customer behaviour, and ROI, helping CMOs identify which efforts to prioritise. For instance, analysing customer journey data might reveal that organic search drives a significant portion of conversions, prompting the team to invest in SEO rather than paid search.

Similarly, understanding the cost-per-lead across different channels enables marketing leaders to allocate budgets more effectively.

Streamlining processes is another critical strategy for managing resource constraints. Automation tools such as **Marketo**, **Pardot**, and **Mailchimp** can handle repetitive tasks like email marketing, social media scheduling, and lead nurturing, freeing up team members to focus on strategic initiatives. For example:

- An e-commerce company might use automation to segment and target customers based on purchase history, ensuring personalised communication without requiring manual effort.

- Automated performance dashboards can reduce the time spent on reporting, allowing marketers to spend more time on optimisation.

Cross-functional collaboration can also help alleviate resource pressures. By working closely with other departments, such as sales, product development, or customer service, marketing teams can leverage shared resources and expertise. For example:

- Partnering with the product team to create co-branded materials reduces the burden on marketing while ensuring consistent messaging.

- Collaborating with customer service can provide valuable insights into common pain points, enabling the marketing team to develop targeted campaigns without conducting separate research.

When facing budget constraints, **leveraging existing assets** becomes essential. Repurposing content, for instance, can maximise the value of prior investments. A single blog post can be transformed into multiple assets, such as a series of social media posts, an email newsletter, or an infographic. Similarly, a webinar recording can be edited into short video clips for use on different platforms. This approach extends the lifespan of existing content and reduces the need for additional production.

Negotiating with vendors and partners is another way to stretch budgets. Many marketing vendors are willing to renegotiate contracts, offer discounts, or provide extended payment terms during periods of financial difficulty. For example, a CMO might negotiate a reduced rate for advertising spend in exchange for committing to a longer-term partnership. Similarly, barter arrangements, such as exchanging promotional opportunities with complementary brands, can help maintain visibility without incurring additional costs.

Despite the need for cost-cutting, it's important not to lose sight of **long-term goals**. A common mistake during budget reductions is to eliminate brand-building efforts entirely in favour of short-term revenue generation. While immediate results are critical, neglecting long-term strategies can harm the organisation's competitive position. For example:

- Continuing to invest in customer retention programs ensures that existing customers remain engaged, reducing churn and increasing lifetime value (CLV).

- Maintaining a consistent presence on key platforms helps preserve brand awareness, ensuring the company remains top-of-mind when spending rebounds.

Transparency and communication are key to maintaining team morale and stakeholder confidence during periods of constraint. CMOs must be upfront with their teams about the challenges they face, outlining clear priorities and providing regular updates on progress. Engaging employees in brainstorming sessions to find creative solutions can also foster a sense of ownership and collaboration. For example, inviting team members to suggest cost-saving ideas or propose innovative low-cost campaigns can uncover untapped potential.

Finally, navigating budget cuts requires a **resilient and resourceful mindset**. CMOs must remain adaptable, continuously reassessing strategies and adjusting tactics as new challenges and opportunities arise. By embracing constraints as an opportunity for innovation, marketing leaders can demonstrate their value to the organisation while ensuring that their teams remain motivated and focused.

In conclusion, **handling budget cuts and resource constraints** is a challenging but manageable aspect of marketing leadership. By prioritising high-impact initiatives, leveraging data and technology, fostering collaboration, and maintaining a balance between short- and long-term goals, CMOs can navigate financial pressures while delivering measurable results. These strategies not only sustain marketing efforts during difficult times but also position the organisation for success when resources are restored.

9.5 - Dealing with Market Crises and PR Nightmares

One of the most daunting challenges a **Chief Marketing Officer (CMO)** can face is navigating a **market crisis** or **PR nightmare**. These situations can arise suddenly and have far-reaching consequences, including reputational damage, loss of customer trust, and financial repercussions. Whether triggered by external factors such as economic downturns or internal missteps like product failures, a crisis demands swift, strategic, and transparent responses to mitigate harm and rebuild credibility.

Understanding the nature of the crisis is the first and most critical step in managing it effectively. Crises can take various forms, such as:

- **Product-related issues,** such as recalls, safety concerns, or defects.
- **Brand controversies** involving negative media coverage or customer backlash.
- **Market disruptions**, including supply chain breakdowns, competitor actions, or regulatory changes.

For example, a food company facing a recall due to contamination must prioritise customer safety and communicate promptly to minimise harm. Alternatively, a tech brand experiencing backlash over user data breaches must focus on restoring trust by addressing security concerns transparently.

Swift and proactive communication is essential during a crisis. Customers, stakeholders, and employees must feel informed and reassured, even if the situation is still unfolding. CMOs should craft messaging that acknowledges the issue, outlines steps being taken to address it, and provides a clear timeline for updates. For instance:

- A retail brand experiencing a data breach might issue a statement within 24 hours, apologising to customers, explaining the extent of the breach, and detailing measures being implemented to enhance security.

- A transportation company dealing with a service disruption might use social media to provide real-time updates on progress, ensuring customers are not left in the dark.

Empathy and accountability are key to effective crisis communication. Customers are more likely to forgive a brand that takes responsibility and demonstrates genuine concern for those affected. For example, a healthcare company responding to a defective product complaint might highlight the specific actions it is taking to prevent similar incidents, such as enhanced quality control measures or independent audits.

The **choice of communication channels** plays a crucial role in managing a crisis. While traditional press releases remain effective for addressing the media, direct channels such as email, social media, and the company website are often more efficient for reaching customers quickly. For instance:

- Social media platforms like Twitter are ideal for real-time updates, allowing brands to engage directly with their audience and address concerns as they arise.
- Dedicated crisis landing pages on the company website can centralise information, providing FAQs, official statements, and contact details for customer support.

Internal alignment is just as important as external communication during a crisis. Employees, particularly those in customer-facing roles, must be briefed on the situation and trained on how to respond to inquiries. For example, if a travel company experiences a system outage affecting bookings, customer service representatives should be equipped with clear instructions on how to assist impacted travellers.

Monitoring and adapting responses is another critical element of crisis management. Public sentiment can evolve rapidly, particularly on social media, and CMOs must stay attuned to how their messaging is being received. Tools like **Brandwatch**, **Hootsuite**, or **Sprinklr** can help track customer sentiment and identify emerging concerns. For instance, if a company's initial response is perceived as insincere, swift adjustments to tone and content can help mitigate further backlash.

Leveraging external expertise is often necessary during high-stakes crises. Partnering with PR agencies, legal counsel, or crisis management firms provides access to specialised skills and insights. For example, a luxury brand facing allegations of unethical sourcing might engage a crisis PR firm to help shape its narrative and ensure compliance with industry standards.

Once the immediate crisis is under control, the focus must shift to **rebuilding trust** and learning from the experience. Transparency remains crucial in this phase. For instance, a logistics company that faced public criticism for delivery delays might issue a follow-up report detailing the root causes of the issue, the corrective actions taken, and the results of those efforts.

Rebuilding trust often involves **demonstrating a long-term commitment** to improvement. For example:

- A financial services firm criticised for a data breach might introduce advanced encryption technology and promote customer education on cybersecurity.
- A food brand recovering from a recall might highlight new safety certifications and invest in campaigns showcasing its dedication to quality.

Turning crises into opportunities is another hallmark of effective leadership. CMOs who approach crises as moments for reflection and improvement can emerge stronger. For example, a fitness brand that faced backlash over body-shaming ads could pivot to launching an inclusive campaign celebrating diversity, transforming criticism into a renewed sense of purpose.

Finally, **preparing for future crises** is an integral part of recovery. Developing a comprehensive crisis management plan ensures the organisation is better equipped to respond to future challenges. Key elements of a robust plan include:

- Establishing a crisis response team with clear roles and responsibilities.
- Creating communication templates that can be quickly adapted for different scenarios.

- Conducting regular simulations and training exercises to test preparedness.

In conclusion, **dealing with market crises and PR nightmares** requires a combination of swift action, strategic communication, and long-term planning. By responding with empathy, transparency, and accountability, CMOs can minimise damage, rebuild trust, and position their brands for future success. While crises are inevitable, they also offer an opportunity to demonstrate resilience, strengthen relationships, and reinforce a commitment to excellence.

9.6 - Keeping Pace with Technological Advancements

For a **Chief Marketing Officer (CMO)**, keeping pace with **technological advancements** is not just a matter of staying competitive; it is essential for driving innovation, improving efficiency, and meeting evolving customer expectations. The rapid pace of change in technology, from artificial intelligence (AI) and machine learning (ML) to blockchain and augmented reality (AR), has transformed how marketing teams operate, interact with audiences, and measure success. However, adopting and leveraging these technologies effectively requires strategic foresight, adaptability, and a clear understanding of organisational goals.

The first step in keeping up with technological advancements is **monitoring trends and emerging tools**. CMOs must stay informed about the latest developments in martech (marketing technology) and evaluate which tools align with their organisation's needs. Resources like **Gartner's Magic Quadrant** or industry conferences such as **CES** and **HubSpot's INBOUND** provide valuable insights into emerging technologies. For instance, keeping an eye on AI-driven tools like **ChatGPT**, which enable automated yet human-like customer interactions, helps CMOs identify opportunities to enhance customer service and engagement.

Prioritising investments in technology is another critical consideration. With countless tools and platforms available, CMOs must focus on those that address specific pain points or deliver the highest ROI. For example:

- If customer data is siloed across multiple platforms, investing in a Customer Data Platform (CDP) like Segment or BlueConic can consolidate data and enable personalised marketing at scale.

- For teams struggling with lead nurturing, tools like Marketo Engage or HubSpot can automate email workflows and provide actionable insights into customer behaviour.

CMOs must also balance the **adoption of new technologies with the effective use of existing systems**. Shiny new tools can be tempting, but they may not always deliver incremental value. Conducting a technology audit helps identify gaps and redundancies in the current stack, ensuring that new investments are truly necessary. For instance, if an organisation already uses a robust CRM system, integrating additional tools for customer segmentation or analytics might enhance its utility rather than replacing it entirely.

Training and upskilling teams is a vital component of keeping pace with technology. Marketing teams need to understand how to use new tools effectively and integrate them into their workflows. Offering training sessions, certifications, or access to online courses ensures that employees can fully leverage the capabilities of emerging technologies. For example, a team adopting **Google Analytics 4** might benefit from certification programmes that teach advanced techniques for tracking customer journeys and conversion rates.

Collaboration with **IT and data teams** is essential when implementing complex technologies. Many advancements, such as AI-driven analytics or programmatic advertising platforms, require robust data infrastructure and seamless integration with existing systems. For instance, deploying an AI-powered recommendation engine for e-commerce requires coordination between marketing and IT to ensure that algorithms are trained on accurate and comprehensive customer data.

Testing and piloting new tools is a low-risk way to evaluate their potential impact before full-scale implementation. CMOs can run controlled experiments to measure the effectiveness of a new technology. For example:

- A retail brand might pilot an AR tool that allows customers to "try on" clothing virtually, measuring engagement and conversion rates before rolling it out across all product lines.
- A financial services firm could test blockchain-powered loyalty programmes in a single region to gauge customer response and operational feasibility.

Managing Challenges as a CMO

One of the biggest challenges in adopting new technologies is **managing costs and proving ROI**. Advanced tools often come with significant upfront costs, and demonstrating their value can take time. CMOs must build strong business cases for technological investments, linking them directly to organisational objectives such as increasing revenue, improving efficiency, or enhancing customer satisfaction. For instance, investing in an AI chatbot might reduce the cost of customer support while simultaneously improving response times and customer satisfaction scores.

Another critical factor is **ensuring ethical and compliant use of technology**. With increasing scrutiny around data privacy and security, CMOs must ensure that new tools adhere to regulations like **GDPR** and **CCPA**. For example:

- When implementing predictive analytics, ensuring that algorithms are transparent and free of bias builds trust and avoids reputational risks.

- Using consent-driven data collection methods for personalisation demonstrates respect for customer privacy while complying with legal requirements.

Staying agile and adaptable is key to navigating the constant evolution of technology. Not every innovation will deliver long-term value, and some tools may become obsolete as newer, more effective solutions emerge. CMOs should adopt an iterative approach, regularly evaluating the performance of existing tools and remaining open to change. For example, a company that invested heavily in third-party data platforms may need to pivot towards first-party data solutions as privacy regulations tighten.

Finally, **fostering a culture of innovation** within the marketing team helps organisations embrace technological change more effectively. Encouraging employees to experiment with new tools, share ideas, and stay curious ensures that the team remains forward-thinking and adaptable. For instance, organising internal hackathons or innovation challenges can spark creative ways to use emerging technologies in campaigns.

In conclusion, **keeping pace with technological advancements** is a continuous process that requires vigilance, strategic prioritisation, and a willingness to adapt. By staying informed, investing wisely, upskilling teams, and collaborating across departments, CMOs can harness the power of technology to drive innovation, efficiency, and competitive advantage. While the pace of change can be overwhelming, those who embrace it with agility and purpose will position their organisations for sustained success.

9.7 - Managing Burnout and Building Resilience

For a **Chief Marketing Officer (CMO)**, the demands of the role, balancing strategy, execution, and leadership, can be overwhelming. The high-pressure environment of modern marketing, coupled with rapid technological change, constant data analysis, and stakeholder expectations, makes **burnout** a significant risk for both the CMO and their team. Addressing burnout proactively and fostering **resilience** is essential for sustaining long-term success, creativity, and motivation.

Understanding burnout is the first step in managing it effectively. Burnout is not just about being tired; it's a state of emotional, physical, and mental exhaustion caused by prolonged stress. For CMOs, this stress can come from tight deadlines, budget constraints, or the pressure to demonstrate ROI on marketing initiatives. Symptoms include reduced productivity, difficulty concentrating, and a sense of detachment or cynicism about work. Recognising these warning signs early, both in oneself and in team members, is critical.

One of the most effective strategies for managing burnout is **prioritising tasks and setting realistic expectations**. CMOs often juggle multiple responsibilities, from overseeing campaigns to liaising with the C-suite. Learning to delegate effectively ensures that the workload is distributed fairly, allowing the CMO to focus on high-value strategic initiatives. For example:

- Assigning day-to-day campaign management to senior team members allows the CMO to concentrate on long-term planning.
- Empowering teams to make certain decisions independently reduces bottlenecks and encourages ownership.

Establishing **clear boundaries** between work and personal time is another essential practice. The always-on nature of modern marketing, amplified by digital tools and remote work, can blur the lines between professional and personal life. CMOs should model healthy work-life boundaries by avoiding unnecessary after-hours communication and encouraging their teams to do the same. For instance:

- Scheduling emails to be sent during working hours instead of late at night sets a precedent for balanced work habits.

- Promoting the use of "focus time" blocks allows employees to work without constant interruptions.

Fostering a supportive culture within the marketing team is equally important. Burnout often arises in environments where employees feel undervalued or unsupported. Regular check-ins, constructive feedback, and recognition of achievements help create a positive atmosphere. For example:

- Hosting monthly "win meetings" where team members share successes fosters a sense of accomplishment.
- Offering flexible working arrangements, such as remote work options or adjusted hours, accommodates diverse needs and reduces stress.

Resilience-building practices are crucial for sustaining energy and creativity over the long term. Resilience is not just about enduring challenges but thriving despite them. For CMOs, this involves cultivating a mindset of adaptability and learning. Techniques include:

- **Mindfulness and stress management practices:** Incorporating meditation, journaling, or breathing exercises into the workday helps clear the mind and improve focus.
- **Continuous learning:** Staying curious and engaged with new marketing trends, tools, or leadership techniques keeps the CMO motivated and forward-thinking.

Encouraging resilience within the team is equally important. Providing access to professional development opportunities, such as training courses or industry conferences, helps employees feel empowered and valued. For example, a marketing analyst learning advanced data visualisation techniques not only grows professionally but also contributes more effectively to the team.

Monitoring workload and capacity is essential for preventing burnout. Overloaded teams are more likely to experience stress, errors, and diminished creativity. CMOs should regularly assess team capacity and redistribute resources as needed. For instance:

- If a team handling a high-stakes product launch appears overstretched, reallocating tasks to another group or hiring temporary support can alleviate pressure.
- Using project management tools like **Asana** or **Monday.com** provides visibility into workloads, enabling better planning and prioritisation.

In times of high pressure, such as during crises or major campaigns, CMOs must also recognise when to **pause and reset**. Encouraging breaks, team-building activities, or even wellness initiatives like yoga sessions or mental health days helps recharge energy and maintain morale. For example:

- Implementing a no-meeting day each week allows employees uninterrupted time to focus on their work.
- Offering access to mental health resources or employee assistance programmes provides crucial support during stressful periods.

Leading by example is perhaps the most impactful way for CMOs to address burnout and build resilience. By demonstrating healthy habits, such as taking breaks, managing stress constructively, and celebrating achievements, the CMO sets the tone for the entire team. For instance:

- Sharing personal stories of overcoming challenges or managing stress can inspire employees to adopt similar strategies.
- Openly acknowledging the importance of mental health destigmatises the issue and encourages employees to seek help when needed.

Finally, **seeking support and mentorship** is vital for CMOs themselves. Leadership can be isolating, and connecting with peers, coaches, or mentors provides valuable perspective and guidance. Participating in professional networks or industry forums, such as **CMO-specific groups on LinkedIn**, creates opportunities to share experiences and learn from others facing similar challenges.

In conclusion, **managing burnout and building resilience** are essential for CMOs navigating the complexities of modern marketing. By prioritising self-care, fostering a supportive team culture, and embracing adaptability, marketing leaders can maintain their effectiveness and creativity. These practices not only sustain individual well-being but also create a resilient, high-performing team capable of thriving in the face of challenges.

9.8 - Balancing Creativity and Data-Driven Decisions

For a **Chief Marketing Officer (CMO)**, striking the right balance between **creativity** and **data-driven decisions** is one of the most critical aspects of effective marketing leadership. Creativity fuels compelling campaigns, builds emotional connections with audiences, and drives innovation, while data ensures that these efforts are strategically aligned, measurable, and optimised for impact. Managing this balance requires a nuanced understanding of both approaches and the ability to integrate them seamlessly.

Creativity in marketing is the art of storytelling, problem-solving, and engaging audiences in ways that resonate on a personal level. Iconic campaigns often stand out because of their creative genius, such as memorable taglines, striking visuals, or innovative use of media. For example, a luxury automotive brand might create an aspirational campaign that positions its cars as symbols of sophistication and success, using emotional appeal to connect with its audience.

On the other hand, **data-driven marketing** focuses on analytics, performance metrics, and customer insights to inform strategies and optimise outcomes. By leveraging tools like **Google Analytics**, **HubSpot**, or **Power BI**, CMOs can identify what works, what doesn't, and how to allocate resources efficiently. For instance, tracking customer behaviour on an e-commerce platform might reveal that personalised product recommendations significantly boost conversion rates, guiding future campaigns.

While creativity and data are often seen as opposing forces, they are most powerful when used together. Data provides the foundation for creativity by offering insights into customer preferences, behaviours, and pain points. Creativity then transforms these insights into engaging narratives and innovative solutions. For example:

- A streaming platform might use data to identify that its audience is interested in thrillers and then launch a creatively designed campaign promoting its new suspense series.

- A cosmetics brand could analyse engagement metrics to identify the most popular social media content formats, using this data to create visually striking, high-performing campaigns.

The challenge for CMOs lies in ensuring that data enhances creativity rather than stifling it. Over-reliance on metrics can lead to risk-averse decision-making, where teams focus solely on what has worked in the past rather than exploring new ideas. To avoid this, CMOs must foster a culture that values experimentation and embraces the possibility of failure as a learning opportunity. For example, testing a bold new concept through a small-scale pilot campaign allows the team to gauge its impact while mitigating risk.

Integrating creativity and data requires clear processes and collaboration across teams. Creative professionals and data analysts often speak different "languages," so bridging this gap is essential. Encouraging regular communication, joint brainstorming sessions, and cross-functional teams helps align efforts. For instance:

- A content marketing team might work closely with data analysts to understand which topics or formats resonate most with their audience, using these insights to develop more targeted content.

- Similarly, creative designers might collaborate with performance marketers to ensure that visuals and messaging are optimised for conversion.

One of the most valuable tools for balancing creativity and data is **A/B testing**. This approach allows teams to test different creative elements, such as headlines, images, or calls-to-action, and measure their effectiveness. For example:

- A retail brand might test two versions of an ad: one focusing on emotional storytelling and another highlighting product features. Analysing the results helps the team determine which approach drives higher engagement and sales.

While data provides critical guidance, CMOs must also recognise its limitations. Metrics often focus on short-term outcomes, such as click-through rates or immediate sales, and may not capture the long-term value of brand-building initiatives. Creativity, on the other hand, plays a crucial role in shaping brand perception, fostering loyalty, and driving sustained growth. For instance, a campaign that doesn't deliver immediate conversions may still contribute to increased brand awareness and customer trust over time.

Leadership plays a crucial role in maintaining this balance. CMOs must champion both creativity and data, ensuring that neither dominates at the expense of the other. By setting clear expectations and fostering a culture that values both art and science, marketing leaders can create an environment where innovative ideas thrive alongside analytical rigour.

Technology is also an enabler of this balance. AI-powered tools, such as **Adobe Sensei** or **Canva's design automation features**, can assist creative teams by generating ideas or streamlining production, while advanced analytics platforms provide the data needed to evaluate performance. For example:

- AI tools might help a creative team generate multiple ad variations, allowing them to test and iterate quickly.
- Predictive analytics can help CMOs identify future trends, guiding the development of campaigns that are both creative and relevant.

Ultimately, **balancing creativity and data-driven decisions** requires a mindset that embraces both intuition and evidence. Creativity should be informed by data but not constrained by it, while data should be used to validate and refine creative ideas without replacing human ingenuity. By integrating these approaches, CMOs can deliver marketing strategies that are not only impactful and engaging but also measurable and scalable.

In conclusion, the fusion of creativity and data is what sets exceptional marketing leaders apart. By leveraging the strengths of both, CMOs can create campaigns that captivate audiences, achieve business objectives, and drive long-term brand success. This balance is not static but dynamic, evolving with each campaign and adapting to the ever-changing needs of the market.

9.9 - Ethical Dilemmas in Marketing Leadership

For a **Chief Marketing Officer (CMO)**, navigating **ethical dilemmas** is an increasingly prominent part of the role. As marketing grows more sophisticated and data-driven, the ethical implications of decisions, ranging from customer privacy and inclusivity to truth in advertising, have become more complex. CMOs must balance the pressure to deliver results with the need to maintain integrity, transparency, and trust, both within their organisations and with their audiences.

One of the most significant ethical dilemmas in modern marketing revolves around **data privacy**. The collection and use of customer data enable personalised experiences, targeted campaigns, and predictive analytics, all of which are essential for competitive success. However, mishandling or overstepping privacy boundaries can erode customer trust and lead to severe consequences, including legal penalties under regulations like **GDPR** and **CCPA**. For instance, while it may be tempting to use third-party data to improve ad targeting, doing so without explicit customer consent could violate privacy laws and ethical standards.

To address this, CMOs must ensure that their organisations adopt **privacy-first marketing practices**. Transparency is key: customers should know what data is being collected, why, and how it will be used. Consent-driven approaches, such as opt-in forms and clear privacy policies, help build trust and comply with regulations. For example:

- A retail brand might implement a preference centre where customers can manage their communication and data-sharing preferences.
- A streaming service could highlight its anonymisation practices, reassuring users that their viewing habits are protected.

Another common ethical dilemma is related to **truth in advertising**. Marketing often walks a fine line between persuasion and misrepresentation, and exaggerating claims can damage brand credibility. For example, a skincare company promising "instant results" without scientific backing risks alienating customers who feel misled. To uphold ethical standards, CMOs should prioritise transparency and honesty in messaging. This includes substantiating claims with evidence and avoiding misleading visuals or language.

Inclusivity and representation present another critical area of ethical consideration. Marketing campaigns have the power to shape cultural narratives, and failing to represent diverse perspectives can alienate audiences or perpetuate stereotypes. For instance, an ad campaign that unintentionally excludes certain demographics may face public backlash. To avoid this, CMOs should foster a culture of inclusivity within their teams and ensure that creative outputs reflect the diversity of their customer base. Practical steps include:

- Conducting focus groups with diverse participants to ensure campaigns resonate across different audiences.
- Establishing review processes to identify and address potential biases in messaging, imagery, or tone.

Greenwashing, or making false or exaggerated claims about environmental sustainability, is another ethical pitfall. As consumers increasingly prioritise eco-conscious brands, the temptation to overstate a company's green credentials can lead to ethical lapses. For example, labelling a product as "sustainable" without verifiable proof risks damaging credibility.

CMOs should ensure that sustainability claims are backed by evidence, such as certifications or third-party audits. For instance, a fashion brand highlighting its use of recycled materials should provide transparent details about sourcing, production, and impact.

Targeting vulnerable audiences also raises ethical concerns. While segmentation and targeting are integral to effective marketing, exploiting insecurities or vulnerabilities crosses ethical boundaries. For example:

- Predatory advertising for payday loans targeted at low-income individuals can harm rather than help.
- Overly aggressive marketing to children, such as in-app purchases in games, may exploit their lack of financial understanding.

To navigate such dilemmas, CMOs should establish **ethical guidelines** for targeting, ensuring that campaigns respect audience sensitivities and promote positive outcomes. For example, a financial services brand targeting low-income households could focus on educating customers about budgeting or financial literacy rather than solely pushing products.

Internal ethical dilemmas can also arise within organisations. For instance, CMOs may face pressure from leadership to prioritise short-term gains over long-term brand integrity. A CMO might be asked to approve a campaign that stretches ethical boundaries to achieve aggressive revenue targets. In such cases, strong ethical leadership is essential. CMOs must advocate for integrity, demonstrating how ethical practices contribute to sustainable growth and customer loyalty.

Building an **ethical framework** within the organisation helps CMOs navigate these challenges. This includes:

- Establishing a code of conduct for marketing practices.
- Conducting regular training sessions on ethical decision-making.
- Encouraging employees to voice concerns without fear of retaliation.

Technology also plays a role in addressing ethical dilemmas. Tools like **AI-driven bias detection** can identify and mitigate biases in content or targeting. For example, a recruitment platform using AI might flag language in job ads that unintentionally discourage applications from certain groups, enabling the team to make necessary adjustments.

Finally, CMOs must **lead by example**. Ethical leadership involves not only making principled decisions but also fostering a culture of accountability and transparency. Sharing ethical dilemmas and their resolutions with the team can help build trust and reinforce the importance of integrity. For instance:

- If a campaign concept is rejected due to ethical concerns, explaining the decision-making process to the team highlights the organisation's commitment to its values.
- Recognising employees who prioritise ethical considerations in their work reinforces a positive culture.

In conclusion, **ethical dilemmas in marketing leadership** require CMOs to navigate complex challenges with integrity, transparency, and foresight. By prioritising honesty, inclusivity, and respect for customer rights, CMOs can build trust and loyalty while safeguarding their organisations against reputational and legal risks. In a competitive landscape, ethics are not just a moral imperative; they are a strategic advantage that sets brands apart and fosters long-term success.

9.10 - Case Study: Overcoming a Major Marketing Challenge

To illustrate the complexities and strategies involved in addressing significant marketing challenges, this case study focuses on how a global **consumer electronics company**, **BrightTech**, navigated a PR crisis and rebuilt trust after a major product failure. The company faced immense backlash when one of its flagship products, a high-end smartphone, experienced widespread battery malfunctions shortly after launch. This crisis threatened BrightTech's reputation, customer loyalty, and financial stability. The steps taken by the **Chief Marketing Officer (CMO)** and their team provide valuable lessons for overcoming a major marketing challenge.

The Challenge

BrightTech had positioned its new smartphone, the **BrightX10**, as a revolutionary device with cutting-edge features and superior battery life. The product launch generated significant buzz, with pre-orders exceeding expectations. However, within weeks of the launch, reports surfaced of overheating batteries causing damage to devices, in some cases leading to minor injuries. News outlets, social media, and tech blogs quickly amplified the issue, sparking public outrage and a wave of negative coverage.

Key challenges included:

- **Reputational damage:** Customers and media questioned BrightTech's quality control and trustworthiness.
- **Financial losses:** The company faced costly recalls, declining sales, and a plummeting stock price.
- **Customer dissatisfaction:** Many loyal customers felt betrayed and demanded accountability.
- **Internal morale:** Employees were demotivated, fearing long-term consequences for the brand.

The CMO, in collaboration with the executive team, recognised the need for a swift and comprehensive strategy to manage the crisis and rebuild the brand.

The Strategy

1. Transparent Communication

The first priority was to address customer concerns with honesty and clarity. The CMO crafted a public apology acknowledging the issue, taking full responsibility, and outlining immediate steps to rectify the situation. Key actions included:

- Launching a dedicated **crisis microsite** to provide updates, FAQs, and contact details for affected customers.

- Hosting a press conference where BrightTech's CEO and CMO personally apologised and announced the recall plan.
- Leveraging social media channels to engage directly with customers, responding to queries and concerns in real-time.

By emphasising transparency, BrightTech demonstrated accountability and began rebuilding trust.

2. Implementing a Recall and Compensation Programme

The company initiated a global recall of the affected devices, ensuring a seamless and customer-friendly process. Customers were offered multiple options:

- **Free replacements** with upgraded models featuring redesigned batteries.
- **Full refunds** for those unwilling to continue using BrightTech products.
- Extended warranties and loyalty discounts for returning customers.

The marketing team ensured that all messaging surrounding the recall focused on the company's commitment to customer safety and satisfaction.

3. Leveraging Influencer and Media Relationships

To counteract negative sentiment, BrightTech worked closely with tech influencers and journalists who had previously supported the brand. Influencers were invited to test the redesigned devices and share their honest reviews. Positive feedback helped shift the narrative from failure to recovery.

The company also partnered with leading technology publications to highlight the rigorous testing processes implemented for future products. Articles emphasising BrightTech's improvements reinforced the brand's commitment to quality.

4. Employee Engagement

Recognising the importance of internal alignment, the CMO spearheaded initiatives to boost employee morale. These included:

- **Town hall** meetings where leadership addressed employee concerns and shared the company's recovery plan.
- Celebrating milestones, such as the successful completion of the recall programme, to instil a sense of pride and resilience.

Employees were encouraged to become brand ambassadors, sharing the company's recovery story on their personal networks.

5. Long-Term Brand Rebuilding

Once the immediate crisis was under control, BrightTech focused on rebuilding its brand reputation through targeted marketing campaigns. The CMO launched the **"BrightFuture" initiative**, highlighting the company's innovations and commitment to excellence. Campaign elements included:

- **Customer testimonials** showcasing satisfaction with the redesigned products.

- **A focus on sustainability**, with the company pledging to recycle recalled devices responsibly and invest in eco-friendly materials for future models.
- **Collaborating with non-profits** to launch a tech education programme, demonstrating the brand's broader social impact.

The Results

Despite the severity of the crisis, BrightTech's proactive and transparent approach led to a successful recovery:

- **92% of affected customers** participated in the recall programme, with over 70% opting for replacements rather than refunds, indicating retained loyalty.
- The redesigned BrightX10 received positive reviews, earning a **4.7-star average** rating on major e-commerce platforms within six months.
- Brand sentiment improved significantly, with social media sentiment analysis showing a **40% increase** in positive mentions post-recovery.
- Employee engagement surveys revealed a **20% improvement** in morale, reflecting confidence in the company's leadership and direction.

Financially, while the crisis initially led to losses, BrightTech's strong recovery efforts restored profitability within 18 months. The company's stock price rebounded, reaching pre-crisis levels by the end of the following fiscal year.

Lessons Learned

BrightTech's experience highlights several key takeaways for CMOs managing significant marketing challenges:

1. **Transparency is non-negotiable**: Honest communication builds trust, even in the face of failure.

2. **Customer-centricity drives recovery**: Prioritising customer safety, satisfaction, and convenience ensures loyalty.

3. **Media and influencer partnerships matter**: Leveraging trusted voices helps shift narratives and rebuild credibility.

4. **Internal alignment is critical**: Engaged and motivated employees are essential for navigating crises.

5. **Focus on long-term reputation**: Recovery doesn't end with crisis management; sustained efforts are needed to restore and strengthen the brand.

Conclusion

Navigating a major marketing challenge requires a combination of **swift action**, **strategic thinking**, and **customer focus**. BrightTech's recovery demonstrates how CMOs can turn crises into opportunities for growth, learning, and brand reinforcement. While no organisation is immune to challenges, those that respond with transparency, accountability, and innovation can emerge stronger and more resilient.

Chapter 10

The Future of Marketing Leadership

> "The future will reward CMOs who are not only fluent in technology but fluent in humanity, able to connect data to desires and strategies to stories."
>
> **Robert N. Jacobs**

As the business landscape transforms at an unprecedented pace, marketing leadership stands at a pivotal crossroads. Chapter 10 delves into the evolving role of the Chief Marketing Officer (CMO), emphasising their emergence as a linchpin in driving innovation, aligning organisational strategy, and championing customer-centricity. Gone are the days when CMOs were confined to the realms of advertising and brand awareness; today, they navigate complex terrains where data analytics, cross-functional collaboration, and technological integration converge. This chapter highlights how the modern CMO is not just a marketer but a strategic business leader with the agility to adapt and the vision to lead.

The chapter also explores the technologies shaping the future of marketing, including artificial intelligence (AI), hyper-personalisation, and automation. With consumer expectations at an all-time high, CMOs must become architects of seamless customer experiences while maintaining ethical practices and fostering diversity and inclusion. As you journey through this chapter, you'll discover not only the skills and strategies essential for the next generation of marketing leaders but also the profound impact they can have on organisational growth, innovation, and societal change.

10.1 - The Evolving Role of the CMO

The role of the **Chief Marketing Officer (CMO)** has evolved dramatically over the past decade, and it will continue to transform as businesses adapt to new challenges, technologies, and customer expectations. Today's CMO is no longer solely responsible for advertising and brand awareness; instead, they are at the nexus of customer experience, data analytics, and organisational strategy. To remain effective, CMOs must embrace their position as both creative visionaries and strategic business leaders.

One of the most notable changes in the role of the CMO is the shift towards being a **customer experience champion**. Modern consumers expect seamless, personalised, and value-driven interactions with brands across every touchpoint. CMOs must oversee not just marketing campaigns but the end-to-end customer journey, from discovery to post-purchase. This requires collaboration with multiple departments, including product, sales, and customer service. For example, a CMO might implement a strategy that integrates customer feedback from support teams into marketing efforts to ensure messaging aligns with customer needs.

The **expansion of technology** within marketing has also redefined the CMO's responsibilities. From artificial intelligence

(AI) to data analytics and marketing automation, CMOs must have a deep understanding of how to leverage technology to drive efficiency and results. For instance, leading organisations increasingly expect CMOs to oversee martech stacks, ensuring that tools like **CRM platforms** and **AI-driven analytics** align with broader business goals.

Another key aspect of the evolving role is the **focus on revenue growth and ROI.** CMOs are now seen as key drivers of business outcomes, accountable for measurable contributions to the bottom line. This requires a blend of creative insight and financial acumen. For instance, a successful CMO might develop a performance-driven strategy that links campaign investments directly to lead generation and sales metrics.

To navigate these changes effectively, CMOs must develop **strong leadership skills**, including the ability to foster collaboration, inspire innovation, and build resilient teams. As the CMO role becomes more integrated with other executive functions, such as the Chief Technology Officer (CTO) or Chief Revenue Officer (CRO), the ability to communicate and align with diverse stakeholders becomes paramount. The modern CMO must excel at balancing short-term objectives, such as quarterly sales targets, with long-term strategies like brand positioning and market expansion.

In conclusion, the **evolving role of the CMO** requires adaptability, technological fluency, and a customer-centric approach. By embracing these responsibilities, CMOs can position themselves as indispensable leaders who not only drive marketing success but also contribute significantly to organisational growth and innovation.

10.2 - Preparing for the AI-Driven Future

As marketing enters the era of artificial intelligence (**AI**), **Chief Marketing Officers (CMOs)** must prepare to harness its transformative potential while navigating its complexities. AI is reshaping the way marketers interact with customers, optimise campaigns, and measure success, making it a cornerstone of the future of marketing. To thrive in this evolving landscape, CMOs need to adopt a proactive approach, leveraging AI not just as a tool but as a strategic enabler.

Understanding AI's potential in marketing is the first step. AI enables capabilities such as hyper-personalisation, predictive analytics, and automated decision-making, which were previously unattainable at scale. For example:

- **Hyper-personalisation**: AI-powered systems can analyse vast amounts of customer data to deliver highly customised experiences. A streaming platform might use AI to recommend content based on individual viewing habits, increasing engagement and retention.

- **Predictive analytics**: AI can forecast future trends, such as identifying which products are likely to see increased demand, allowing marketers to adjust campaigns proactively.

- **Automation**: Tools like **chatbots** and **email automation platforms** use AI to handle routine interactions, freeing up human resources for more complex tasks.

The Future of Marketing Leadership

To fully leverage these capabilities, CMOs must invest in the right **technology infrastructure**. This includes tools like **machine learning (ML) platforms**, **natural language processing (NLP) systems**, and AI-powered analytics software. For example:

- **Google Cloud AI** can be used to build models for customer segmentation and behaviour prediction.
- **Adobe Sensei** enhances content creation by suggesting optimised designs, layouts, and messaging based on data-driven insights.

However, adopting AI requires more than just tools; it demands a **cultural shift** within the marketing organisation. Teams must embrace experimentation, learn to work alongside AI and develop new skills to maximise their potential. For instance:

- Training employees to interpret and act on AI-generated insights ensures that human judgment complements machine intelligence.
- Encouraging collaboration between data scientists and creative teams fosters innovative applications of AI in campaigns.

Ethical considerations are another critical aspect of preparing for the AI-driven future. As AI systems make decisions based on algorithms, ensuring that these algorithms are unbiased and transparent is essential. CMOs must establish guidelines for ethical AI usage, particularly in areas like targeting and data collection. For example:

- A retailer using AI for personalised ads must ensure that targeting does not reinforce stereotypes or exclude certain demographics unfairly.

- Consent-driven data collection practices are essential to maintain customer trust and comply with privacy regulations like **GDPR**.

Overcoming challenges is an inevitable part of AI adoption. One common hurdle is the integration of AI tools with existing marketing systems. CMOs must work closely with IT and data teams to ensure seamless implementation. Another challenge is the fear of job displacement among marketing staff. To address this, CMOs should emphasise that AI is a tool to enhance human creativity and efficiency, not replace it. For example, **AI** can handle **repetitive tasks** like A/B testing, allowing marketers to focus on strategy and storytelling.

Measuring the impact of AI is essential for demonstrating its value. CMOs should track metrics such as cost savings, increased efficiency, and improved campaign performance. For instance, an e-commerce company might measure how AI-driven recommendations boost average order value or reduce cart abandonment rates.

Looking ahead, **AI will continue to evolve**, offering even more sophisticated capabilities. For example:

- **Generative AI**, which creates original content like text, images, or videos, is already being used to automate ad creation and content production.
- **Voice search optimisation**, driven by AI, is becoming increasingly important as smart speakers and voice assistants gain popularity.

In conclusion, **preparing for the AI-driven future** requires CMOs to embrace technology, foster a culture of innovation, and prioritise ethical considerations. By leveraging AI strategically, marketing leaders can not only improve efficiency and personalisation but also position their organisations at the forefront of a rapidly changing industry. The key is to view AI as a collaborative partner that enhances human capabilities, paving the way for more impactful and creative marketing strategies.

10.3 - Mastering Cross-Functional Collaboration

For a **Chief Marketing Officer (CMO)**, **cross-functional collaboration** is a cornerstone of success in an increasingly interconnected business environment. Modern marketing is no longer confined to its own department; it intersects with sales, product development, IT, finance, and even human resources. By mastering collaboration across these functions, CMOs can ensure alignment with organisational goals, drive innovation, and deliver a seamless customer experience.

Understanding the importance of cross-functional collaboration begins with recognising that marketing impacts and is influenced by multiple areas of the business. For example:

- **Sales** relies on marketing to generate high-quality leads and support conversions with targeted campaigns.
- **Product teams** depend on marketing insights to guide development and positioning.
- **IT departments** enable marketing strategies through technology infrastructure and data integration.

The ability to break down silos and foster communication ensures that all departments work together toward shared objectives.

Establishing clear goals and metrics is a key first step in building effective collaboration. Each department often has its own priorities, which can lead to misalignment. For instance, marketing might focus on increasing brand awareness, while sales prioritise closing deals. A CMO can bridge this gap by creating shared goals, such as increasing conversion rates or improving customer retention, and defining metrics that reflect contributions from both teams. For example:

- Sales and marketing might agree on a target number of marketing-qualified leads (MQLs) that meet specific criteria.
- Collaboration with product teams might focus on achieving a successful product launch, measured by adoption rates and customer feedback.

Effective communication channels are essential for fostering collaboration. Regular meetings, shared platforms, and collaborative tools ensure that teams remain aligned and informed. For example:

- Weekly joint meetings between marketing and sales can provide updates on campaign performance, lead quality, and feedback from prospects.
- Tools like **Slack**, **Microsoft Teams**, or **Asana** facilitate real-time communication and task management across departments.

Leveraging data and insights strengthens cross-functional collaboration by providing a common foundation for decision-making. Marketing teams can share customer insights, survey data, and campaign performance metrics with other departments to guide strategy. For instance:

- Data on customer preferences can help the product team prioritise features or refine designs.
- Insights from marketing campaigns can inform sales strategies, such as which messaging resonates most with prospects.

Building strong relationships is another critical component of successful collaboration. CMOs must foster trust and mutual respect among teams, encouraging open dialogue and valuing diverse perspectives. For example:

- A collaborative workshop involving marketing, sales, and product teams can generate innovative ideas for a new campaign or product launch.
- Celebrating joint successes, such as meeting a revenue target or achieving a successful launch, reinforces the value of teamwork.

One of the challenges in cross-functional collaboration is managing conflicting priorities. For example, the finance team may prioritise cost control while marketing advocates for increased budget allocation to support growth initiatives. In such cases, the CMO must act as a mediator, presenting data-driven arguments that align with broader organisational goals. For instance:

- Demonstrating the ROI of a proposed campaign can persuade finance to approve additional funding.

- Highlighting how marketing initiatives directly support sales objectives can resolve conflicts between the two departments.

Technology integration plays a pivotal role in enabling seamless collaboration. Tools like **Customer Relationship Management (CRM) systems** and **data visualisation platforms** create shared dashboards that provide visibility into performance metrics across departments. For example:

- A shared CRM like **Salesforce** allows marketing and sales to track leads, monitor engagement, and measure conversion rates collaboratively.
- Platforms like **Tableau** or **Power BI** can consolidate data from multiple sources, offering insights that benefit all teams.

Leadership is critical in driving collaboration. As the head of marketing, the CMO must lead by example, demonstrating a commitment to teamwork and inclusivity. This involves actively participating in cross-departmental initiatives, addressing conflicts constructively, and advocating for the shared success of all teams. For instance:

- A CMO might collaborate with HR to align internal branding efforts with external marketing campaigns, creating a cohesive brand identity.
- Working closely with the IT team to implement a new martech solution ensures that both technical and marketing requirements are met.

Finally, CMOs must focus on **long-term relationship building** rather than viewing collaboration as a one-off effort. This involves establishing ongoing processes for alignment, such as quarterly strategy reviews, cross-departmental task forces, or integrated workflows. By institutionalising collaboration, CMOs ensure that teamwork becomes a consistent part of the organisational culture.

In conclusion, **mastering cross-functional collaboration** is essential for CMOs seeking to maximise the impact of their marketing strategies. By fostering communication, aligning goals, leveraging data, and building strong relationships, marketing leaders can create synergies that drive innovation, improve efficiency, and enhance customer experience. Collaboration is not just a strategy, it is a mindset that empowers organisations to thrive in a competitive and interconnected world.

10.4 - Global Marketing: Strategies for International Growth

For a **Chief Marketing Officer (CMO)**, expanding into international markets is one of the most complex and rewarding challenges in marketing leadership. **Global marketing** requires a nuanced approach that balances standardisation with localisation, navigates cultural and regulatory differences, and leverages economies of scale while respecting local nuances. Success in international growth depends on a well-planned strategy that aligns with the company's overarching goals while adapting to the unique needs of diverse markets.

Understanding market dynamics is the foundation of global marketing. Each market operates with its own set of cultural, economic, and behavioural factors that influence how customers perceive and interact with brands. Conducting thorough **market research** is essential before entering any new territory. This includes:

- Analysing customer behaviour, preferences, and pain points specific to the region.
- Identifying competitors and their positioning within the local market.
- Evaluating economic factors, such as purchasing power, growth potential, and pricing sensitivity.

For example, a global fashion retailer expanding into Southeast Asia might discover that customers in this region prioritise affordability and value over luxury. This insight would inform the brand's pricing strategy and product selection for that market.

Cultural adaptation is another critical component of international growth. Messaging, imagery, and even product offerings that resonate in one region may fail, or worse, offend, in another. For instance:

- A marketing campaign that uses humour might need to be adapted to suit the cultural tone of a particular region.
- Product names, taglines, or slogans may require localisation to avoid unintended meanings in different languages.

A notable example is how **Coca-Cola** successfully localises its campaigns while maintaining a consistent global brand image. By tailoring advertisements to reflect local values and traditions, the brand connects with diverse audiences while preserving its core identity.

Balancing standardisation and localisation is a key strategic decision for CMOs in global marketing. Standardisation ensures brand consistency, economies of scale, and operational efficiency, while localisation addresses specific market needs and preferences. For instance:

- A global cosmetics brand might maintain consistent packaging and branding across markets but adapt its advertising to highlight different product benefits based on regional preferences (e.g., anti-ageing in Europe versus hydration in Asia).

- Similarly, a fast-food chain might keep its core menu items standard while introducing region-specific dishes to cater to local tastes.

Navigating regulatory landscapes is another important aspect of global marketing. Different countries have varying laws governing advertising, data privacy, and product labelling. CMOs must work closely with legal and compliance teams to ensure campaigns meet local regulations. For example:

- In the European Union, marketing initiatives must comply with **GDPR**, requiring explicit customer consent for data collection and usage.

- In China, social media marketing strategies must align with government restrictions on certain platforms and content types.

Digital platforms play a pivotal role in international marketing. Social media, search engines, and e-commerce sites provide scalable ways to reach global audiences. However, the platforms used may differ significantly by region. For instance:

- In Western markets, **Facebook**, **Instagram**, and **Google** dominate digital marketing.
- In China, platforms like **WeChat**, **Weibo**, and **Baidu** are essential for reaching consumers.

CMOs must tailor their digital strategies to the platforms popular in each market, ensuring that content and messaging resonate with local audiences.

Building local partnerships can accelerate international growth. Collaborating with local influencers, distributors, or agencies provides valuable insights into the market and enhances credibility. For example:

- Partnering with a local distributor ensures that products reach customers efficiently while benefiting from the distributor's established networks.
- Engaging local influencers allows brands to connect authentically with target audiences, leveraging the influencers' cultural understanding and follower trust.

Maintaining brand consistency across markets is another challenge in global marketing. While localisation is necessary, CMOs must ensure that all adaptations align with the brand's core values and identity. Establishing global brand guidelines helps maintain this balance. For instance, a global brand like **Nike** ensures consistency in its "Just Do It" ethos while tailoring campaigns to reflect local sports culture and athletes.

Measuring performance in international markets requires a combination of global and local metrics. CMOs should track overall performance indicators, such as revenue and market share, while also monitoring region-specific metrics like customer engagement, brand awareness, and campaign ROI. Tools like **Google Analytics** and **Tableau** can provide insights into global trends, while local market research firms may offer a deeper understanding of specific regions.

Overcoming operational challenges is also critical. Expanding internationally often involves logistical complexities, such as managing supply chains, hiring local talent, and adapting customer service processes. For example:

- An e-commerce brand entering a new market might need to establish partnerships with local delivery providers to ensure timely and cost-effective fulfilment.
- Recruiting local marketing teams ensures campaigns are culturally relevant and effectively executed.

In conclusion, **global marketing** requires a delicate balance of strategy, cultural awareness, and operational excellence. By conducting thorough research, leveraging local insights, and maintaining a consistent yet adaptable brand presence, CMOs can successfully navigate the complexities of international growth. The key lies in understanding that while global strategies drive scalability, localised execution ensures relevance, authenticity, and connection with diverse audiences.

10.5 - The Importance of Diversity and Inclusion in Marketing

In today's interconnected and socially conscious world, **diversity and inclusion (D&I)** are no longer optional in marketing; they are essential for building trust, fostering brand loyalty, and staying relevant in an increasingly diverse marketplace. For a **Chief Marketing Officer (CMO)**, embracing D&I goes beyond representation in campaigns; it requires embedding inclusive practices into every aspect of marketing, from strategy and creative development to hiring and audience engagement.

Understanding diversity and inclusion in marketing begins with recognising the importance of reflecting the diverse identities, cultures, and perspectives of customers. Representation in campaigns should not be tokenistic but authentic, ensuring that all audiences feel seen, valued, and respected. For example:

- A skincare brand targeting a global audience should feature models of different ethnicities, ages, and skin types to reflect the variety of its customer base.
- A financial services company might create campaigns in multiple languages to engage non-native speakers, demonstrating a commitment to inclusivity.

One of the key benefits of prioritising D&I in marketing is its impact on **customer trust and loyalty**. Research shows that customers are more likely to support brands that align with their values and champion inclusivity. For instance:

- A study by Adobe revealed that 61% of consumers are more likely to purchase from brands that show diversity in their advertising.
- Inclusive campaigns can resonate deeply with underrepresented groups, fostering emotional connections and long-term loyalty.

Authenticity is critical when implementing D&I strategies. Consumers are quick to spot insincerity or performative efforts, such as campaigns that use diverse imagery without backing it up with inclusive practices. For example, a retailer that promotes diversity in its advertising but fails to implement fair hiring practices risks alienating customers. CMOs must ensure that their brand's commitment to D&I is consistent across both external messaging and internal operations.

Building inclusive marketing teams is an essential step in creating authentic campaigns. A diverse team brings a variety of perspectives, experiences, and ideas, reducing the risk of bias and ensuring that campaigns resonate with a broader audience. For instance:

- Hiring creatives from underrepresented backgrounds can lead to fresh insights and innovative storytelling.
- Establishing employee resource groups (ERGs) allows marketers to seek input from colleagues who represent different demographics.

Research and audience insights play a crucial role in developing inclusive campaigns. Understanding the needs, preferences, and cultural nuances of different customer segments ensures that messaging is relevant and respectful. For example:

- Conducting focus groups with diverse participants can reveal how specific communities perceive a brand and its offerings.
- Social listening tools like **Brandwatch** or **Hootsuite Insights** can help identify topics, trends, and sentiments that matter to diverse audiences.

Avoiding stereotypes and biases is another critical aspect of inclusive marketing. Campaigns should celebrate diversity without reducing individuals to clichés or perpetuating harmful narratives. For example:

- A campaign celebrating cultural festivals should ensure accuracy and respect for traditions, avoiding oversimplifications or misappropriations.
- Marketing materials should avoid caricatures or oversimplified depictions of specific demographics, ensuring authenticity and sensitivity.

Measuring the impact of inclusive marketing involves tracking both quantitative and qualitative metrics. CMOs should monitor how D&I initiatives influence brand perception, customer engagement, and market share. For example:

- Analysing customer sentiment on social media can reveal how audiences respond to inclusive campaigns.
- Tracking sales growth in underrepresented segments can demonstrate the business impact of inclusive strategies.

Challenges in implementing D&I often stem from organisational inertia or fear of getting it wrong. Some brands avoid inclusive efforts due to concerns about backlash or controversy. However, taking a stand on inclusion, even in the face of challenges, can strengthen a brand's reputation. For example, a brand that recognises previous shortcomings in diversity may address them transparently while launching an updated campaign, earning praise for its commitment to improvement.

Partnerships and collaborations can amplify inclusive marketing efforts. Working with organisations, influencers, or non-profits that represent diverse communities helps brands connect authentically. For instance:

- Partnering with local community leaders or cultural experts ensures messaging is accurate and respectful.
- Collaborating with regional artists allows brands to celebrate cultural diversity through creative, locally inspired campaigns.

In conclusion, **diversity and inclusion in marketing** are not just ethical imperatives but strategic advantages. By prioritising authentic representation, building inclusive teams, and fostering a culture of respect and empathy, CMOs can create campaigns that resonate deeply with audiences. Embracing D&I is not a one-time effort but an ongoing commitment to understanding and celebrating the richness of human diversity. As markets continue to evolve, brands that champion inclusivity will stand out as leaders in both innovation and integrity.

10.6 - The Role of Purpose-Driven Marketing

In an era where consumers increasingly prioritise brands that align with their values, **purpose-driven marketing** has emerged as a vital strategy for building meaningful connections with customers. For a **Chief Marketing Officer (CMO)**, integrating a brand's purpose into marketing efforts is more than a trend; it's a strategic approach to driving customer loyalty, differentiation, and long-term growth. Purpose-driven marketing focuses on highlighting a company's mission and commitment to making a positive impact, whether socially, environmentally or within its industry.

Defining a clear and authentic purpose is the foundation of this approach. A brand's purpose goes beyond selling products or services; it reflects its core values and the positive change it aims to create. For example:

- A technology company may centre its purpose around advancing digital accessibility for underserved communities.
- An agricultural brand might focus on sustainable farming practices that benefit the environment and local farmers.

It's critical that the brand's purpose aligns with its actions and is not perceived as superficial. Authenticity is essential, as customers can quickly identify insincerity or "purpose-washing," where a company promotes values it does not genuinely uphold.

Purpose-driven marketing also strengthens emotional connections with customers. Consumers are more likely to support brands that share their values and demonstrate a commitment to causes they care about. For instance, a company that takes a strong stance on environmental sustainability by implementing eco-friendly practices and supporting reforestation initiatives can inspire loyalty among eco-conscious consumers. This emotional connection often translates into advocacy, as customers are more likely to recommend purpose-driven brands to others.

Integrating purpose into marketing efforts involves more than occasional campaigns or one-off initiatives. The brand's mission should be woven into every aspect of its strategy, from messaging and content to partnerships and product development. For example:

- An outdoor gear company with a purpose centred on environmental conservation might highlight its efforts in reducing waste through upcycled products while partnering with organisations that protect natural habitats.
- A financial institution with a focus on empowering small businesses could spotlight real stories of entrepreneurs it has helped through grants or low-interest loans.

Storytelling plays a crucial role in purpose-driven marketing. Sharing authentic narratives about the brand's impact and the people or communities it supports creates a relatable and compelling connection with audiences. For example:

- A beverage company might showcase the journey of local farmers whose livelihoods have improved due to the company's ethical sourcing practices.
- A software company could create a video series highlighting how its tools have empowered non-profits to scale their impact.

The Future of Marketing Leadership

Measuring the success of purpose-driven marketing requires both quantitative and qualitative metrics. CMOs should evaluate the business impact, such as increased customer loyalty, market share, or revenue growth, alongside measures of social or environmental impact. For instance:

- Tracking metrics like customer retention rates or the number of new customers acquired due to purpose-driven campaigns provides insight into their effectiveness.
- Monitoring the tangible outcomes of initiatives, such as the number of trees planted or scholarships funded, demonstrates the brand's commitment to its mission.

Partnerships amplify the reach and impact of purpose-driven marketing. Collaborating with reputable organisations, non-profits, or other businesses that share similar values enhances credibility and broadens the brand's influence. For example:

- A retail brand committed to ending hunger might partner with a global charity to donate a percentage of every purchase to food programmes.
- A tech company focused on education could work with schools and educators to provide free training and resources in underserved areas.

Purpose-driven marketing also resonates strongly with employees. A brand's mission can become a source of pride and motivation, fostering engagement and loyalty within the organisation. For instance:

- Employees of a renewable energy company may feel more inspired and committed, knowing their work contributes to combating climate change.

- Organisations that involve their employees in purpose-driven initiatives, such as volunteer programmes or community projects, strengthen their internal culture and alignment with the brand's values.

Challenges in purpose-driven marketing often revolve around authenticity and execution. Brands must avoid overpromising or focusing too heavily on promoting their efforts at the expense of real impact. For instance:

- A company claiming to prioritise sustainability but failing to address waste in its supply chain risks damaging its reputation.
- Overly polished campaigns that appear more focused on marketing than on genuine action can lead to scepticism among consumers.

To overcome these challenges, CMOs should ensure that purpose-driven marketing efforts are grounded in transparency and accountability. Regular reporting on progress, including successes and areas for improvement, builds trust and demonstrates a commitment to continuous growth.

In conclusion, **purpose-driven marketing** is a powerful strategy that enables brands to differentiate themselves in a crowded marketplace while making a meaningful impact. By defining an authentic mission, integrating it across all aspects of the business, and measuring both business and social outcomes, CMOs can create campaigns that resonate deeply with customers and employees alike. In an age where consumers increasingly demand that brands stand for something greater, purpose-driven marketing offers a path to relevance, loyalty, and long-term success.

10.7 - Lifelong Learning and Professional Development

For a **Chief Marketing Officer (CMO)**, the journey of learning and professional development does not end upon reaching a senior leadership position. In fact, it becomes even more crucial as the role evolves in response to new technologies, shifting consumer behaviours, and emerging industry trends. Lifelong learning is a mindset and a strategy that allows CMOs to remain relevant, innovative, and effective in a dynamic business environment.

Understanding the importance of lifelong learning begins with recognising the rapidly changing nature of marketing. Advances in **artificial intelligence (AI)**, **big data**, and **personalisation technologies** are constantly reshaping the marketing landscape. A CMO who stops learning risks falling behind competitors and losing the ability to drive impactful campaigns. For example:

- A CMO who invests in understanding AI applications in marketing can identify opportunities for automation, such as predictive analytics or personalised customer journeys, which drive efficiency and results.
- Staying updated on emerging platforms, like the metaverse or blockchain-based advertising, ensures that the CMO can evaluate their relevance and potential impact.

The Future of Marketing Leadership

Commitment to continuous education involves actively seeking out opportunities to expand knowledge and refine skills. This can take several forms, including:

- **Executive education programmes**: Institutions like Harvard Business School and INSEAD offer specialised courses tailored to senior executives, focusing on leadership, innovation, and strategy.
- **Certifications in niche areas**: Enrolling in courses on topics like data analytics, digital marketing, or behavioural economics can help CMOs deepen their expertise in critical areas.
- **Attending industry conferences**: Events like **Cannes Lions**, **SXSW**, or **HubSpot's INBOUND** provide insights into the latest trends, tools, and case studies from industry leaders.

Staying informed through thought leadership is another vital aspect of professional development. CMOs should regularly engage with books, articles, podcasts, and webinars from experts in their field. For instance:

- Reading books by marketing pioneers like **Seth Godin** or **Byron Sharp** provides valuable perspectives on consumer behaviour and brand strategy.
- Following platforms such as **Harvard Business Review** or **Marketing Week** ensures CMOs stay updated on industry developments and best practices.

Networking and peer learning offer invaluable opportunities for growth. Engaging with other CMOs and industry professionals enables the exchange of ideas, experiences, and solutions to common challenges. This can be achieved through:

- Joining professional organisations like **The CMO Club** or **AMA (American Marketing Association)**, which provide forums for discussion and collaboration.
- Participating in roundtables or panel discussions to gain insights from peers facing similar challenges.
- Seeking mentorship from experienced leaders or offering mentorship to rising talent, fostering mutual learning.

Developing leadership skills is an integral part of professional development for CMOs. As marketing leaders, they must navigate complex stakeholder relationships, inspire creativity, and drive organisational change. Skills such as emotional intelligence, strategic thinking, and conflict resolution are essential for long-term success. For example:

- A CMO leading a global team must hone their cross-cultural communication skills to foster collaboration across diverse markets.
- Building resilience and adaptability helps CMOs guide their teams through crises or rapidly changing business conditions.

Staying open to cross-disciplinary learning is another valuable strategy. Marketing intersects with fields such as psychology, technology, and economics, and gaining knowledge in these areas enhances a CMO's ability to innovate. For instance:

- Understanding behavioural psychology can inform more effective messaging strategies.

- Gaining insights into supply chain logistics might help a CMO better align marketing campaigns with product availability and distribution timelines.

Investing in team development is also an essential aspect of a CMO's lifelong learning journey. By fostering a culture of learning within their team, CMOs ensure that the entire marketing function remains forward-thinking and agile. For example:

- Encouraging team members to pursue certifications or attend workshops strengthens collective expertise.
- Hosting internal knowledge-sharing sessions allows employees to present key takeaways from conferences or training sessions, benefiting the broader team.

Balancing self-reflection and external feedback helps CMOs identify areas for growth. Regularly assessing one's own performance and seeking input from colleagues, mentors, or team members provides valuable perspectives on strengths and areas for improvement. For instance:

- A CMO might solicit feedback on their communication style during stakeholder presentations and adjust accordingly to improve clarity and impact.
- Reflecting on past campaigns and analysing what worked, or didn't, can guide future strategies.

The challenges of lifelong learning often stem from time constraints and the risk of information overload. CMOs juggle demanding schedules, making it difficult to prioritise education. To address this, they should create structured learning plans that align with their goals. For example:

- Setting aside dedicated time each month for professional development activities ensures consistent progress.
- Focusing on specific areas of interest or relevance, rather than trying to learn everything at once, prevents overwhelm.

In conclusion, **lifelong learning and professional development** are essential for CMOs to stay at the forefront of their industry, inspire their teams, and drive meaningful results. By embracing a growth mindset, seeking out new knowledge, and investing in their leadership capabilities, CMOs can continue to thrive in an ever-changing marketing landscape. As marketing evolves, those who remain committed to learning will lead the way in innovation, adaptability, and impact.

10.8 - Becoming a Thought Leader in Your Industry

For a **Chief Marketing Officer (CMO)**, becoming a **thought leader** is an opportunity to build credibility, influence industry conversations, and elevate both personal and organisational reputation. Thought leadership extends beyond self-promotion; it involves sharing insights, driving innovation, and contributing to the broader development of the marketing field. For CMOs, this not only strengthens their professional brand but also reinforces the organisation's position as a leader in its industry.

Understanding thought leadership begins with recognising its value. A thought leader is someone whose opinions and expertise are sought after and respected within their industry. For a CMO, this can mean being the voice of authority on topics such as marketing innovation, customer experience, or digital transformation. By positioning themselves as a thought leader, CMOs can:

- Attract top talent by showcasing the organisation as a forward-thinking workplace.
- Strengthen relationships with stakeholders by demonstrating expertise and foresight.
- Enhance the organisation's brand reputation, creating a competitive edge.

Defining your niche is a key first step in building thought leadership. CMOs should focus on topics where they have deep expertise or unique perspectives, ensuring their contributions are meaningful and impactful. For example:

- A CMO with extensive experience in digital marketing might share insights on leveraging AI to drive personalisation.
- Another might focus on sustainability in marketing, discussing strategies for reducing environmental impact while maintaining profitability.

Content creation is at the heart of thought leadership. Publishing high-quality, insightful, and actionable content allows CMOs to share their expertise and engage with their audience. This can take various forms, including:

- **Articles and blogs**: Writing for industry publications or the organisation's blog helps establish authority. For instance, a CMO could pen an article for **Marketing Week** on the future of data-driven decision-making.

- **Books and eBooks**: Publishing a book consolidates expertise and positions the author as a leading voice in their field.

- **Case studies**: Sharing detailed accounts of successful campaigns or strategies provides practical value to peers and followers.

Speaking engagements and events are another powerful way to establish thought leadership. Conferences, webinars, and panel discussions offer platforms to share insights, network with peers, and gain visibility. For example:

- Participating as a keynote speaker at **Cannes Lions** or **HubSpot's INBOUND** demonstrates authority and builds connections with industry professionals.

- Hosting webinars or roundtable discussions on emerging trends allows CMOs to engage directly with their audience.

Leveraging social media is essential for amplifying thought leadership efforts. Platforms like **LinkedIn** and **Twitter** are ideal for sharing content, engaging in conversations, and building a professional network. For example:

- Regularly posting insights, trends, or reflections on LinkedIn positions the CMO as a knowledgeable and approachable leader.

- Engaging with other industry leaders by commenting on or sharing their posts fosters collaboration and mutual recognition.

Building relationships with media and influencers can further enhance visibility and credibility. CMOs can work with journalists to contribute to articles, offer expert commentary, or provide data-backed insights for industry reports. For instance:

- Being quoted in a major publication like **Harvard Business Review** reinforces authority and reach.
- Collaborating with industry influencers on joint projects or interviews introduces the CMO's expertise to new audiences.

Staying authentic and accessible is crucial in thought leadership. Audiences value leaders who are genuine, relatable, and transparent. For example:

- Sharing personal experiences, challenges, or lessons learned humanises the CMO and fosters trust.
- Acknowledging mistakes or failures, along with the steps taken to address them, demonstrates accountability and continuous learning.

Consistency is key to building and maintaining thought leadership. CMOs should commit to a regular cadence of content creation and engagement to keep their audience informed and interested. For instance:

- Publishing a monthly blog post or hosting a quarterly webinar ensures ongoing visibility.
- Setting aside time each week to engage with social media followers maintains relevance and connection.

Thought leadership also involves giving back to the industry. Mentoring rising talent, supporting industry initiatives, or contributing to educational programmes demonstrates a commitment to the broader community. For example:

- Volunteering as a guest lecturer at universities or marketing associations helps shape the next generation of leaders.
- Participating in industry awards as a judge underscores expertise and fosters recognition.

Challenges in becoming a thought leader often include time constraints and balancing personal and organisational branding. CMOs must prioritise thought leadership efforts alongside their responsibilities, focusing on areas where they can provide the most value. Additionally, ensuring that personal thought leadership aligns with the organisation's values and objectives is essential to avoid conflicts of interest.

In conclusion, **becoming a thought leader in your industry** is a strategic way for CMOs to build credibility, influence, and impact. By sharing expertise, engaging with peers, and staying authentic, CMOs can shape industry conversations and inspire others. Thought leadership is not just about individual recognition; it's about contributing to the advancement of marketing as a discipline and driving meaningful change.

10.9 - Key Predictions for the Next Decade

The role of the **Chief Marketing Officer (CMO)** is poised to undergo significant transformation over the next decade, driven by technological advancements, evolving consumer behaviours, and shifting market dynamics. To remain effective, CMOs must anticipate these changes, adapt strategies, and embrace innovation. Here are key predictions that will shape the future of marketing leadership in the coming years.

1. AI Will Dominate Marketing Operations

Artificial intelligence (**AI**) will become even more integral to marketing, automating processes, generating insights, and enabling hyper-personalisation at scale. Tools powered by AI will handle everything from content creation and predictive analytics to customer segmentation and chatbots. For example:

- AI-driven platforms like **ChatGPT** will assist in crafting tailored content and messaging for specific audience segments.
- Predictive analytics will allow marketers to forecast trends, optimise campaigns in real-time, and deliver personalised experiences based on behavioural data.

However, as AI takes on a larger role, CMOs must balance automation with human creativity, ensuring that campaigns retain authenticity and emotional resonance.

2. First-Party Data Will Reign Supreme

With increasing regulations around data privacy, such as **GDPR** and **CCPA**, and the phasing out of third-party cookies, CMOs will need to prioritise first-party data collection. Building direct relationships with customers will become essential for gathering actionable insights. For example:

- Loyalty programmes and personalised offers will incentivise customers to share their preferences and behaviours directly with brands.
- Tools like **Customer Data Platforms (CDPs)** will consolidate first-party data into unified profiles, enabling more effective targeting and personalisation.

Brands that invest in ethical, transparent data practices will gain a competitive edge by earning customer trust.

3. Marketing Will Drive Sustainability Efforts

Sustainability will no longer be an optional initiative but a core pillar of marketing strategies. Consumers increasingly expect brands to demonstrate environmental responsibility, and CMOs will play a key role in communicating these efforts. For instance:

- Companies will highlight sustainable practices, such as reducing carbon footprints or adopting circular economy models, in their messaging.
- Certifications and third-party audits will be prominently featured to validate claims and build credibility.

Beyond campaigns, CMOs will collaborate with operations and product teams to align marketing efforts with broader sustainability goals.

4. Personalisation Will Reach New Heights

Advancements in AI, machine learning (**ML**), and data analytics will enable unprecedented levels of personalisation. Customers will expect brands to anticipate their needs and deliver highly relevant experiences across all touchpoints. For example:

- E-commerce platforms might use AI to recommend products based on real-time browsing behaviour and past purchases.
- Streaming services could create personalised content playlists that evolve based on viewing habits.

While personalisation will drive engagement, CMOs must ensure these efforts respect privacy boundaries and avoid crossing into invasive territory.

5. The Metaverse Will Redefine Customer Engagement

The rise of the metaverse will create new opportunities for immersive and interactive brand experiences. CMOs will need to explore how virtual reality (VR), augmented reality (AR), and other metaverse technologies can enhance customer engagement. For example:

- Fashion brands might host virtual fashion shows where customers can "attend" using VR headsets and purchase items directly.
- Automotive companies could offer virtual test drives in realistic digital environments.

As the metaverse evolves, early adopters will gain a competitive advantage by establishing a presence and experimenting with creative activations.

6. Content Marketing Will Evolve into Experiential Storytelling

Traditional content marketing will shift towards **experiential storytelling**, where brands engage customers through interactive and participatory content. For example:

- Interactive video campaigns could allow viewers to choose their own storyline, creating a more engaging and memorable experience.
- Gamification elements, such as quizzes or challenges, will be integrated into campaigns to drive deeper engagement.

CMOs will need to invest in innovative content formats and platforms that capture attention in increasingly crowded digital spaces.

7. Diversity and Inclusion Will Be Non-Negotiable

Diversity and inclusion (**D&I**) will continue to be a critical focus for brands. Customers will demand authentic representation in advertising and a genuine commitment to inclusivity. CMOs will need to:

- Ensure campaigns reflect the diverse identities and experiences of their audience.
- Build inclusive marketing teams that bring a variety of perspectives to creative development.

Authenticity and transparency in D&I efforts will be essential to avoid backlash or accusations of tokenism.

8. CMOs Will Be Key Drivers of Digital Transformation

As organisations undergo digital transformation, CMOs will play a central role in guiding these efforts. Marketing is often the first department to adopt new technologies, making CMOs natural leaders in driving broader organisational change. For instance:

- CMOs may oversee the integration of advanced martech tools across departments, ensuring alignment with business objectives.
- They will collaborate with IT and data teams to improve customer experience through seamless digital touchpoints.

This expanded role will position CMOs as strategic leaders beyond their traditional marketing remit.

9. Real-Time Marketing Will Become the Norm

The ability to respond to events and trends in real-time will become a critical differentiator for brands. Social media platforms, AI-powered analytics, and automation tools will enable marketers to react instantly to customer behaviours and external events. For example:

- A food delivery app might launch a campaign within hours of a trending event, using humour or cultural relevance to connect with audiences.
- Sports brands could create real-time activations tied to live games or tournaments.

CMOs will need agile teams and streamlined processes to capitalise on these opportunities.

10. Ethical Marketing Practices Will Define Success

Ethical considerations will take centre stage as consumers increasingly hold brands accountable for their actions. CMOs will need to prioritise transparency, fairness, and authenticity in every aspect of their strategies. For example:

- Campaigns should avoid manipulative tactics, such as creating false urgency or exploiting customer insecurities.
- Brands must ensure their supply chains align with ethical standards, avoiding associations with exploitative labour or unsustainable practices.

CMOs who lead with integrity and purpose will not only win customer loyalty but also strengthen their organisation's long-term reputation.

The next decade will bring profound changes to marketing, challenging CMOs to adapt, innovate, and lead with purpose. By embracing technological advancements, prioritising personalisation and sustainability, and maintaining a strong ethical foundation, CMOs can navigate these shifts successfully. The marketing leaders who anticipate and prepare for these trends will be well-positioned to shape the future of their organisations and industries.

10.10 - Case Study: A Visionary CMO's Legacy

In this case study, we explore the journey of a visionary **Chief Marketing Officer (CMO), Rebecca Hartwell**, whose strategic leadership and forward-thinking approach transformed her organisation, **EcoSphere Technologies**, from a niche sustainability startup into a global market leader. Rebecca's ability to anticipate industry trends, embrace innovation, and instil a purpose-driven culture left a lasting legacy that serves as a blueprint for future marketing leaders.

The Challenge

When Rebecca joined EcoSphere Technologies, the company was struggling to gain traction in a competitive market dominated by established players. EcoSphere's mission was to provide sustainable energy solutions, but its brand lacked visibility, its messaging was inconsistent, and its marketing budget was limited. Key challenges included:

- **Limited brand awareness**: EcoSphere was overshadowed by larger competitors with deeper pockets.

- **Skepticism about sustainability claims**: Many potential customers viewed the company's promises as too ambitious or unattainable.

- **Internal misalignment**: The marketing team operated in silos, leading to inefficiencies and missed opportunities for collaboration.

Rebecca recognised that overcoming these challenges required a bold, integrated strategy that would differentiate EcoSphere while staying true to its purpose.

The Strategy

1. Establishing a Clear and Purpose-Driven Brand Identity

Rebecca began by redefining EcoSphere's brand identity, ensuring it aligned with the company's mission and resonated with its target audience. She introduced the tagline, **"Powering Tomorrow, Sustainably Today,"** which encapsulated the brand's commitment to innovation and environmental responsibility. This messaging was reinforced across all marketing channels, creating a consistent and compelling narrative.

Rebecca also invested in **certifications and transparency** to validate EcoSphere's sustainability claims. By obtaining recognised certifications and sharing detailed reports on the company's environmental impact, she built trust with customers and stakeholders.

2. Leveraging Data and Technology for Precision Marketing

Rebecca adopted a data-driven approach to optimise EcoSphere's marketing efforts. She implemented a **Customer Data Platform (CDP)** that consolidated data from various touchpoints, providing a unified view of customer behaviour. This enabled the marketing team to:

- Identify high-value customer segments for targeted campaigns.
- Tailor messaging based on customer preferences and purchasing behaviours.
- Track campaign performance in real-time and adjust strategies accordingly.

For example, data analysis revealed that small-to-medium-sized enterprises (SMEs) were particularly interested in affordable solar solutions. Rebecca's team launched a targeted campaign highlighting cost savings and government incentives for adopting solar energy, resulting in a 40% increase in lead generation within this segment.

3. Embracing Digital Transformation

Rebecca recognised the power of digital platforms to amplify EcoSphere's reach. She spearheaded the company's entry into social media, focusing on platforms like **LinkedIn** and **Twitter** to engage with B2B audiences. Her team created thought leadership content, such as blog posts, whitepapers, and webinars, that positioned EcoSphere as an authority in sustainable energy.

Rebecca also introduced **interactive tools** on the company's website, such as a solar savings calculator that allowed customers to estimate their potential cost and energy savings. This tool not only educated users but also captured valuable leads for follow-up by the sales team.

4. Building Strategic Partnerships

Rebecca forged partnerships with non-profits, industry associations, and governments to enhance EcoSphere's credibility and expand its reach. For instance:

- Collaborating with environmental organisations provided access to advocacy networks and aligned the brand with trusted voices in sustainability.
- Partnering with government agencies enabled joint initiatives, such as workshops educating SMEs about renewable energy adoption.

These partnerships not only increased visibility but also reinforced EcoSphere's reputation as a purpose-driven leader in its industry.

5. Fostering Internal Collaboration and Innovation

To address internal misalignment, Rebecca reorganised the marketing team to encourage collaboration and agility. She introduced regular cross-departmental brainstorming sessions and established clear goals that aligned with the company's overarching strategy. Rebecca also invested in professional development, ensuring her team stayed ahead of industry trends.

Her leadership inspired a culture of innovation. For example, one brainstorming session led to the idea of creating a mobile app that allowed users to monitor their energy consumption in real-time. The app became a key differentiator for EcoSphere, enhancing customer engagement and loyalty.

The Results

Rebecca's efforts had a transformative impact on EcoSphere Technologies:

- **Revenue growth**: Annual revenue increased by 150% within five years, driven by a surge in customer acquisition and retention.

- **Global expansion**: The company entered new markets across Europe and Asia, supported by tailored marketing strategies for each region.

- **Brand recognition**: EcoSphere's brand awareness doubled, with the company earning industry awards for innovation and sustainability.

- **Customer loyalty**: The introduction of personalised campaigns and interactive tools boosted customer satisfaction scores by 30%.

Internally, Rebecca's leadership revitalised the marketing team. Employee engagement surveys showed a 25% improvement in morale, and turnover rates decreased significantly. Her focus on collaboration and professional growth created a cohesive and motivated team.

Lessons Learned

Rebecca's journey offers valuable insights for CMOs aiming to leave a lasting legacy:

1. **Purpose drives success**: Aligning marketing efforts with a clear and authentic mission creates a strong foundation for growth.

2. **Data fuels precision**: Leveraging customer insights ensures that campaigns are targeted, relevant, and impactful.

3. **Collaboration fosters innovation**: Breaking down silos and encouraging diverse perspectives unlocks creative potential.

4. **Adaptability is key**: Embracing digital transformation and evolving strategies to meet market demands ensures sustained competitiveness.

Conclusion

Rebecca Hartwell's legacy as a visionary CMO demonstrates the power of purpose-driven marketing, strategic foresight, and effective leadership. By aligning EcoSphere Technologies with its mission, embracing innovation, and fostering a culture of collaboration, she not only transformed the company but also set a benchmark for marketing excellence. Her journey serves as an inspiration for CMOs seeking to navigate challenges, seize opportunities, and create meaningful impact in their industries.

Thinking About a CMO as a Career Path – Here's What You Need to Do

If you aspire to become a **Chief Marketing Officer (CMO)**, you'll need a unique combination of leadership, technical expertise, creativity, and strategic thinking. The modern CMO must master digital marketing, understand diverse business functions, and remain a lifelong learner to stay competitive in an ever-evolving landscape. Below, we outline the qualifications, skillsets, software mastery, and fields of expertise required to build a successful path to this pinnacle marketing role.

Qualifications and Education

1. Foundation Degrees
   - A bachelor's degree in marketing, Business Administration, Communications, or related fields.
   - Supplemental courses in psychology, sociology, or behavioural economics for consumer insights.
2. Advanced Degrees:
   - An MBA (Master of Business Administration) with a focus on Marketing, Leadership, or Data Analytics provides strategic and financial acumen.
   - Master's degrees in digital marketing, Data Science, or Customer Experience (CX) offer specialised expertise.
3. Certifications:
   - Google Analytics Certification (GA4) for audience and performance insights.

Thinking About a CMO as a Career Path – Here's What You Need to Do

- HubSpot Academy: Inbound marketing, content marketing, and email marketing certifications.
- SEO and SEM Certifications: SEMrush Academy, Moz SEO Essentials, or Google Ads certifications.
- PMP (Project Management Professional) or Agile Scrum Certification for mastering campaign workflows.
- Courses in advanced tools like Tableau, Power BI, and marketing automation platforms.

4. Key Learning Platforms:
   - LinkedIn Learning: Marketing and leadership courses.
   - Coursera: Specialisations in data science, innovation, and effective communication from top universities.
   - Skillshare: Focused training on creative storytelling, video editing, and brand design.

Skillsets Required and Where to Learn Them

1. **Digital Marketing Mastery:** Proficiency in SEO, SEM, content marketing, PPC, and social media marketing is non-negotiable.
   - Where to Learn:
     I. **Google Digital Garage:** Free foundational courses.
     II. **SEMrush Academy:** SEO and PPC certifications.
     III. **Meta Blueprint:** Facebook and Instagram advertising.
     IV. **HubSpot Academy:** In-depth training on inbound and content marketing.
2. Leadership and Strategic Thinking

Strong decision-making, team alignment, and long-term vision development.

- Where to Learn:
    I. Harvard Business School Online: Leadership programmes.
    II. INSEAD: Executive education on strategy.
    III. LinkedIn Learning: Leadership and strategic thinking courses.

3. Data Analysis and Decision-Making

Ability to analyse campaign performance, interpret KPIs, and forecast trends.

- Where to Learn:
    I. **Google Analytics Academy:** Free training in Google Analytics 4.
    II. **Tableau Training:** Courses on building dashboards and visualisation.
    III. **Coursera:** Data Science for Marketing from Johns Hopkins.

4. Creative and Storytelling Skills

Crafting compelling narratives that resonate with audiences and enhance brand equity.

- Where to Learn:
    I. **Skillshare:** Courses on storytelling and creative writing.

II. **Canva Design School:** Tutorials for creating visual content.

III. **The Copywriter Club:** Advanced copywriting and storytelling resources.

5. Communication and Collaboration

Effective verbal and written communication to influence stakeholders and build partnerships.

- Where to Learn:
    I. **Toastmasters International:** Public speaking workshops.
    II. **LinkedIn Learning:** Courses on communication and stakeholder management.

6. Project and Team Management

Overseeing multi-channel campaigns and managing cross-functional teams.

- Where to Learn:
    I. **PMP Certification** (Project Management Institute).
    II. **Asana Academy:** Tutorials for managing workflows.
    III. **Agile Scrum Training:** Courses from Scrum Alliance.

Software, Platforms, and Tools to Master

1. Analytics and Reporting Tools
    - **Google Analytics 4 (GA4)**: Website performance and audience insights.

- **Crazy Egg** and **Hotjar**: Heatmaps and user behaviour tracking.
- **Tableau** and **Power BI**: Data visualisation and executive reporting.

2. SEO and SEM Tools
   - **SEMrush** and **Ahrefs**: Keyword research, site audits, and competitor analysis.
   - **Google Ads**: Paid search campaigns.
   - **BrightEdge**: Advanced content optimisation.

3. Social Media Management
   - **Hootsuite** and **Sprinklr**: Social media planning and analytics.
   - **Meta Ads Manager**: Facebook and Instagram ad management.
   - **TikTok Ads**: Emerging platform for younger demographics.

4. Creative and Content Marketing Tools
   - Adobe Creative Suite:
     - Photoshop and Illustrator for design.
     - Premiere Pro and After Effects for video editing and motion graphics.
     - InDesign for layout and publishing.
     - Canva: Easy-to-use design tool for quick visual creation.

5. Marketing Automation and CRM

- **HubSpot**, **Marketo**, and **Pardot**: Personalised workflows and email campaigns.
- **Salesforce**: CRM management for customer relationships.
- **ActiveCampaign**: Advanced automation and email marketing.

6. CRO and User Experience Tools
   - **Optimizely** and **VWO**: A/B testing and CRO optimisation.
   - **Crazy Egg**: Heatmaps to track user interactions.

Fields to Gain Experience In

1. **Content Marketing**: Writing, designing, and distributing high-value content to attract and retain customers.
2. **Social Media Marketing**: Building communities, managing campaigns, and leveraging platforms for brand awareness.
3. **Performance Marketing**: Managing PPC campaigns, analysing ad spend, and improving ROI.
4. **Product Marketing**: Positioning products in the market and crafting go-to-market strategies.
5. **Customer Experience (CX)**: Enhancing the end-to-end customer journey for satisfaction and loyalty.

Practical Steps to Build Your Career Path

1. **Gain Broad Marketing Experience**: Work across SEO, branding, analytics, and social media to build a well-rounded skillset.

2. **Specialise, Then Generalise**: Focus on a niche (e.g., digital marketing, content marketing) and then expand your expertise into broader marketing functions.
3. **Network Actively**: Attend industry events, join marketing forums, and connect with mentors for guidance and opportunities.
4. **Stay Ahead of Trends**: Follow industry publications like **Marketing Week** or **Harvard Business Review**. Learn emerging platforms like **TikTok**, **blockchain marketing**, and **metaverse campaigns**.
5. **Build Leadership Capabilities**: Take on team management roles and develop cross-functional collaboration skills.

Conclusion

To become a **world-class CMO**, you need a combination of advanced education, mastery of technical tools, and expertise across key marketing functions. Pursue specialised certifications, hone your creative and analytical abilities, and focus on leadership development. By continuously learning and evolving, you can prepare yourself for the dynamic and rewarding challenges of leading marketing at the highest level.

Printed in Great Britain
by Amazon

f903dd19-2c1c-4f35-abb4-702e635c013aR01